FIRST
TEMPLAR
NATION

"In this well-told story, author Freddy Silva has filled a long-standing need for a real understanding of the Templars' early history, their search for treasure in the Temple of Solomon, and the creation of an independent Portugal with a Templar knight as king. *First Templar Nation* is a fascinating contribution to the body of knowledge of the Order."

STEVEN SORA, AUTHOR OF
THE LOST TREASURE OF THE KNIGHTS TEMPLAR,
THE LOST COLONY OF THE TEMPLARS, AND
SECRET SOCIETIES OF AMERICA'S ELITE

ALSO BY THIS AUTHOR

The Divine Blueprint
Temples, Power Places, and the Global Plan
to Shape the Human Soul

The Lost Art of Resurrection
Initiation, Secret Chambers, and the
Quest for the Otherworld

Chartres Cathedral
The Missing or Heretic Guide

Secrets in the Fields
The Science and
Mysticism of Crop Circles

FIRST
TEMPLAR
NATION

How Eleven Knights
Created a New Country
and a Refuge for the Grail

FREDDY SILVA

Destiny Books

Rochester, Vermont • Toronto, Canada

Destiny Books
One Park Street
Rochester, Vermont 05767
www.DestinyBooks.com

Text stock is SFI certified

Destiny Books is a division of Inner Traditions International

Copyright © 2012, 2017 by Freddy Silva

Originally published in 2012 by Invisible Temple under the title *First Templar Nation: How the Knights Templar Created Europe's First Nation-State*
Revised edition published in 2017 by Destiny Books

Library of Congress Cataloging-in-Publication Data
Names: Silva, Freddy, 1961- author.
Title: First Templar nation : how eleven knights created a new country and a refuge for the grail / Freddy Silva.
Description: Revised edition. | Rochester, Vermont : Destiny Books, 2017. | Includes bibliographical references and index.
Identifiers: LCCN 2017011504 (print) | LCCN 2017037726 (e-book) | ISBN 9781620556542 (pbk.) | ISBN 9781620556559 (e-book)
Subjects: LCSH: Templars—History. | Military religious orders—History.
Classification: LCC CR4743 .S489 2017 (print) | LCC CR4743 (e-book) | DDC 255/.7913—dc23
LC record available at https://lccn.loc.gov/2017011504

Printed and bound in the United States by Lake Book Manufacturing, Inc. The text stock is SFI certified. The Sustainable Forestry Initiative® program promotes sustainable forest management.

10 9 8 7 6 5 4 3 2 1

Text design and layout by Freddy Silva and Debbie Glogover
This book was typeset in Garamond Premier Pro with Gill Sans, Ruritania, and Engravers used as display typefaces

To send correspondence to the author of this book, mail a first-class letter to the author c/o Inner Traditions • Bear & Company, One Park Street, Rochester, VT 05767, and we will forward the communication, or contact the author directly at **invisibletemple.com**.

For my goddess

AUTHOR'S NOTE

Over a decade of research went into this book, by which time I felt as though I could feel the people and events involved. Which is just as well, because although there are many good books on history, so many are dry and lack a human touch. I have therefore written this work in a style that is closer to that of a novel to make the reading experience more enjoyable for you. However, all the people, events, and facts portrayed are true, as the copious bibliography will testify.

If you are not familiar with the geography of Europe, do not be troubled; I have included numerous maps to help you keep track of where you are.

Just a few points to bear in mind: In this era Europe is a cornucopia of duchies, counties, and kingdoms. There is no Spain, no Italy, and France is still fragmented and mostly made up of autonomous duchies and provinces, including the kingdom of the Franks; Germany is part of the Holy Roman Empire. And in place of today's Portugal there is the county of Portucale, named after its main city, Porto. So whenever I refer to France or French or Spanish I use the terms as generalizations and to avoid lengthy explanations.

Provinces often pledged allegiance to a neighboring king or duke. Thus, a *suzerain* was a sovereign or state having control of another state that was internally autonomous. A *vassal* was a person or country subordinate to another. A *fief* was land held under a nobleman's sphere of control or a person under such control.

People's names were often spelled in different ways and different languages. I have tried to keep most names as they would have generally appeared in the twelfth century, except where they cause confusion in the text.

As for the Knights Templar, the terms Procurator, Commander, Preceptor, Master, and Brother were regularly used terms referring to members of the Order in Europe. All were subordinate to the Grand Master, Hugues de Payns.

CONTENTS

EPILOGUE

Lusitania. Where knowledge is stored, guarded
by a goddess whose symbol is a triangle . . . *352*

ACKNOWLEDGMENTS

The late André Jean Paraschi, who inspired me to ask more questions. Wendy Craig for the oversights. My overworked editor, Mindy Branstetter. And to the fact-checks. The librarians I overworked, particularly those in the Houghton and Widener Libraries at Harvard University; Jessica Thomas at the Portland Public Library; the archivists in Sintra and Tomar; Torre do Tombo in Lisbon; the Library of Congress, Washington, D.C.; John Reid, Malcolm Barber, and Susan Gonzales; the helpful people in Tomar. Sorry if I've forgotten everyone else. I'm over fifty, I'm allowed.

May this work finally bring me home and peace.

EUROPE
and the
NEAR EAST
1080 A.D.

KINGDOM
OF
HUNGARY

Belgrade

BULGARIA

MACEDONIA

Constantinople

ANATOLIA

Troy

DOMINIONS OF THE
SELJUK TURKS

GREECE

SYRIA

Antioch

THE LEVANT

bria

DOM

PALESTINE

Jaffa   Jerusalem

MEDITERRANEAN SEA

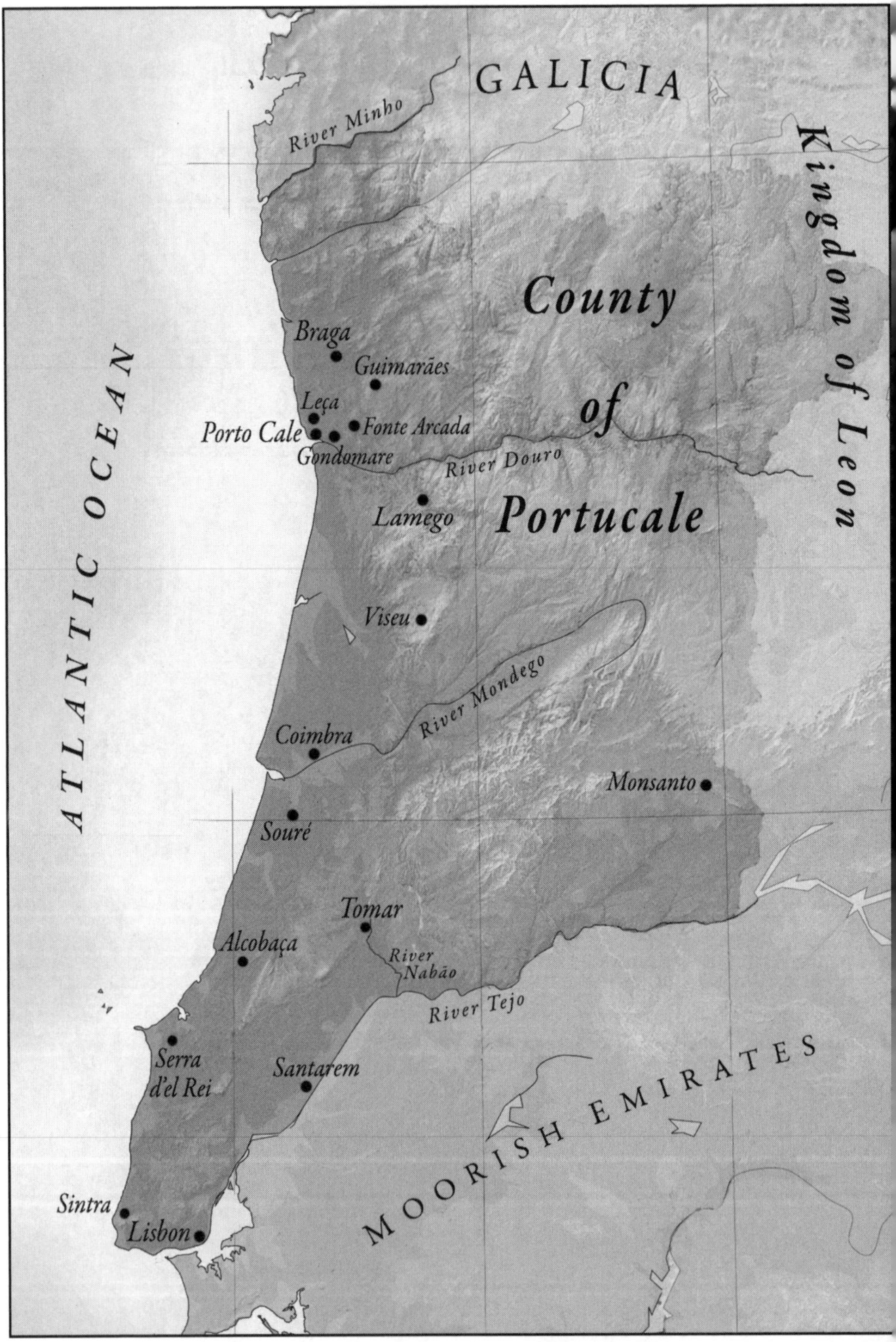

GALICIA

Kingdom of Leon

ATLANTIC OCEAN

River Minho

County

of

Portucale

Braga
Guimarães
Leça
Porto Cale
Fonte Arcada
Gondomare
River Douro

Lamego

Viseu

River Mondego

Coimbra

Monsanto

Souré

Tomar

Alcobaça
River Nabão

River Tejo

Serra
d'el Rei
Santarem

MOORISH EMIRATES

Sintra
Lisbon

If one does not understand how the body he wears came to be, he will perish with it . . . whoever does not understand how he came will not understand how he will go.

GOSPEL OF TRUTH,
NAG HAMMADI LIBRARY

I pray to the end of the universe and the beginning of the beginning, to the object of man's quest, the immortal discovery.

DISCOURSE ON THE EIGHTH AND THE NINTH,
NAG HAMMADI LIBRARY

1

1125.

**AN OAK TABLE IN A LARGE HALL
IN A SMALL COUNTY NAMED
PORTUGALE . . .**

The aged velum parchment is a donation of a small town near the city of Braga.

It reads, "I, Queen D. Tereja give to God and the Knights of the Temple of Solomon the village called Fonte Arcada . . . with all its rights and benefits, for the good of my soul."[1]

The generous donation includes no less than seventeen additional land grants by local families.[2] Meticulously written in pen and ink, it is signed, "I, Guilherme, Procurator of the Temple in this territory, receive this document."

The signatory holds the key to a mystery. As Procurator of the Temple, Guilherme Ricard is invested with the power and authority to conduct transactions on behalf of the Grand Master of the Knights Templar in Jerusalem, Hugues de Payns. But he is much more than that. His name appears on a second grant—this time as Magister Donus Ricardus—for half the estate of Villa-nova, donated by Affonso Annes "to God, and the brotherhood of the Knights Templar."[3]

This Guilherme Ricard is also the first Master of the Knights Templar in a small county named Portugale.[4]

These events are extraordinary because the year is 1125 and no members of the Knights Templar are known to exist outside Jerusalem, least of all in a region on the opposite side of Europe. Stranger still, in 1111, seven years before the Templar brotherhood came into existence, the knights were awarded a strategic property in this same territory.

Three things are certain.

One: the Knights Templar pledged allegiance not to the pope but to an influential monk in the French county of Champagne.

Two: in a document addressing the Templars, a young man destined to be king of a land that will be known as Portugal reveals that "within your Brotherhood and in all your works I am a Brother."

And three: during interrogation by the Holy Inquisition, a Templar knight made a cryptic statement: "There exists in the Order a law so extraordinary on which such a secret should be kept, that any knight would prefer his head cut off rather than reveal it to anyone."

And virtually all captured Templars proved this by being burned alive at the stake.

What follows is the true and untold story behind the first Templar nation.

The growing assembly of abbots, bishops, archbishops, princes, nobles, lords, and laymen gathered inside the great church hall in Clermont and awaited the arrival of the pope. When they finally caught sight of his tonsured head ambling down the aisle, it was clear that Urban II was less than happy. The long year of touring had carried the pontiff to several French and Mediterranean regions, then to northern Italy, where an ecclesiastical conclave at Piacenza tested his patience and the results were far from what he had expected. And besides, Piacenza in the spring had been far more climatically rewarding than the bitter November cold of Clermont, in this the year of our Lord 1095.

Urban II rose from his seat and addressed the council, beginning with his report on the church's situation in the Near East. Aside from the problem of the Seljuk Turks having overrun Asia Minor and seizing control of much of the Levant—including the city of Jerusalem—these troublesome people had also shut off access to the Christian holy places, contrary to their more tolerant Arab predecessors.

And he was not finished. Urban also had a problem with the Christians. He had seen clerics trafficking in church property, nobles

and monarchs, at home and abroad, who, wallowing in luxury, constantly violated the laws of the church on peace by picking fights with Arabs purely for material gain. And as for their knights, well, they were behaving more like mercenaries.

After his rant—some would argue a justifiable one—Urban worked up enough zeal among the assembled throng to initiate a crusade and reclaim the Christian holy places from the infidels and thus channel all this destructive energy into something worth fighting for: "I, or rather, the Lord, beseech you as Christ's heralds to publish this everywhere and to pursue all people of whatever rank, foot-soldiers and knights, poor and rich, to carry aid promptly to those Christians and to destroy that vile race from the lands of our friends. I say this to those who are present, it is meant also for those who are absent. Moreover, Christ commands it."[1]

Having warmed up, the pope then made his way out of the church, ascended a wooden platform, and began to address an even larger gathering whose numbers had strained the available meeting area of the Champet and the services the town was able to provide: "This land which you inhabit, shut in on all sides by the seas and surrounded by the mountain peaks, is too narrow for your large population; nor does it abound in wealth; and it furnishes scarcely food enough for its cultivators. Hence it is that you murder one another, that you wage war, and that frequently you perish by mutual wounds. Let therefore hatred depart from among you, let your quarrels end, let wars cease, and let all dissensions and controversies slumber. Enter upon the road to the Holy Sepulcher, wrest that land from the wicked race, and subject it to yourselves . . . God has conferred upon you above all nations great glory in arms. Accordingly undertake this journey for the remission of your sins, with the assurance of the imperishable glory of the Kingdom of Heaven."[2]

Shouts of "Deus vult, Deus vult" rose agreeably above the frozen fields of Clermont.[3] "God wills it, God wills it." Soon this would fester into a purulent propaganda slogan for the recruitment of thousands of foot soldiers.

Despite the languid air, Urban's motivational speech seemed to be having a far more resuscitating effect than it had had back in Piacenza. So he continued, with an added flourish of rabble-rousing: "They overturn and desecrate our altars . . . they will take a Christian, cut open his stomach, and tie his intestine to a stake; then stabbing at him with a spear, they will make him run, until he pulls out his own entrails and falls dead on the ground."[4]

The pope then employed bait guaranteed to rally the swelling of participants to his cause.

All who die by the way, whether by land or by sea, or in battle against the pagans, shall have immediate remission of sins. This I grant them through the power of God with which I am invested. O what a disgrace if such a despised and base race, which worships demons, should conquer a people which has the faith of omnipotent God and is made glorious with the name of Christ! With what reproaches will the Lord overwhelm us if you do not aid those who, with us, profess the Christian religion! Let those who have been accustomed unjustly to wage private warfare against the faithful now go against the infidels and end with victory this war which should have been begun long ago. Let those who for a long time, have been robbers, now become knights. Let those who have been fighting against their brothers and relatives now fight in a proper way against the barbarians. Let those who have been serving as mercenaries for small pay now obtain the eternal reward. Let those who have been wearing themselves out in both body and soul now work for a double honor. Behold! On this side will be the sorrowful and poor, on that, the rich; on this side, the enemies of the Lord, on that, his friends. Let those who go not put off the journey, but rent their lands and collect money for their expenses; and as soon as winter is over and spring comes, let them eagerly set out on the way with God as their guide.[5]

Curiously, for all of the pope's talk addressing the liberation of the Holy Lands, including his letters that followed, hardly any mention was made of two of its most important holy places. The chronicler Fulcher de Chartres, who was present during the speech at Clermont, makes no mention of Urban II discussing the liberation of Jerusalem or its holiest temple, the Church of the Holy Sepulcher—the site of Christ's burial—only of him asking to "aid promptly those Christians and to destroy that vile race [the Turks] from the lands of our friends."[6]

But exactly how much aid did those Christians need? Following the conquest of Palestine by the Arabs in AD 637, only a quarter of Jerusalem, including the Church of the Holy Sepulcher, was left in the hands of Christians. Naturally, this only swelled the numbers of Christian pilgrims to this and other sites associated with the life of the avatar Jeshua ben Joseph, otherwise known as Jesus. However, not only was access to the sacred sites allowed and maintained under the Arabs, Christian worship was tolerated too; even Mohammed directed his followers to face the site of Solomon's Temple during prayer,[7] for it was also respected by Muslims as a place of great sacredness. This tolerance prevailed into the tenth century under the caliphs of Egypt, who solemnly promised protection for travelers. In fact, life under the infidel was not as tough as expected; even the tax burden was lighter than under previous Christian rule.

But in 1065 this optimistic picture changed when the Arabs' unruly Turkish neighbors, led by the barbaric Emir Ortok, conquered and plundered the city of God, whereupon three thousand citizens were massacred. Ortok violently suppressed any remaining Christians, and then for sport imprisoned or killed visiting pilgrims unless each paid one piece of gold as the price of admission into the Church of the Holy Sepulcher.

That is assuming any pilgrim even reached the city alive. Due to the political destabilization, bands of lawless brigands roamed the plains of Palestine seeking hapless tourists, while Bedouin horsemen led desultory attacks on pilgrims from beyond the River Jordan. Not surprisingly, such behavior engendered strong sympathy and fervor from many of the European bishops and barons stirred by Urban II's impassioned speech to assemble vast armies on a crusade to wrestle formerly Christian sites from the Seljuk Turks and give safe passage to pilgrims.

And yet for all the pope's rhetoric, there may have been those present who perceived an ulterior motive. Five months earlier, one of the few highlights at the Council of Piacenza—at least for Urban II— was the reception by the pope of envoys sent from Constantinople by Emperor Commenus. The Byzantine emperor had a big problem: for a number of years the Turks had been eating away at his empire, having already gobbled up most of Anatolia, Syria, and Palestine. The council proved a most opportune moment for Commenus: Urban was close by, geographically speaking, and seven years earlier, this promising new pope had overturned Commenus's excommunication from the church. So the portents looked fortuitous for another small favor from one of Commenus's few friends, particularly if it included dispatching an army of new knights by way of Constantinople.

Commenus was a shrewd manipulator. His ambassadors not only exaggerated the need for an army, but just in case the pope faltered, they also were to remind him that Jerusalem was presently under restrictive

The Council of Clermont.

Seljuk control, with the rights of visitation of pilgrims at stake. In any event, Urban's performance at Clermont succeeded beyond both men's wildest dreams, and within months tens of thousands volunteered to rid the Near East of Turks and recapture the holy places.

One person who required little excuse to embark on this Crusade was an ardent monk of small stature from Amiens named Peter the Hermit. In his lifetime Peter had been a soldier and a married father of five children, as well as a noble and a vassal of Count Eustache of Boulogne.[8] And yet Peter renounced everything to become a reclusive monk, except for the one time he made a pilgrimage to Jerusalem. He was horrified at the treatment of pilgrims there, so much so that he was granted an audience with Simeon, the city's patriarch, during which Peter promised to canvass nobles across the whole of Europe, even the pope, on his behalf: "I shrink not from taking upon me a task for the salvation of my soul; and with the help of the Lord I am ready to go and seek out all of them, solicit them, show unto them the immensity of your troubles, and pray them all to hasten on the day of your relief."[9]

Simeon could hardly turn down such an offer of help, especially given Peter's character references. His contemporary Guibert de Nogent said of him:

> His outside made but a very poor appearance; yet superior powers swayed this miserable body; he had a quick intellect and a penetrating eye, and he spoke with ease and fluency. We saw him at that time scouring city and town, and preaching everywhere; the people crowded round him, heaped presents upon him, and celebrated his sanctity by such great praises that I remember not that like honor was ever rendered to any other person. He displayed great generosity

Peter the Hermit.

in the disposal of all things that were given him. He restored wives to their husbands, not without the addition of gifts from himself, and he re-established, with marvellous authority, peace and good understanding between those who had been at variance. In all that he did or said he seemed to have in him something divine.[10]

So generous was Peter the Hermit to the poor and so honored for his great piety was he that even the hairs of his mule were plucked as holy relics.

Encouraged by Peter's eagerness, Simeon accepted the pilgrim's offer and handed him some letters prior to his departure.

Peter, dressed in his woolen tunic and serge cloak, with arms and feet bare, succeeded in meeting with Urban II in Rome and handed him Simeon's letters discussing the dire situation in the Holy Land. This was just the beginning of his recruitment drive along the arduous route back to the French lands. Years of errant preaching while living on nothing but a little bread, wine, and some fish finally paid off, and on this frigid November afternoon in Clermont he now stood on a sturdy wooden platform beside Urban II.

The frail hermit spoke first, his skin and skeleton precariously held together by his zeal, but still he addressed the open space, now carpeted by an endless ragtag army of followers whom he had converted to march on the Holy Land. Guibert de Nogent would comment that Peter looked much like his donkey and smelled considerably worse. Peter shared with the crowd the tortures, tribulations, miseries, and humiliations suffered by the Christian pilgrims, himself included, at the hands of the Turks.

"God wills it, God wills it."

There was little left for Urban II to stoke the fervor of the mob aside from an obviously overpatriotic speech capped by a unique selling proposition: "Take ye, then, the road to Jerusalem for the remission of your sins, and depart assured of the imperishable glory which awaits you in the kingdom of heaven."

"God wills it, God wills it."

Pope Urban II.

Drunk on hope and religion, it is doubtful that few remained behind in the freezing drizzle to hear the coordinated date of departure for the entire Crusade, which was to be led by knights and commence the following August on the Feast of the Assumption. Or for that matter, to take in the final portion of Urban's speech, requesting restraint: "We ordain not, and we advise not, that the journey be undertaken by the old or the weak, or such as be not suited for arms, and let not women set out without their husbands or their brothers . . . and no layman shall commence the march save with the blessing of his pastor."[11]

But in times characterized by an economy based on plunder, the promise of a remission of sins and the glory of the kingdom of heaven was sufficient to incite three armies combining some 120,000 poorly equipped peasants. No sooner was the winter snow replaced by spring than in March 1096 central Europe was one long, unprepared, unorganized swarm of men, women, children, farmers, even the infirm, marching in three, sometimes five "armies" of nonmilitary personnel. Peter the Hermit headed one. A second was led by another colorful character, a former lord from the Île-de-France who, like Peter, sought a truer, mystical experience of God and thus renounced his worldly possessions to march to Jerusalem. He would be known as Walter the Penniless.

This was the People's Crusade.

Along the punishing road east to Constantinople many inquired desperately upon arriving at every new village, "Is this Jerusalem?"

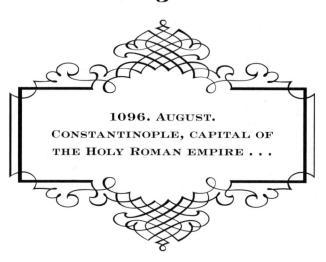

1096. AUGUST.
CONSTANTINOPLE, CAPITAL OF
THE HOLY ROMAN EMPIRE . . .

It was a miracle, and Emperor Commenus rubbed his hands with glee at the sight of it: a vast column of people approaching the city. Here at last, the reward for his efforts to prize out of the pope a fresh army that would certainly restore his faded power over a dwindling empire.

But this sublime vision of a mighty and shining fighting force slowly decayed as one after another of thousands of soiled, unsanitary, and hungry peasants pressed up to the city gate, expecting hospitality from the Holy Roman emperor.

This was not an army of knights but of locusts.

The trouble with a large mass of disorganized medieval zealots marching from village to village on little more than a vision of hope and the charity of local villagers is that no leadership can adequately provide for their physical needs, and by the time the People's Crusade had crossed Hungary it was not just taking charity so much as devouring it. Many resorted to pilfering from the initially hospitable Christian populations, eventually turning to stealing local wives, raping women, burning granaries, and generally embarking on plunder, some of it at the behest of one of the "leaders," Count Emerico, who

"himself took part in the plunder and incited his comrades to crime."[1]

They murdered four thousand in Hungary alone before setting the Serbian city of Belgrade ablaze. But not before looting it.

Commenus saw nothing but having to provide sustenance for a band of paupers, vagabonds, and opportunists. The city gates remained firmly bolted, and the People's Crusade made do by pitching tents outside the insurmountable walls.

Emperor Commenus.

Weeks of idleness ensued, and with their noses pressed to the window of riches inside Constantinople, the pilgrims took to pillaging homes on the outskirts of the capital. Despite the very best efforts of Peter the Hermit and Walter the Penniless to set examples of decorum, brigandage replaced discipline: "They were not held back by the decency of the people of the province, nor were they mollified by the Emperor's affability, but they behaved very insolently, wrecking palaces, burning public buildings, tearing the roofs off churches that were covered with lead, and then offering to sell the lead back to the Greeks."[2]

A seething Commenus eventually made the sensible decision to gather provisions and deliver his capital from this swarm, even furnishing the People's Crusade with boats to take them across the narrow strait of the Bosphorus and into Anatolia.

And off his hands.

4

1096. AUGUST.
WITH THE NORTHERN ARMY,
PREPARING TO DEPART . . .

he Feast of the Assumption came soon enough for the thousands of knights persuaded either by conscience or Urban II's rhetoric to stand in the fields of Lorraine and Flanders, adjusting their equipment and waiting the order that would propel a vast column of fighting men toward the Holy Land. The bright August sunshine flittering across their chain mail was a good omen.

En route they were to rendezvous with three other armies of similarly inspired men marching from separate locations throughout Europe, amalgamating at Constantinople to form a fighting unit of four thousand knights and thirty thousand infantrymen. Unlike the People's Crusade, this northern branch of the crusading army was led by Flemish nobles who commanded discipline—three brothers of Merovingian bloodline, sons of Eustace II, Count of Boulogne.[1] The youngest, Baudoin de Boulogne, was a student of the liberal arts; then there was Eustace III, who had inherited the title of Count of Boulogne after his father's death; and finally, tall, blond, bearded, and pious, a model knight named Godefroi de Bouillon.

A chronicler of the Crusades named Raoul of Caen described Godefroi thus: "The lustre of nobility was enhanced in his case by the

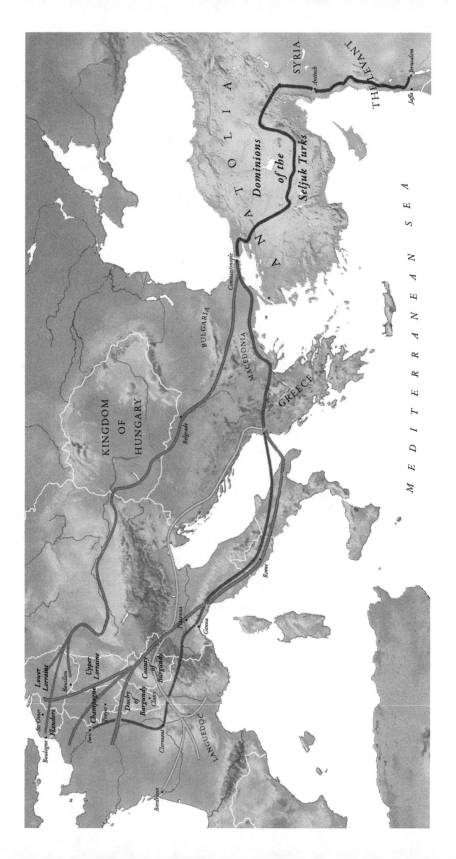

splendor of the most exalted virtues, as well in affairs of the world as of heaven. As to the latter, he distinguished himself by his generosity towards the poor, and his pity for those who had committed faults. Furthermore, his humility, his extreme gentleness, his moderation, his justice, and his chastity were great; he shone as a light amongst the monks, even more than as a duke amongst the knights."

And just as well, because being the second of three brothers, Godefroi stood to inherit little and was thus afforded fewer advantages in life. That is until his uncle Godefroi the Hunchback (son of Godefroi the Bearded) died without an heir and bequeathed the lordship of Bouillon to his young, enlightened nephew.

As the crusading armies threaded their way through the kingdoms of central Europe, they encountered a populace browbeaten but wiser from the marauding behavior of their forerunners, the People's Crusade. Aside from a few skirmishes with the Greeks and an incident in Hungary—in which Baudoin volunteered to be held in ransom by the king to ensure the proper conduct of the armies through his territory—things generally went smoothly.

By November 1096, Godefroi de Bouillon and his mounted knights and infantrymen were within reach of Constantinople when they came under sporadic harassment by troops that later turned out to have been sent by Emperor Commenus. Perhaps after his experience of the People's Crusade the emperor had become suspicious of the help Urban II was sending his way; furthermore, the presence in the arriving army of the emperor's old nemesis, Prince Bohemund, did little to appease Commenus' paranoia.

Nevertheless, within four months all the Crusaders combined at the gates of Constantinople. They required sustenance and expected this simple courtesy from Commenus.

Commenus made promises and then broke them. Advances were betrayed by hostility, further irritating the soldiers. Then he demanded their sworn obedience and fealty. When he received neither he attempted to subdue them by famine while lavishing great feasts on selective knights—a potential candidate for multiple personality disorder. But the year was drawing to a close and winter called. Finally the Crusaders had had enough and resorted to plundering the countryside.

The year 1097 arrived, and still Anatolia beckoned the Crusaders from across the narrow waterway of the Bosphorus. The rocky chasm separating Europe from the East perfectly reflected the impasse between the knights and their neurotic host.

It was at this point that Godefroi de Bouillon must have detected an ulterior motive behind the pope's push for a Crusade. As far as this knight was concerned, his intent was to march to Jerusalem, liberate the Church of the Holy Sepulcher, and reestablish the accord between Christians and Arabs, even if it meant a fragile one. It was a clear plan, yet Commenus provided nothing but obstacles; in fact, he now demanded an oath of obedience from the nobles in charge of the armies. To all intents and purposes, the Crusade appeared like an opportunistic accord between the pope and the Holy Roman emperor to commandeer soldiers and rid the Turks from the emperor's lands.

For Godefroi, the reality of the situation was that tens of thousands of men needed to be ferried across the Bosphorus. They could build their own ships for the short hop, but that would take months. Commenus knew this; he also owned all the vessels in Constantinople. The only way forward was diplomacy and compromise, so Godefroi and the nobles convened with the emperor, whereupon the ever-scheming Commenus proposed a modified oath. In return for the ferrying of troops into Turkish territory the army leaders agreed to assist him by marching on the city of Nicaea, attack the Turks in their stronghold, and liberate the city in the name of Christendom. Godefroi grudgingly agreed to the modified oath; Raimond—another leader of the army— told Commenus politely to go stuff himself, but at least gave a pledge not to attack him.

And so it was that by the spring of 1097 the Crusaders finally made landfall in Anatolia with the help of the emperor's ships. However, even as Godefroi's army prepared to lay siege to Nicaea, they discovered

Godefroi and the other leaders of the Crusade.

Commenus had made a secret treaty with the Turks, in which the surrender of the city was ensured to the emperor, thus making it look as though his Byzantine army, not the Crusaders, had won the conflict.

Following the betrayal, Godefroi and his brothers, along with their respective Crusading armies, turned south toward Jerusalem and resumed their original intent.

5

1098.
ON THE DESERT ROAD
NEAR ANTIOCH . . .

In the distance they resembled blackened matchsticks shimmering in the heat rising off the arid plains of the Levant. By the time the crusading knights caught up with them in Syria, the remnants of the People's Crusade numbered less than ten percent of the original desperate souls who had ventured out from the Frankish kingdoms.

The stories were gruesome. Priests traveling among them provoked the pilgrims by suggesting the Turks swallowed their valuables so as to conceal them from robbers, so whenever they captured one, the pilgrims cut open his belly and eager fingers probed among bloody intestines for hidden treasure.

The pilgrims were butchered in turn by the equally barbaric Turks. Those captured alive were placed in town squares and used for target practice by archers. Those who survived were returned to the desert, where they resorted on occasion to drinking their own urine. Or starved to death.

As for Peter the Hermit, his zeal had finally been foreshortened by the Turks, who tortured him. Godefroi de Bouillon was pleased enough just to find him still alive. The knight dismounted his horse, hugged

the emaciated evangelist like a long-lost friend, and had him nursed back to some sort of health.

During his convalescence Peter recounted in lurid detail "how the people, who had preceded them under his guidance, had shown themselves destitute of intelligence, improvident, and unmanageable at the same time; and so it was far more by their own fault than by the deed of any other that they had succumbed to the weight of their calamities."[1] His vigor renewed, the monk continued the journey with Godefroi's army on the remaining miles of dirt, sand, and rock still standing between them and Jerusalem.

That Godefroi himself appears to have marched to the Holy Land with his own objective right from the start was evident in his engagements with the Turks, for although his role in the army was important, his involvement in the battles and skirmishes in the Levant was minor. And battles there were aplenty.

The remnants of the People's Crusade.

Writing to his wife in France, the knight Étienne Henri de Blois was hopeful that the remaining three hundred miles to Jerusalem would take a mere five weeks to cover.[2] In reality it took the Crusaders two years before they finally caught a glimpse of the city they had so persevered to reach.

previously unstoppable Julius Caesar was vexed: "There exists a civilization in the northern confines of Iberia who refuses to govern itself and will not allow itself to be governed."[1] The tribe giving him and subsequent Roman legions two hundred years of aggravation was the Lusitani, a Celtic tribe whose name translates as "people of the light of Ani."

Ani is one of the primary deities of the Celtic world, a variant of the Sumerian goddess Inanna. In later incarnations she reappears as Saint Anne, grandmother of Jesus. Regardless of her many derivatives—Ana, Anu, Annan, Danu, Dana—she was considered the mother of the gods. Her influence is still reflected in the origin of place names throughout Europe, such as the river Danube, or the Paps of Anu, the fabled sacred hills of Ireland, once venerated by another legendary Celtic race, the Tuadhe d'Anu, the "people of Anu." Like so many ancient races, the Tuadhe are said to have introduced mathematics, agriculture, the arts, and music; they possessed the fine gift of temperament and knowledge that gave them control over the forces of nature, and such attributes had them compared to gods.

The head of the Lusitani, Viriato, was celebrated as a Celtiberian

leader possessing the noblest ancient virtues. He was honest, fair, and faithful to his word, and his brilliant strategizing won many wars against overwhelming Roman forces—to the point where recruitment in the legions dropped significantly.[2] Only through betrayal did the Romans finally become masters of this fiercely independent patch of

Viriato.

soil on the cusp of Europe and the Atlantic. Suffice it to say that a deep-seated resentment, nay hatred, of most things Roman persists to this day in the DNA of its inhabitants.

The Lusitani were also an incredibly spiritual people. They believed in the survival of the soul, in the Otherworld, and that in certain parts of the land there exists a special force that can be harnessed to connect with domains existing beyond the five senses. Such beliefs would find a continuum in that most Celtic of priesthoods, the Druids, who also found a home in Lusitania, as well as Galicia to the north; as did a Celtic tribe in the region of Denmark named Burgundii, who in time would lend their name to the French province of Burgundy.

The Druids shared something else in common with the Lusitani: they were loathed and feared in equal amounts by Julius Caesar, and he made it his mission in life to obliterate both.

After the Romans came, saw, conquered, and inevitably lost, Lusitania changed name and allegiance numerous times depending on the political wind of the month. Mountainous regions are like that: independent of mind, autonomous of spirit, stubborn to the core. Yet by the ninth century AD the political landscape began to stabilize—or comparatively so given that these were the turbulent Dark Ages—and it did so around a village appropriately named Cale.

Cale was located at the mouth of the River Douro (River of Gold), which flows into the Atlantic Ocean in the north of what is today Portugal. The Trojans were possibly one of the first groups to settle in Cale, for the name derives from the Greek word *kallis* (beautiful), referring to the sinuous beauty of the fertile Douro valley. Given how the Trojans did pass through this region on their journey to Britain, the hypothesis is a sound one.[3] *Cale* is also an ethnonym derived from the Celtic tribe who settled in the area, the Callaici, whose own name derives from the source of their veneration, the goddess Cailleach, still to this day present in Irish lore. Thus the Callaici or Gallaeci associated their name with their estuary home, which expanded into Porto Cale (beautiful harbor).[4]

Their name is also found in nearby regions of note: Gaia, Galicia, and later, the *gal* in Portugal.[5] But we are getting ahead of ourselves.

With the evaporation of the Lusitanians and the Romans, local history becomes as easy to explain as the traffic pattern inside a mound of termites. In brief, northwestern Iberia was generally known as Galicia. Sometime around the year 848 AD, between the many conquests and reconquests that characterize the fluid stability of this region, Porto Cale expands from a mere port into the region of Portucale, a strip of coastal land between the rivers Douro and Minho. The territory of Portucale then spends some two hundred years extricating itself from the yoke of Galicia; first it comes under sole governorship by 950 AD, then is governed as a fief until 1050, but twenty years later it is reincorporated into the kingdom of Galicia. Then around 1083, just to add more ingredients to this complex stew, two cousins from the House of Burgundy arrive on horseback from Dijon.

The two noble knights—Henri and his distant but far more ambitious cousin Raimond, son of Guillaume the Great, Count of Burgundy—rode into northern Iberia at the request of Alfonso VI, king of Castilla e León, Galicia e Portucale. Nicknamed "the Brave," Alfonso VI had given himself the thankless task of integrating all the disparate Spanish kingdoms, half of which were currently under Muslim rule, as were parts of his own provinces. But although this required battling with Saracens, Moors, and other Arabs, Alfonso VI appears to have been somewhat enlightened as a ruler, for he made no generalized judgments about his enemies. He still offered protection to Muslims in his territory, minted coins in Arabic, and admitted to his bed the refugee Muslim princess Zaida de Seville.

Alfonso's instructions to the knights Henri and Raimond were straightforward: recapture the parts of Galicia and Portucale that had been stolen by the Moors. Which the two would do admirably, with both Burgundians earning a great reputation for services rendered over the course of eight years by reconquering territory all the way south to the river Tejo, including the city of Lisbon.

As a token of his appreciation to Raimond, Alfonso the Brave offered his daughter Urraca's hand in marriage and bestowed on him the government of Galicia as a personal fief.

As for the equally brave Henri—a descendent of the Frankish kings in the male line, great-grandson of King Robert I, son of Duke Henri of Burgundy, and nephew of Alfonso's second wife—he received the hand in marriage of Alfonso's illegitimate daughter Dona Tareja, along with a dowry of lands in Castilla.

In any other era this would have seemed a straightforward arrangement, but this being the eleventh century, even one's own family could not be trusted, and no sooner had Raimond joined Urraca in matrimony than his father-in-law discovered their ambition to expand their newly acquired Galician territory. And so Alfonso the Brave designed a cunning plan to thwart this, by awarding Henri and Tareja a slice of an adjacent territory—the county of Portucale—which at that moment was under the suzerainty of Raimond. Essentially, Alfonso would undermine the pretensions of his more ambitious son-in-law by making Raimond an immediate neighbor of his cousin Henri, while establishing both their territories as dependencies of his own kingdom of Castilla e León.

And finally some sense of order comes to bear on the region.

At least for now.

Meanwhile, the summer of 1096 was in full bloom, and over in the Flemish kingdoms and French duchies, including Burgundy, armies were assembling, saddling up and heading east on the arduous Crusade to the Holy Land. As news of this most noble enterprise reached Alfonso VI, the Spanish king unreservedly vowed to make a personal contribution, but with the Moors making constant incursions into his kingdom, even retaking Lisbon, Alfonso was otherwise too occupied with his own campaigns at home to venture overseas. Instead, he would send help to the First Crusade by way of his trusted son-in-law Henri, who would act on his behalf.[6]

Here, family relationships worked in Henri's favor (Alfonso's second wife was also Burgundian), not to mention his upbringing within the enlightened House of Burgundy. In this era, the duchy of Burgundy was the epicenter of a renaissance, the commercial and intellectual crossroads of Europe, and since Henri and Alfonso were alumni of its liberal circle, both men no doubt shared intellectual bonds as well as a common view of the world. In return for his commitment to sail the 2,500 miles to Jerusalem—and partly to keep cousin Raimond under control—Henri's newly acquired father-in-law further granted him full governorship of the port city of Porto Cale and its surrounding territory.[7]

For a man who had been born a younger son, and thus stood to achieve little wealth or inheritance by title, Henri of Burgundy did well for himself. Upon acquiring the ancient land of the Lusitanians he was awarded the title of count and took to his new estate of mountains, moorland, coastline, and forests with enthusiasm, adopting the local customs, learning the Portuguese language, even changing his name to Count Dom Henrique as a mark of respect. Rather than staying in the city of Porto Cale, he settled instead for the verdurous hills and the inland city of Guimarães—by his time already venerated as a place of pilgrimage—whereupon he granted a charter for the city and effectively established a de facto capital for the county of Portucale.

With the affairs of state in order, Henri/Dom Henrique paused briefly to enjoy his new and wonderful life before making preparations to embark on the long voyage to Palestine, with the aim of liberating the Church of the Holy Sepulcher.[8] Little did he know that his decision would mark a pivotal moment in the history of Portucale, for the people he'd meet in Jerusalem would shape the destiny of this territory.

Dom Henrique set sail from Porto Cale en route to Genoa on the northern Italian coast and joined forces with one of the Crusader armies—most likely the one led by the son of the French king[9]—then continued with the fleet to the ancient port of Jaffa, disembarking

33 miles to the west of the gates of Jerusalem. His timing could not have been better, coinciding as it did with the arrival of the Crusaders presently descending on the city from the north, dusty from months of the laborious march through the Levant.[10]

Count Dom Henrique's adventure is rarely acknowledged in history, and yet his travels to Palestine are asserted by a chronicler of the Cistercian Order, who also noted how the count was accompanied by a Portuguese monk from the Hermitage of Saint Julian.[11] Further support for this voyage comes from foreign sources—not all of them supporters of the Portuguese at that—such as Father Zapater, chronicler of the Cistercian Order in the Spanish court of Aragon.[12] A later account by a member of the Templar Order goes so far as to state that Dom Henrique "was known by Pope Urban II who named him as one of the twelve leaders of that sacred expedition."[13]

And there's more. The Cistercian monks were consummate scribblers. They wrote copious volumes chronicling the events of their day, and in one account they state that while in Palestine Dom Henrique "venerated the Sacred Places," and in return for his faithful assistance, a grateful king of Jerusalem—a Flemish knight—gave him custody of various holy relics, including the lance used at Christ's crucifixion, samples of the crown of thorns, and the cloak of Mary Magdalene.

By the end of 1099 this same king dispatched Dom Henrique back to Portucale. Upon arrival, he promptly rode to the city of Braga, accompanied by Gerard, the soon-to-be French archbishop of that city, whereupon they placed said holy relics inside its main church.

Dom Henrique subsequently spent the next couple of years traveling between the city of Coimbra (to administer to the affairs of state) and his court in Guimarães (to attend to his neglected wife, Tareja), before embarking on a second voyage to Palestine in 1103, again with the Genoese fleet, this time accompanied by Dom Mauricio, French bishop of Coimbra,[14] together with Guido of Lusitania and other nobles of the region.[15] Three years later Dom Henrique and the bishop are back in Coimbra, as evidenced by the count's signature on a document.[16]

Count Dom Henrique.

So, not only do the accounts place the ever-journeying Count of Portucale in Jerusalem at the time of the Crusade—twice—they also provide another revelation: they list by name the Flemish knight, king of Jerusalem, who originally handed him the religious artifacts for safekeeping in Portucale, for in the description of the movements of Count Dom Henrique it is written that "his valor was esteemed by Godefroi, King of Jerusalem."[17]

Which begs the question: What exactly transpired at the siege of Jerusalem, and how did a Flemish knight of average social rank attain the highest seat of power in the city of God?

7

1099. JUNE.
OUTSIDE THE GATES OF
JERUSALEM . . .

he outline of the city shimmered and refracted in the searing heat of the summer sun. Soldiers openly wept at the sight of this divine apparition, the mirage now only too real. And although they had fared better than the poorly organized People's Crusade, only about twelve thousand of the original thirty-four thousand Crusaders reached their intended destination.[1]

The terrain surrounding the hilltop city was arid from the relentless heat. Men were thirsty and hungry and insufficient in number to lay siege. All-out assault was the only choice.

Five weeks later the city walls remained resilient and impervious to all attacks. Better news arrived on June 17 when ships from Genoa anchored at Jaffa to provide the leaders of the armies with skilled engineers and, critically, with the expertise to built siege engines made from timber cannibalized from their own vessels.[2] The sultry air made haste impossible, until news of impending Arab reinforcements marching from Egypt motivated the Crusaders to act. With one final effort they hurled every projectile at the city walls from the north and south until the stones protecting Jerusalem finally relented. The prize was theirs.

Crusaders upon first sighting Jerusalem.

The conduct of the victors over the vanquished very much depended on who was in charge of which army, and atrocities, as in any war, became standard practice, "the juxtaposition of extreme violence and anguished faith."[3] The air of disgust from some Crusaders was impaled on the odor of depravity of the rest, but the same was true of the Arabs, who massacred all the captives they had held prisoner inside a mosque.

A week after the adrenalin of war subsided, a council was held in the refreshing interior of the Church of the Holy Sepulcher on July 22, the feast day of Mary Magdalene, to deliberate on the election of a king for Jerusalem. Of all the leaders whose names were volunteered, one stood above the others by seniority alone: Comte Raimond de Toulouse, highly admired as a fighter and the first to volunteer for the Crusade back on that fateful November day in Clermont. But in the end the votes were awarded to the one man who had not sought any. By his own deeds Godefroi de Bouillon had proven himself to be valiant, discreet, worthy, and modest. His own servants, in private counsel, testified to his "possession of the virtues which are put in practice without any show." His ideals for the common man impressed even the Arab sheiks, who marveled at the modesty of the Flemish prince, for when they came to make offerings to Godefroi they were surprised by a royal tent bereft of silk and its king content with squatting on a bail of straw. Made aware of their comments, Godefroi elucidated that "man must remember that he is only dust and will return to dust."[4]

Godefroi had marched all the way to the Holy City on one principle: to liberate the Holy Sepulcher. Personal gain had not been his motivation. When presented with the title king of Jerusalem he politely refused to be crowned, accepting instead the alternative title Advocatus Sancti Sepulchri (defender of the Holy Sepulcher) and adopting the informal term *princeps* (first citizen). As he would later state, "I will never wear a crown of gold in the place where the Savior of the world was crowned with thorns."[5]

Urban II, whose words had set these events in motion, for better or worse, would never learn of the developments taking place in Jerusalem, for he died barely two weeks after the siege ended and before news of it reached his ear.

Meanwhile, the indefatigable Godefroi de Bouillon made his way through the southern Gate of Sion and beyond the walls of Jerusalem, to a trail leading up a short incline to a limestone hill where, according to tradition, the Virgin Mary passed into eternity and her son performed the Last Supper. On this sacred space Godefroi observed the shell of a church, the Hagia Sion, the Byzantine Basilica of the Assumption. The dilapidated building was hardly fit for habitation, let alone a king, and its position beyond the protective walls of the city would make it hard to defend, if and when the Arab armies returned. Nevertheless, Godefroi took up residence. But he was not to live there alone, for he was promptly joined by a chapter of Augustinian canons,[6] along with a religious icon in his own right, Peter the Hermit.[7]

It turns out that, far from being some moribund evangelist, Peter was regarded with great esteem, because shortly after the capture of Jerusalem the Crusaders embarked on another military campaign and left the monk temporarily in charge of the entire city. Peter the Hermit eventually returned to France to become prior of a church of the Holy Sepulcher, which he founded before entering into retirement near Huy, where he also founded a monastery.[8] His contemporaries were not ungrateful, nor did they forget his contribution to the purer ideals of Christianity.

The faithful, dwellers at Jerusalem, who, four or five years before had seen the venerable Peter there, recognizing at that time in the same city him to whom the patriarch had committed letters invoking the aid of the princes of the West, bent the knee before him, and offered him their respects in all humility. They recalled to mind the circumstances of his first voyage; and they praised the Lord who had endowed him with effectual power of speech and with strength to rouse up nations and kings to bear so many and such long toils for love of the name of Christ. Both in private and in public all the faithful at Jerusalem exerted themselves to render to Peter the Hermit the highest honors, and attributed to him alone, after God, their happiness in having escaped from the hard servitude under which they had been for so many years groaning, and in seeing the holy city recovering her ancient freedom.[9]

Godefroi de Bouillon.

Curiously, also taking up residence with Peter, Godefroi de Bouillon, and the canons in the tumbledown basilica was a further group of monks from Orval under the direction of an abbot.[10] Somehow Godefroi's odd choice of home on Mount Sion, along with Peter and the monks from Orval, had all the appearances of a premeditated agreement.

n 1070 a group of monks made their way from Calabria in southern Italy to Orval in Upper Lorraine, a grand adventure of 1,200 miles, and appeared on the doorstep of Mathilde de Toscane, Countess de Briey. The monks had come to take charge of a tract of land kindly granted by the countess and her husband.[1]

This graceful land had been a sacred place for centuries, and since at least the ninth century a chapel had stood there. Now it was the monks' turn to leave their mark. They needed a quiet place to do their business and quickly set about building a monastery, thanks to the generosity of their new patrons.

It is a mystery why a group of monks—led by an individual named Ursus (Bear)—should have ventured so far in search of peace and tranquillity. It has been suggested they harbored secret scrolls and other long-suppressed material pertaining to ancient Mysteries, as well as evidence of records relating to a holy bloodline; indeed the land in and around Orval was once associated with a Merovingian bloodline. What is certain is the monks had recently escaped persecution in Jerusalem by sailing to Calabria and the safety of monasteries in Sicily, then made their way north via Burgundy and Champagne to meet with people

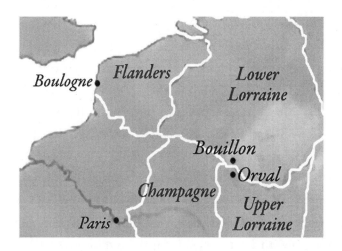

who were friendly to whatever cause they harbored.[2] Perhaps an examination of their patron, Mathilde de Toscanne, will present an answer.

Mathilde was an Italian noblewoman and a fief of the comte de Champagne and, briefly, wife of Godefroi the Hunchback.[3] She was also aunt and foster mother to a ten-year-old nephew who was himself of Merovingian descent and whose name was Godefroi.[4] Some years later this exceptionally pious young man would inherit this land, become a knight, acquire the title de Bouillon, liberate the Church of the Holy Sepulcher, and be king of Jerusalem.

It takes quite an effort to erect a monastery, and yet less than forty years into its construction the monks at Orval just packed up their meager belongings and vanished as mysteriously as they'd appeared. Some say they departed for the Holy Land because their sect already possessed a church in Jerusalem. Indeed, this may be true, for the monks are said to have been associated with a certain Ordre de Sion—the namesake of the hill outside Jerusalem and its run-down basilica, which a grown-up Godefroi de Bouillon would call home after becoming protector of the city.

Of great interest is the identity of one of the original monks at Orval, a noble who renounced his worldly possessions to lead an ascetic life, a certain Peter the Hermit.[5] Peter was a vassal of Eustache de Boulogne, who happened to be the father of Godefroi de Bouillon.[6]

When these two men met at Orval, Godefroi was a mere ten years of age. It is probable that Peter became a tutor to the impressionable young man, and if so, the monk's view of the world must have imprinted itself on young Godefroi, given how their friendship remained true over the course of thirty years, right up to that fateful day when Godefroi's crusading army picked Peter's emaciated body up off the dirt road near Antioch.

The story sounds like a meticulously executed plan, perhaps because it is reasonable to assume it was. Various chroniclers and historians, both contemporary and modern, have suggested that a small, tight-knit enclave of highly influential people lay behind Godefroi's initial motivation to march on Jerusalem to relieve the Holy Sepulcher of infidels, even in installing him as king; at one time this group may even have been involved with restoring the Merovingian bloodline in Lorraine.[7] Albert of Aachen, a historian who traveled with the First Crusade, describes a small group of knights who were separate and close to Godefroi, whom he refers to as *clientele Godefridi* and *domus Godefridi,* consisting of clergymen and close relatives, quite possibly family.

All these connections converged in 1099 in a freshly reconquered Jerusalem.

It is said that Godefroi assisted a group of monks from Orval in taking up residence in the compound of holy buildings on Mount Sion, the high ground barely half a mile from the site of Solomon's Temple, then installed an order of twelve knights to protect it.[8] One account says of this, "There were in Jerusalem during the Crusades . . . knights attached to the Abbey of Notre Dame de Sion who took the name of Chevaliers de l'Ordre de Notre Dame de Sion."[9] The commune became known as Sainte-Marie du Mont Syon et du Saint-Esprit.[10]

But what was so special about Mount Sion—and its dilapidated church in particular—that drew so much attention that monks, knights, even the protector of Jerusalem himself chose it above all other domiciles, despite its exposed location? Were they simply paying homage to their faith, motivated by a promise in the Bible "You come to Mount

Sion, to the city of the living God, the heavenly Jerusalem, and to an innumerable company of angels"?[11]

Indeed, the rock of Sion does receive an unusual amount of attention throughout the Bible, where it is regularly referred to as a stone that is overlooked during the building of the temple that must be retrieved and incorporated as the structure's keystone.* This "precious cornerstone" of the New Jerusalem described in the Book of Isaiah[12] is similarly identified in Islamic scholarship as the cornerstone of the Ka'Ba in Mecca[13]—the holiest of Muslim shrines—and by the prophet Mohammed, who refers to it as Sahyun.[14] The origin of the word *sion* is related to the Arabic *sahi* (ascend to the top)[15] a metaphor that suggests the hill is somehow associated with a process of rising, perhaps where the Mysteries of initiation and resurrection were conducted.

The Arabic interpretation is echoed in Jewish Kaballah, where the reference to Sion assumes an esoteric mantle as Tzion, a spiritual point from which all reality emerges. It is the center of existence, nay, the purpose of existence itself, the underlying goal of life. As Rabbi Heshy Grossman describes it, "There is a purpose and theme that unites all of creation. Just as the center of a sphere, which is the common point unifying every extremity on its surface, so too Tsion is the 'Tachlis' that all of life aspires to . . . and it has the power on earth to wake us from our stupor and remind us of Heaven."[16]

The Byzantine basilica on Mount Sion stood on the site of an earlier community of Essenes who lived there during the era of John the Baptist and who granted Jesus the use of their ritual room in order for him to conduct his own ritual, the Last Supper. Following the

---

*See Psalms 118:22: "The stone which the builders refused is become the head stone of the corner"; in Acts 4:10–11: "By the name Jesus Christ of Nazareth . . . doth this man stand here before you whole. This is the stone which was set at nought of you builders, which is become the head of the corner." And in 1 Peter 2:3–86: "The Lord is gracious. To whom coming, as unto a living stone, disallowed indeed of men, but chosen of God, and precious. Ye also, as lovely stones, are built up a spiritual house, a Holy priesthood, to offer up spiritual sacrifices. . . . Behold I lay in Sion a chief corner stone, elect, precious: and he that believeth on him shall not be confounded."

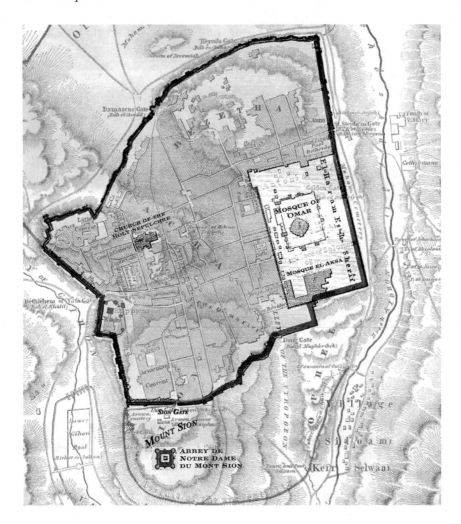

destruction of the city in AD 68, a new sanctuary was erected. Emperor Hadrian saw the tiny building still intact during his visit to the city following the Roman rampage, and even by his time it was already referred to as the Mother of All Churches, built as it was over the tomb of King David and probably an even older temple.*[17] By the fourth century this small church was enlarged into the Byzantine Hagia Sion, but in the waning and waxing political fortunes of subsequent centuries the hon-

---

*These historical accounts were validated by archaeological digs that uncovered the Gate of the Essenes along with the large stone baths used by the sect in their rituals.

orable basilica inevitably fell into disrepair. It was its empty shell that Godefroi de Bouillon recycled when he expressly ordered the reconstruction of the new Abbey de Notre Dame. Interestingly, Godefroi made additions to the original floor plan. One room in particular was named the Chamber of Mysteries. It was supported on a foundation of eight pillars and built right above the tomb of King David, the room associated with the Last Supper.[18]

Godefroi's refurbished abbey became a self-contained community, heavily fortified, with high walls and battlements. Not only was it an unusual deviation from standard ecclesiastical building procedure, it also was totally out of character for a place of worship, as though the architect intended to keep something very secret. A place of veneration, after all, is supposed to beckon the faithful, not scream "go away!" Of all the real estate available to him in Jerusalem, Godefroi not only chose a property outside the city and in a state of total disrepair, he also picked one with a legacy of sacred space spanning at least two thousand years by his time. And now that we know the origin of events surrounding young Godefroi's life in Orval, none of this appears to have been by accident: Peter the Hermit and a group of monks arrive from Calabria to build a monastery on land owned by Godefroi's aunt, claim their seat to be the church on Mount Sion, and during their tenure there, become associated with the name Ordre de Sion.

One document goes so far as to claim the Ordre de Sion was founded in 1090 by Godefroi de Bouillon himself—six years before the Crusaders marched to Jerusalem—while another states the founding date as 1099.[19] Depending on the point of view, both could be right. A plan may have been initially drawn up between Peter the Hermit, the Calabrian monks, and Godefroi, then executed nine years later thanks to the convenient timing of a Crusade marching on Jerusalem, which allowed for the city to become accessible once again to Christians.

If the Ordre de Sion was indeed an echo of a former sect with a long history on Mount Sion—the Essenes—changing circumstances and war would have rendered its *corpus* dormant for a thousand years, and in returning to Jerusalem the brotherhood was merely recovering its original place of veneration. By rebuilding the abbey Godefroi helped the brotherhood reestablish its long-lost physical domicile on that hill.

Whatever went on inside the abbey's compound, it was conducted within a perimeter built more like a fortress than a church and pursued with utmost conviction, tenacity, and secrecy,[20] as though the Ordre de Sion was engaged in some crucial yet undisclosed plan, to all intents and purposes behaving like a secret society pursuing a holy grail.

One of the alleged aims of the Ordre de Sion was to allow eligible Muslims, Jews, and people of other denominations to be allied to a Christian Order that in time would evolve into another equally secretive Order, the Knights Templar.[21] Indeed, it is documented that the closeted brotherhood inhabiting the Abbey de Notre Dame du Mont de Sion did maintain close bonds with the future Templars, the relationship revealed in a ceremony performed at Gisors, France, eighty-eight years after Godefroi de Bouillon exercised his plan in Jerusalem.*[22] And as we shall soon discover, the cooperation between these two brotherhoods became integral to the creation of a nation-state on the other side of the Mediterranean.

The Ordre de Sion had a second stated aim, and it involved the reestablishment of the Merovingian bloodline.[23]

The Merovingian bloodline is a messianic lineage of priest-kings, in the Egyptian and Sumerian tradition, whose history possesses near mythical status and claims direct descent from the Sicambrians, a branch of the Trojan royal family who settled along the river Danube and eventually in the area covered by the duchies of Lorraine and Flanders.[24] Unlike created kings, their succession was automatic by virtue of hallowed appointment.[25] Their name stems from *merovie* or *meruvie*, meaning "sea of life" or "source of life,"[26] and as such, their kings were considered vessels of a sacred water that was transmitted

---

*This was the Cutting of the Elm in 1188, when the two Orders made a formal split following an unspecified betrayal by the then Templar Grand Master, Gerard de Richfort.

down a lineage of priest-kings known as the People of the Bear. Their practices were similar to those of the Druids, Sumerian magi, even early Nazarites; like the Celts of Porto Cale they followed the goddess Anu. They were regarded as highly spiritual people, teachers, and healers; they were well versed in the esoteric sciences, and possessed clairvoyant ability. Their principal interests were education, agriculture, and maritime trade, and their belief in wisdom, insight, and the divine harmony in nature was represented by their adopted symbol, the bee—the same sacred emblem of ancient Egyptian and Sumerian royalty.

These attributes will be of central interest in the development of our story, but for now the following five points are of prime concern:

- After migrating to central Europe, the Sicambrians/Merovingians became closely associated with the Burgundians.
- One of their most important cities was named in honor of their Trojan heritage: Troyes, in Champagne.
- Their revered model was King Solomon and his temple.
- The Roman Catholic Church's focus on eradicating their bloodline bordered on the fanatical.
- According to legend, people of their lineage bore a distinctive "birthmark" in the form of a red cross on their chest.[27]

It has long been claimed that the Ordre de Sion was instrumental in electing the kings of Jerusalem, and if so, such an organization would have been invested with enormous power, for in those days the appointment of kings was the sole domain of the pope. The Ordre de Sion may have asserted that power, for shortly after the conquest of Jerusalem, a secret conclave, featuring a bishop from Calabria, met in the Church of the Holy Sepulcher to elect a king of the city[28]—Godefroi de Bouillon, a knight of the Merovingian bloodline.[29]

Sadly, Godefroi's enjoyment of his tenure as patriarch was brief, for he died a year after conquering the city, poisoned by Muslim leaders at a banquet under the ruse of a peace treaty: "The Muslim leaders . . . brought supplies and served them in his presence. Godefroi accepted and unsuspectingly ate the dishes they presented, which were poisoned. He died several days later along with forty other people."[30] The crown he never wore was immediately passed to his younger brother, Baudoin, who was crowned first Latin king of Jerusalem on the winter solstice, a highly symbolic pagan celebration of the day when the sun begins its triumphant journey over the days of darkness.

A foremost authority on the Crusades states that Baudoin I, like his brother, came from a royal tradition founded on the rock of Sion that was equal to the reigning dynasties of Europe, a kind of holy bloodline.[31] As with the appointment of Godefroi, the Ordre de Sion appears to have been behind his brother's election, for it was claimed that Baudoin I "owed his throne" to the Ordre, whose seat was the Abbey de Notre Dame du Mont de Sion.[32]

But the creation of kings was not the only thing to come out of

Abbey de Notre Dame du Mont de Sion.

the abbey that Godefroi rebuilt and the Ordre de Sion inhabited. The abbey was also the domicile of a man whose background would form a bridge between the nascent Templars and their involvement in the creation of a nation-state on the opposite side of Europe. An original document bears the seal of the Ordre de Sion, "represented on one side by the Pentecost with the phrase *sigil. spe. sci. de monte syon* and on the other side, an image of the death of the Virgin . . . with the inscription *transitus dei genitricis.*"[33] The document is signed by the prior of Notre Dame du Mont de Sion, a certain Arnaldus, or as he was better known in the Portuguese city of Braga, Arnaldo da Rocha.[34]

1114.
BRAGA. A VERY OLD CITY IN
PORTUGALE . . .

long line of lords, townspeople, and country folk stood on either side of the nine miles of dirt road connecting Guimarães with the cathedral city of Braga. It was the beginning of May and the Celtic fertility feast of Beltane, but there was little to celebrate. Along the final stretch of gray cobblestones leading to the cathedral, a solemn procession carried the casket of a dignified Burgundian knight who had been born in Dijon and died in the small territory he carefully cultivated eight hundred miles from his birthplace, deeded to him by his father-in-law, King Alfonso VI of Castilla e León.

At fifty-five years of age Count Dom Henrique the Good, father of the county of Portucale, was dead.

In his time he had been much admired by his subjects, whose quality of life he raised by making a priority of education and the husbandry of the land. He would leave behind his wife, Tareja, to act as regent for their five-year-old son, Afonso Henriques, who, with good fortune, would complete his father's dream: the establishment of an independent state of Portucale, an idea the count had set in motion a few years earlier while taking advantage of the civil war raging in Castilla e León following the death of its king, the very man who awarded Dom Henrique

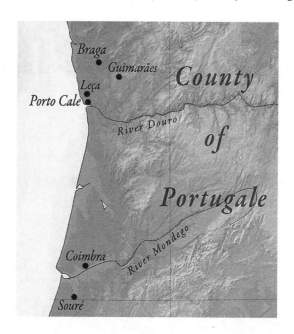

his territory. Even now the county was referred to in the softer local
dialect—Portugale.

And so on this somber day in 1114 began the adult life of the child
Afonso, surrounded by the austere granite of the cathedral of Braga.[*1]

Afonso could not have imagined he would rise to power with
the help of a fraternity of spiritual knights with whom his father had
become involved—in their embryonic stage—during his voyages to
Jerusalem or that the activities of the brotherhood would be centered
unequivocally around the city of Braga.

By all surviving accounts, Braga is the oldest Portuguese city and
one of the oldest in Iberia, allegedly founded by Teukros, son of the
Greek king Telamon, who fought in the Trojan War even though he
was related to the royal family of Troy. The legends may well be correct.
After the war Teukros moved to Cyprus and founded the city of Salamis
before departing westward along the Mediterranean, sailing through the
Pillars of Heracles, then turning north along the Lusitanian coast before

---

*The author Herculano posits that Count Dom Henrique died naturally in 1114, and
that his official death of 1112 was popularized to coincide with his injuries in battle.

Count Dom Henrique at rest.

disembarking in the town of Porto Cale. This dates the founding of nearby Braga to around 1190 BC.[2] Hellenistic presence in this part of the world is strong, with other Greek settlements founded nearby at Tuy and Hellene.[3] Brutus of Troy is also known to have sailed here circa 1100 BC with a large contingent of fellow countrymen on his way to southern Britain, where by the banks of the river Isis, or Tammuz, he founded the city of Caer Troyus, later renamed Llandin. We know these landmarks today as the river Thames and the city of London.[4] Certainly, there still lingers a great kinship between the Greek/Trojan and Portuguese cultures to this day, but little love for the Romans. Much to the embarrassment of Rome, during a forty-year siege of Braga even the women joined in to defeat its legions, leaving six thousand soldiers dead.[5]

Myths also link the founding of Braga with the Egyptian god of resurrection, Osiris, and a temple dedicated to his wife Isis still existed in AD 44. The cult of Isis was venerated throughout the region and

Stone in Braga cathedral marking the temple of Isis.

partly lent its name to the nearby province of Gallissa.[6] There was also a temple in the city dedicated to the god of two faces, Baal-Ianus, symbolizing the balance of opposing forces; a street still honors the location today.[7] Indeed, ancient esoteric roots run very deep here, as they do along much of northern Iberia through to Gaul, for it was an area where the teachings of Priscillian were held in high esteem.

Priscillian was a fourth-century bishop, mystic, and theologian, and the first person in the history of Christianity to be executed for heresy— or to be legally precise, for the practice of magic. As with later characters such as Walter the Penniless and Peter the Hermit, Priscillian was a rich noble who renounced his material possessions in favor of ascetic mysticism, and through a classical pagan education came to the understanding that true Christian principles require a mystical and continual intercourse with God.[8] To prove it he upheld the esoteric Christian ethos, "Know ye not that ye are the temple of God?" and argued that to make itself a vessel fit for the habitation of the divine a person must renounce material goods, do works of love, and above all—and this will come as no surprise—practice a hard asceticism.[9]

Priscillian founded a group that subsisted for several centuries despite persistent persecution. Naturally, his growing appeal among large numbers of followers threatened the growing authority of the Catholic Church, which led to trumped up charges of heresy. Priscillian responded with an appeal to both the Holy Roman emperor and the pope, for which he and six of his followers were beheaded—the first Christian heretics murdered by Christians. Thus Priscillianism was quite at home in Portugale and Braga, places with a long appetite for the independent of spirit.

Ancient Braga suffered heavily throughout the Dark Ages, when waves of barbarian Sueves, Vandals, and Visigoths swooped in from central Europe to rob, pillage, desecrate, violate, murder, rape, and generally lay waste to any land they touched. The Catholics who followed appear to have behaved no better, as did the Saracens and Moors afterward, who in their ignorance and savagery turned much of the ancient city into rubble. Only during the eighth century did some sense of civilization return to the region when Affonso I, king of Asturias, won back the cathedral cities and ordered the new bishops to reform the depraved ways of the Christians, that good laws be passed for the people of the land, and most astonishing of all, that the old pagan temples be venerated once more.[10]

Then, thanks to an enlightened Burgundian knight who became count of Portucale, Braga experiences a renaissance.

In 1089 Count Dom Henrique and Bishop Gerald de Moissac consecrated the ground occupied by the former temple of Isis and continued the honoring of the divine feminine by constructing a new church and chapel dedicated to Notre Dame.* Among several treasures placed inside is the arm of Saint Luke that Dom Henrique himself brought back from one of his two journeys to Jerusalem.[11] And so by his deeds

---

*In Portuguese, Nossa Senhora de Santa Maria

the count raised Braga to become one of the most important bishoprics in the Iberian Peninsula, and the humble church eventually soared into a grand cathedral.

Whether or not the count was feeling homesick, his suggestion of architectural style was modeled on the monastery church of Cluny back in his Burgundian homeland. The ultimate irony is that in erecting this good work for the love of God and paying for it out of his own pocket, Dom Henrique was eventually laid to rest inside its solid granite walls.[12]

Given the local inhabitants' deep-rooted penchant for independence and respect of pagan traditions (*pagan* meaning "countrydweller"), it is not surprising that the city of Braga and its surrounding area should have become a magnet for people sharing similar ideals and wishing to practice them in relative peace—such as a small brotherhood of monks and spiritual knights who in time became known as the Knights Templar.

At the time of Count Dom Henriques' death in 1114 the Order of the Temple was still in its embryonic stage in Jerusalem, but according to historical accounts the Templars were already present in Portugale by his date: "After D. Affonso VI married his daughter to Count Dom Henrique, they [the Templars] always came to his aid, and did not stop doing so even after the death of his son."[13] An independent German source also states categorically that the proto-Templars forged a working relationship with Count Dom Henrique: "The acquisition of an important property, such as that of the castle of Souré, which was given to them [the Order of the Temple] by Count Henrique in 1111 proves that these knights had already rendered some services, and that he was convinced of their usefulness."[14]

These statements are told by historians with no ax to grind, so there is no reason to believe the claims were invented out of thin air, and yet the repercussions are explosive given what is historically accepted about the foundation of the Templars. If Dom Henrique donated a castle to the Templars in 1111 it establishes their presence in the county of Portugale seven years prior to their founding date and a full seventeen before their acknowledgment by the pope—the point at which the brotherhood of nine original knights became official in the eyes of the world.

The presence of the Knights Templar in Portugale, years before their accepted creation, makes for all kinds of tantalizing conjectures: for instance, what business could a small band of knights possibly be conducting in a faraway county when their base of operation lay at the opposite end of the Mediterranean?

A close examination of surviving documents shows how this brotherhood is sometimes referred to as Templars and sometimes as Order of the Temple or Knights of Solomon, and these titles were often interchangeable. And they were by no means the only group of knights residing in Jerusalem, but one of four.

As we already know, after the battle of Jerusalem, Godefroi de Bouillon installed a group of knights in the Abbey of Mount Sion, and they were appropriately named the Chevaliers de l'Ordre de Notre Dame de Sion, that is, the Knights of the Order of Our Lady of Sion.[15] Of these, virtually no information survives; the knights and their movements remain as mysterious as the monks of the Ordre de Sion whom they protected. Even so, this fraternity was preceded by another group of knights. Toward the end of the eleventh century, Italian merchants from Amalfi purchased a piece of land in the Christian quarter of Jerusalem, where they built two hospitals and two chapels to care for the sick and the poor. After the reconquest, the growing numbers of pilgrims flocking to Jerusalem required an infrastructure to meet their needs for food and lodging. This was provided by the Amalfi Hostelry, and within the compound of this hospital there grew a body of horsemen and foot soldiers who took it upon themselves to protect the pilgrims, giving rise to the Knights Hospitaller.

Then there was a third group, also nonmilitary in nature, comprising twenty monks, along with twelve knights to protect them, a total of thirty-two,[16] also installed by Godefroi de Bouillon in the church where Christ was interred. It became known as the Order of the Knights of the Holy Sepulcher. According to the thirteenth-century chronicle by

Bernard the Treasurer, within this rapidly expanding Milities Sancti Sepulchi[17] there was said to exist a small fraternity of knights with far different ideals, a brotherhood within a brotherhood,[18] and although their liturgy was that of the church—l'ordinaire del Sepulchre—their practices were far more spiritual in nature compared with the rest of the knights. These men were led by a man named Hugues de Payns, and they later built octagonal churches inspired by the church in which they resided.[19]

Hugues de Payns was a noble from Burgundy who spent a considerable part of his life traveling throughout Asia Minor. According to a contemporary account, this man:

> went to Jerusalem on pilgrimage. Having heard that at a cistern just outside Jerusalem, Christians watering their horses were frequently ambushed and killed in pagan attacks, he took pity on them. Moved by a strong feeling of justice, he defended them to the best of his ability, often lying in ambush himself and then coming to their aid, killing several of the enemy. The pagans were shaken by this and they set up camp in such numbers that nobody would be able to counter the attacks. The result was that the cistern had to be abandoned. But Payns, who was a man of energy and not easily defeated, obtained help for himself and for God after a lot of effort. From the Regular Canons of the Temple of the Lord [the Holy Sepulcher] he acquired by means at his disposal a large house within the precincts of the Temple. He lived there poorly dressed and ill-fed, spending everything he had on horses and arms, using all means of persuasion and pleading to enlist whatever pilgrim-soldiers he could either for permanent service there to the Lord or at least for temporary duty. Then, strictly according to rank and duty he fixed for himself and his fellow knights the insignia of the cross or the shield, imposing on his men a regime of chastity and sobriety.[20]

This brotherhood lived among the Knights of the Holy Sepulcher for about fourteen years before something compelled them to move a few blocks away to Temple Mount. At that moment, the fourth group, the Knights Templar, were born.

Portuguese chroniclers make very clear distinctions between the Knights Templar, Knights Hospitaller, and Knights of the Holy Sepulcher, that they were co-dependent and cooperative entities, and that all three were either influential or directly involved in the creation of Portugal as a nation-state.*[21]

The Knights Hospitaller[†] were the first group to appear in Portugale, in 1104,[22] shortly after Count Dom Henrique returned from his first voyage to the Holy Land. It is reasonable to assume they came at his invitation, and their residence would have been near the royal household. Indeed, the Hospitallers' first recorded conventual house in 1112 was located by the river in Leça,[23] a small town one league from the city of Porto Cale and twenty-five from the royal household in Guimarães. Built on the site of a previous Roman temple dedicated to Jupiter, it became the Hospitallers' primary chapter house and consisted of a hospital, a monastery, and several homes where the monks lived as regular canons.

Like the Knights Hospitaller, the Knights of the Holy Sepulcher were also present in Portugale from an early date; in fact, the Order expanded considerably thanks to properties donated by the widow Countess Tareja during her reign as regent, in continuation of the tradition begun by her late husband,[24] as well as from private donations such as the one by "Emisa Trastemiriz, wife of D. Egas Mendes, of the convent of Pendorara with all its rights to the Saint Sepulcher."[25] Two decades later, the Order of the Holy Sepulcher was still residing near Porto Cale, in a monastery under the ownership of the Knights Hospitaller.[26]

The glaring anomaly in the story is the aforementioned donation of the castle of Souré by Count Dom Henrique in 1111 to the Order of

---

*A *nation-state* is defined as a political unit consisting of an autonomous state inhabited predominantly by a people sharing a common culture, history, and language. According to Jenkins and Sofos (*Nation and Identity, 155*), "Portugal lays claim to be the oldest nation-state in Europe, usually dated from as early as 1139."
†Also referred to as the Order of the Hospital.

the Temple. At that time the Knights Templar simply did not exist, that name was still seven years in the future. And yet Dom Henrique would hardly have awarded a castle to a nonexistent entity.

There is one possibility. It has been repeatedly suggested that Hugues de Payns, together with his partner, the Flemish knight Godefroi de Saint-Omer, had designs on Temple Mount from the moment they took up residence in the Church of the Holy Sepulcher. Is it possible they and their small group of nine knights were secretly addressing themselves as the Order of the Temple in anticipation of the day they moved to Temple Mount? Hugues de Payns arrived in Jerusalem the same year Count Dom Henrique was stationed there, and it is natural to assume the two Burgundian knights established a friendship. If so, Dom Henrique was privy to inside information on Hugues de Payns' plans, and if these two leaders established an accord, Dom Henrique's awarding of a castle to Hugues and his proto-Templars makes perfect sense.

The donation of Souré gave the proto-Templars a foothold in Portugale. But shortly before he passed away Dom Henrique signed another document providing them with a second, a residence in the city of Braga donated by a member of the clergy. It is very simple to locate this property because it is described as being "beside a Templar hospital," which would be the hospital for the poor founded by Archbishop Payo Mendes of Braga, "annexed to the main houses he had earlier donated to the Templars in the hermitage."[27]

That's a lot of properties donated to the proto-Templars by a high-ranking clergyman. In those days it was customary to give property *to* the church, not the other way around! What is even more interesting is that said hospital in Braga had previously been in the possession of the Knights Hospitaller, who transferred ownership to said archbishop; two days later, Payo Mendes donated it to the Order of the Temple.[28] In the glacially moving world of real estate deals, this is an extraordinarily rapid series of transactions. Why the haste?

Mendes had the deed countersigned by Dom Henrique. A head of

Templar font, Cathedral of Braga.

state would hardly be called into to a real estate transaction unless he had a vested interest in one of its parties or stood to gain from such a deal, and given how the count was already in the late stages of the illness that ultimately claimed his life, the latter motive can be ruled out.[29] However, with the property underwritten by the Count of Portugale, the Order of the Temple was guaranteed a domicile regardless of whether Dom Henrique lived or died. In the end, this transaction served the proto-Templars well, for it would become their center of operations, a fact openly asserted by a later Templar Master in his own words, "De Domo Templi, quae est in Bracharensi Civitate (the home of the Temple, which is in the city of Braga)."[30]

Whatever elaborate plans were made in Jerusalem between Count Dom Henrique, his friend Godefroi de Bouillon, Hugues de Payns, and the Order of the Temple, they were most likely put on hold following the count's untimely death. With his five-year-old son Afonso far too young to rule, the opportune moment to set things in motion would have to wait.

10

1100.
JERUSALEM. IN THE PALACE
OF THE NEW KING . . .

Just as the sultry days in the holy city were replaced by the cooler climes of November, so the deceased Godefroi de Bouillon was succeeded by his colder and tougher Burgundian brother, Baudoin. The new king was described as "very tall and much larger than his brother . . . of rather light complexion, with dark-brown hair and beard. His nose was aquiline and his upper lip somewhat prominent. The lower jaw slightly receded, although not so much that it could be considered a defect. He was dignified in carriage and serious in dress and speech. He always wore a mantle hanging from his shoulders. . . . [He] was neither stout nor unduly thin, but rather of a medium habit of body. Expert in the use of arms, agile on horseback, he was active and diligent whenever the affairs of the realm called him."[1]

From the start, Baudoin I's attention was focused more on logistical problems of state that on ecclesiastical pursuits. He inherited a kingdom more isolated than before, cut off from the north and the sea by minor Moslem emirates and by the failure to establish a permanent overland route from Europe. The fortress towns remained scattered among a countryside made more hostile by brigands, arrogant Crusaders, and local mercenaries.[2]

Throughout his reign Baudoin I would deal with countless attempts by small Muslim armies to retake Jerusalem while chipping away at outlying settlements suffering from a lack of trained men to adequately garrison castles and towns. There was the problem of depopulation after the conquest, and many Crusaders returned to their homelands now that their vows were fulfilled, leaving too few remaining citizens to adequately defend the entire city.[3] To add to the king's civic woes, the city's treasury was bankrupt.

Meanwhile, the perils of the pilgrim trail did not diminish, and various firsthand accounts describe the insecurity of walking the 33-mile route from the port of Jaffa to Jerusalem. The Norse pilgrim Saewulf, who attempted the journey in 1102, described corpses of attacked victims rotting by the side of the road due to the soil being too hard to dig and the people willing to bury them being wise not to linger lest they too should be attacked.[4] Ambushes were frequent, by Saracens, by brigands, sometimes by mountain lions; survivors would then have to contend with sunstroke and restricted access to well water.

Still, behind all the drama, Baudoin played an important role in nurturing the seed of the future Knights Templar that had been planted in the Church of the Holy Sepulcher by his late brother Godefroi. At some point there came the need for this brotherhood, set up by Hugues de Payns, to leave the church. Perhaps there was a gulf dividing the ethics of the knights following Hugues's moral example, and the others who grew bored from lack of fighting and got drunk. Such misconduct was sufficient for Hugues, along with his colleague Godefroi de Saint-Omer and a small band of knights, to go visit Baudoin and ask the king for assistance.[5]

11

1100.
BRAGA. HEARING FOREIGN
VOICES . . .

It was not uncommon to hear people in the streets of Braga speaking in their native French tongue. By the mid-eleventh century there already existed a conclave of Burgundians living in and around the city,[1] as though the area was their medieval holiday resort.[2] One of these people was Pedro Arnaldo da Rocha, son of the family de la Roche from the Burgundian county of Roche, which they owned.*

At some point the smell of the ocean enticed two family members to relocate from Burgundy to a small coastal village not far from Braga.[3] En route Madame de la Roche gave birth to Pierre Arnolde in the Portuguese riverside city of Santa Erea.†[4]

Pierre Arnolde became Pedro Arnaldo in his new home, and his role in the creation of a Portuguese nation-state begins with a short, casual statement made in the archives of the Cistercian monastery of Alcobaça, in a black book with a white border titled *Second Part of the Codex Alcobaciensis,* where exists the following entry: "Hujus tempore moritur Arnandus, qui juvenis ivit ad bellum Syriae cum bono Comite

---

*Now the community of La Roche Vanneau.
†Today known as Santarém.

Henrico, e multa fortia egerat" (This is the time of Arnando's death, who as a young man went to war in Syria with good Count Henrique, and many great deeds he has done).[5]

Arnaldo da Rocha would have been between twenty and thirty years of age when he accompanied the Count of Portugale to the Holy Land, and for such a situation to have taken place there must have existed a close bond between the two men. Obviously, they shared the same Burgundian heritage, with the de la Roche property actually situated within the district of Dijon, Dom Henrique's birthplace; one family member was even employed as a steward of the Duke of Burgundy, from whom Dom Henrique was descended.[6] When the de la Roche family settled in Portugale they chose the town of Vianna, 33 miles from the royal seat in Guimarães. With the city of Braga in-between, both families would have moved in the same social circles, even attended mass in the same cathedral.

On the journey to Jerusalem, Count Dom Henrique would no doubt have introduced Arnaldo to Godefroi de Bouillon. The count was obviously on very good terms with the princeps, seeing as how Godefroi entrusted him with holy relics such as the arm of Saint James and the cloak of Mary Magdalene. What better way than for three knights, all far from their ancestral domiciles in Burgundy and Lorraine, to spend an afternoon discussing matters of common interest, such as the improvement of the human condition, the importance of faith, and the reconquering of lands and holy places usurped by infidels. It only requires a tiny leap of imagination to see that close bonds were established between the three men, and given the intricate family ties then existing within the French nobility, it is even conceivable all three may have been related.

Arnaldo's presence in Jerusalem was very opportune, for he arrived at the moment Godefroi de Bouillon was installing members of the Ordre de Sion in the rebuilt abbey on its namesake hill. To say he made a favorable impression on the monks is an understatement, because by 1116 Pedro Arnaldo resurfaces as a full member of the Ordre, his signature inscribed on an original document from the abbey, in which he is addressed in Latin as Prior Petrus Arnaldus.[7]

Whether Prior Arnaldo became a member of the Ordre de Sion by being at the right place at the right time or whether he sailed with Count Dom Henrique with the intent to join the monks from Orval who constituted said brotherhood, we shall never know for sure, but the thread stitching all these people and events together is thick enough as to be beyond mere coincidence.

Such a position imbued Arnaldo with immense political leverage. The abbey established close ties with the nearby Church of the Holy Sepulcher right from the time both fraternities were installed by Godefroi de Bouillon. It therefore afforded its prior direct access to two people in particular—Hugues de Payns and Godefroi de Saint-Omer, the nucleus of the Order of the Temple. That relationship was revealed on July 19, 1116, when a document signed by both Prior Arnaldus and Hugues de Payns declares "good relations are assured between the two Orders."[8]

In the relationship between the Order of the Temple, the House of Burgundy, the Ordre de Sion, and the incipient Portuguese kingdom, Arnaldo da Rocha would prove to be the lynchpin. He was Portuguese by birth. His friendship with Count Dom Henrique granted him favor within the Portuguese court and, through his family's status, connections with the nobles and ecclesiasts in and around the city of Braga and the royal seat in Guimarães, many of whom were of Burgundian heritage.

But Portuguese chroniclers going back at least five centuries give Prior Arnaldo even more credit. They cite him as a key founder of the Knights Templar in Portugal, as well as one of the *original* Templars in Jerusalem: "Arnaldo da Rocha, who was a Templar knight, was one of the first nine originators of this illustrious Order of the Temple in Jerusalem,"[9] wrote the historian Alexandre Ferreira in 1735, quoting an earlier seventeenth-century source, Manuel de Faria e Sousa.[10] And Sousa would have been in an excellent position to state the facts, for not only did he study original documents in Braga—which places him in the perfect geographical location for source material—he was himself a Templar knight.*

Arnaldo da Rocha as one of the original Templars is both provocative and explosive, at the very least historically, because it brings into sharp focus an unsettling proposition: Were there really only nine original Templar knights? Or was this number merely a symbol, a talisman, the kind of flourish employed by secret societies throughout that period?

We may never know the truth for certain; however, an esteemed chronicler of the seventeenth century, the monk Bernardo de Brito, categorically stated in the Cistercian chronicles of Portugal that the original Templars consisted of "Hugues and Godefroi *and* nine other knights"[11] (emphasis added). This raises the original core group of proto-Templars to eleven.[12]

Did Brito misinterpret?

What would his motive have been?

To what end?

The point is worth considering. And so is this: throughout the ancient Mysteries schools, the number nine has represented the gnostic concept of utmost perfection. It is personified by the gestation period of the egg inside the female womb, a Holy Trinity to the power of three. In relation to our quest, there exists an arcane system of knowledge encoded within the Tarot, and although for most people the Tarot is nothing more than a set of decorative playing cards, in reality it is modeled on Kaballah, an ancient system of knowledge whose ideology is enshrined within most pagan and esoteric societies from remote times to the Middle Ages, and into the eighteenth century through speculative Freemasonry and its 33 degrees of initiation.

To the point, the ninth card in the deck of the Tarot is The Hermit. And as we have already seen, it was a hermit named Peter who, with a

---

*He was a knight of the Order of Christ, the name by which the Knights Templar would be known in Portugal after the fourteenth century.

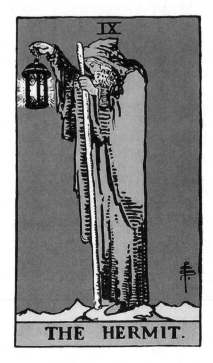

The Hermit card.

group of monks addressing themselves as the Ordre de Sion, traveled to Orval, home of Godefroi de Bouillon, the protector of the Holy Sepulcher, who subsequently installed this fraternity in the abbey he rebuilt atop Mount Sion.

And by 1116 the head of this organization is a Portuguese prior and friend of Hugues de Payns, the emerging Grand Master of a group of knights soon to be known as the Knights Templar.

12

1117.
BETHLEHEM.
AT A CEREMONY . . .

t has always been a mystery why Baudoin I also "owed his throne" to the Ordre stationed in the Abbey de Notre Dame du Mont de Sion, unless the same people who installed his late brother on the throne reconvened soon after the knight's untimely death to appoint another member of the Merovingian bloodline, thereby assuring its continuity. Part of the answer materialized in 1117 when Baudoin I negotiated one of history's most important events: the constitution of the Order of the Temple, which effectively legitimized a breakaway group of knights stationed in the Church of the Holy Sepulcher. The ceremony was performed at the site of Saint Leonard of Acre in Bethlehem, a fief belonging to the Ordre de Sion.

Baudoin is said to have undertaken this ceremony under "obligation," suggesting he owed the Ordre de Sion a big favor. In any event, the monarch's actions were timely seeing as his health was deteriorating by the day.[1] A few months later, following a march in Egypt, Baudoin fell ill once again when "he went walking along the river which the Greeks call the Nile and the Hebrews the Gihon, near the city, enjoying himself with some of his friends. Some of the knights very skillfully used their lances to spear the fish found there and carried them to their

camp near the city and ate them. Then the king felt within himself the renewed pangs of an old wound and was most seriously weakened."[2] Baudoin contracted food poisoning and was carried back to Jerusalem on a litter but died along the way. "The Franks wept, the Syrians, and even the Saracens who saw it grieved also," wrote the chronicler Fulcher de Chartres, who described him as another Joshua, "the right arm of his people, the terror and adversary of his enemies."[3]

And so on Easter Sunday 1118, yet another king of Jerusalem was chosen, Baudoin de Bourcq, cousin of Godefroi de Bouillon. Like his former family members, he too had served on the First Crusade.

Barely had Baudoin II gotten used to his newly appointed seat when he received a visit from Hugues de Payns and Godefroi de Saint-Omer, as though the two intrepid knights were presenting their credentials. They may have received a less enthusiastic reception than from his predecessor: Baudoin II was in desperate need of warrior knights above spiritual warriors. The king's position may have created an ethical dilemma for Hugues, as the contemporary account by Michael the Syrian describes how "Baudoin advised this Hou de Payn to serve in the militia as a fighter instead of taking holy orders."[4]

Hugues was a well-traveled man; he had been tested for the better part of a decade in the Near East and was familiar with the works of influential moral writers such as Guigo, prior of La Grande Chartreuse, who would warn him of the dangers of mixing military and monastic life, and no doubt the pious Hugues paid attention to such sound spiritual advice:

It is indeed pointless for us to attack exterior enemies if we do not first conquer those inside ourselves. If we are unable first to subject our own bodies to our wills, then it is extremely shameful and unworthy to wish to place under our control any sort of military force. Who could tolerate our desire to extend our domination broad over vast tracts of land abroad while we put up with the most

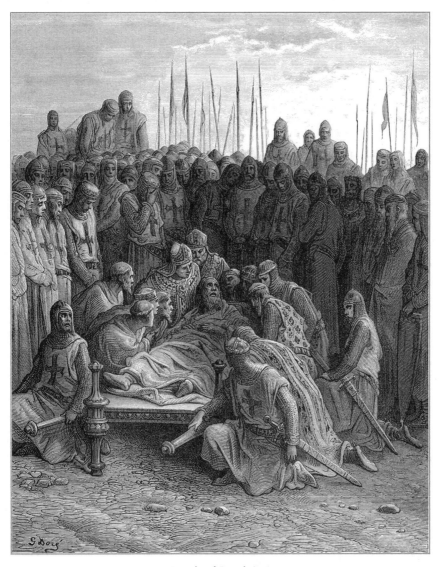

Death of Baudoin I.

ignominious servitude to vices in those minute lumps of earth that are our bodies? Let us therefore first of all conquer ourselves so that we may then go forth in safety to combat external foes; let us purge our souls of vices before we rid the lands of barbarians.[5]

And so it fell on Hugues de Payns, together with Godefroi de Saint-Omer, to repitch to the new king the importance of the mission of this "brotherhood within a brotherhood" living among the Knights of the Holy Sepulcher. Perhaps they argued the case convincingly because there is no account of this core group of knights ever having battled alongside Baudoin II.

The king mulled over Hugues's proposal. He possessed several properties in Jerusalem, one being his residence, the al-Aqsa Mosque, at the southern end of the platform of Temple Mount, the site previously occupied by Solomon's Temple. Only recently had the mosque and its adjacent buildings been converted to suit his needs. The location even held for him a certain sentimental value: a banquet had been offered there following his coronation, and a thousand years before him, it had been the place where Jesus himself had been offered. What favor, then, did these obscure knights carry that led Baudoin II to agree to vacate the holiest of sites in Jerusalem, the very rock on which Mohammed had "climbed to heaven," the site where Solomon's Temple once had stood?[6]

And that is not all. In addition to the Temple of Solomon, "The lord king together with his nobles, granted temporarily or in perpetuity certain benefices from their own holdings to cater for their food and clothing."[7] Certainly Hugues de Payns and his group were powerful. They already had the authority to appoint their own priests, a right exclusive only to the pope, and these priests not only formed the nucleus of the Order, they also were directly descended from the offices of the canons of the Holy Sepulcher.[8]

Whatever Hugues de Payns pitched to Baudoin, it sold him. Hugues and Godefroi de Saint-Omer humbly accepted the offer to move to

Baudoin II receives Hugues de Payns and Godefroi de Saint-Omer.

Temple Mount, and as a gesture of gratitude they built for the king "a splendid manor next to the Temple so that the King could reclaim his own to stay in if he wanted."[9] And so the brotherhood of knights gained independence from the Church of the Holy Sepulcher. From this moment, thirty knights, including a nucleus of nine, possibly eleven men, took up residence and became forever known as the Knights Templar.

The specific premises granted them was Solomon's stables, a space so cavernous even the German Crusader and eyewitness Jean de Würtzburg remarked, "One sees a stable of such marvelous capacity and extent that it could house more than two thousand horses or fifteen hundred camels."[10] Why did Hugues de Payns and Godefroi de Saint-Omer request a residence so grossly disproportionate to the number of knights? And why should Baudoin have unquestionably submitted to their request?

The common point of contact between the Templars and Baudoin was the Ordre de Sion: What influence did it exert on this event? We can only speculate. However, it is worth reminding ourselves of the accepted story of the origin of the Knights Templar, how they wished to serve the Christian ideal by protecting pilgrims traveling the perilous, bandit laden road from sea to shrine. The fact that this was to be accomplished by nine knights is logical proof that the legend is both preposterous and unenforceable and was thus provided as a smoke screen masking an ulterior and undisclosed motive. Besides, right from the very start, the protection of pilgrims had been entrusted to the Knights Hospitaller, who were far better equipped for the task.

During the years that followed, the Templars resided on Temple Mount and hardly left the premises, much less took an interest in safeguarding pilgrims. They were said not to have had the material resources to maintain the upkeep of their own premises, and in time the building looked as dilapidated as their clothing.[11] It is as though they adopted a monastic lifestyle or spent their time purposefully studying or planning something of such importance that demanded complete concentration. Just like that of the Ordre de Sion on the neighboring hill, the Templar's work was carried out with pathological secrecy. Archaeological accounts confirm the knights dug tunnels beneath Temple Mount, and they left behind several items that can be positively identified as Templar artifacts.[12] This has led to speculation that their real task "was to carry out research in the area in order to obtain certain relics and manuscripts which contain the essence of the secret traditions of Judaism and ancient Egypt."[13]

Baudoin I's most famous last act as king established 1118 as the founding date of the Knights Templar, at least as a coherent entity. And yet rumors persist that the concept of the Knights Templar had been around much earlier. The hypothesis is supported by a number of sources: Ernoul, a squire of the Templar knight Balian d'Ibelin, claimed the date to be earlier than 1118, as did Simon, a monk of Saint Bertin of Sith, who placed the event at 1099;[14] the eighteenth-century historian André Mende even traces the origin of the Knights Templar to 1096.[15] All of the above may in fact be correct in their own right if we stand back and look at the facts presented so far.

The seed of the idea to create an elite group of spiritual knights may have been planted in 1096 at Orval, born of discussions between Peter the Hermit, the monks from Calabria, and Godefroi de Bouillon. Upon the declaration of the first Crusade to free the city of God, this idea was given forward motion, and following the successful reconquest of Jerusalem, the plan took material form when Godefroi rebuilt the Abbey de Notre Dame du Mont de Sion and installed the monks, along with a brotherhood of twelve knights. At the same time, he installed an additional group of knights in the Church of the Holy Sepulcher, within which was planted a spiritual brotherhood led by Hugues de Payns. Like looping a circuit, this group subsequently established good relations with the Ordre de Sion.

A number of key associates and supporters of the Order of the Temple all converged in Jerusalem around this formative period, and not necessarily to take part in the reconquest of the city. For instance, the executive owner of the land at Orval and one of the Templars' original supporters, Comte Hugh de Champagne, visited the Holy Land with a group of knights, friends, and vassals as early as 1104, staying for four years before returning home.[16] Clearly something impressed him because he returned in 1114. Shortly before his second departure he received a letter from the bishop of Chartres, who wrote, "We have heard that . . . before leaving Jerusalem you made a vow to join the Militia of Christ, that you will enrol in this evangelical soldiery."[17]

If Hugh de Champagne made a vow before his return home in 1108, either there must have been a coherent group of knights already established by Hugues de Payns or the comte made contact with these knights (most of whom originated from his own duchy and those adjacent), who intended to form one by the time of his second voyage.

It is his first trip that is of interest. Comte Hugh de Champagne and Hugues de Payns were no strangers to each other; Hugues was the comte's cousin and vassal,[18] and on at least two occasions in 1100 both men were cosignatories in property transactions in the duchy of Champagne, the domicile of Hugues de Payns.[19] Besides,

Hugh de Champagne would have been privy to Hugues de Payns's intentions in the Holy Land, least of all because they spent a month together aboard a ship bound for Jerusalem. Once he set foot there, Hugues de Payns, like so many of his countrymen, made his pilgrimage to the place over which so much blood had been spilled, the Church of the Holy Sepulcher. He met with its resident knights and monks and soon after took up residence in the church's compound.

His arrival in this compact city could not have been better timed, because another Burgundian knight had recently arrived from an equally arduous sea voyage, the Count of Portugale. Dom Henrique and Hugues de Payns would have had ample time to get acquainted—two years, in fact—and this circle of friendship would inevitably have included the man traveling with the count, Prior Arnaldo da Rocha.

And so in 1104, the principal figures in the story linking the Knights Templar, the Ordre de Sion, and the county of Portugale appear together in the same location.

By 1106 Dom Henrique returns to Portugale—with or without Arnaldo we do not know—but Hugues de Payns remains behind in Jerusalem for the next six years.[20] During that time he is joined by the other cofounder of the Knights Templar, Godefroi de Saint-Omer. This knight not only originated from the same duchy as the first patriarch of Jerusalem, he was also identified as one of the entourage that originally accompanied Godefroi de Bouillon, the so-called *domus Godefridi,* meaning that at least one cofounder of the Knights Templar was part of the patriarch's inner circle. And if this tightly knit group of advisers included members of the Ordre de Sion—which by all accounts it did—it may explain why documents cryptically refer to the Ordre de Sion having been instrumental in the creation of the Templar Order.[21]

Needless to say, the proto-Templars existed in one form or another at least eighteen years before Baudoin I gave them a king's blessing at the ceremony at Saint Leonard of Acre.

And in this sequence of events we can also appreciate how it was possible for the Order of the Temple to have been present in Portugale far earlier than previously known.

After establishing himself on Temple Mount, Hugues de Payns remained in close contact with the canons at the Holy Sepulcher.[22] As he did with the monks of the Ordre de Sion: nine years after his signature appeared on the document alongside that of Prior Petrus Arnaldus,[23] a second document was made on May 2, 1125 (the Celtic feast of Beltane), again bearing both men's signatures, once more declaring "good relations are established between the two Orders."[24]

A continuous collaboration between the Templar Grand Master and the Portuguese prior of the Ordre de Sion? To what end?

One thing is certain. If a relationship existed between Prior Arnaldus and Hugues de Payns, so by implication it existed between the Ordre de Sion, the Knights Templar, and the nascent Portuguese nation-state.

1117.
GUIMARÃES. IN THE COURT
OF COUNTESS TAREJA . . .

With her son and heir to the throne of Portugale a mere eight years of age, the thirty-two-year-old widow Tareja found herself with the responsibility of governance, yet the years she would endure as a mere countess were brief. After her military victory defending her southernmost city of Coimbra against the Moors in 1117, she began addressing herself as queen—an unrealistic expectation given how she was an illegitimate daughter and her late husband had been a mere count. Nevertheless, her delusions of grandeur were assisted by a papal decree recognizing her as such, Rome being more than delighted to award her a token title for having dispatched many Arab infidels back to Allah.

Whether this promotion rose to her head is hard to say, but soon she sought to expand her territory and pursue a larger share of her family's Leónese inheritance. Unfortunately, this meant "Queen" Tareja found herself at war with a real queen—her half sister Urraca of Castilla e León—or forming alliances with her enemies, whichever proved the most expedient or convenient.

A simpler solution was to find a close and stable ally. He materialized in the form of Count Fernán Péres de Traba, the most powerful Galician

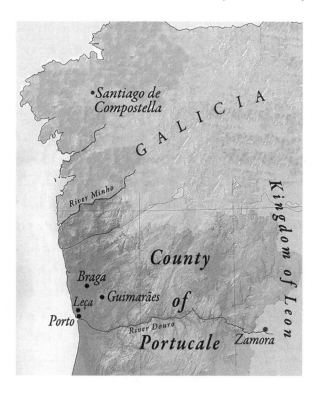

nobleman, a sensitive fellow who took a brief moment to consider the widow's proposal, then, upon assessing her ample Portuguese property, promptly dumped his own wife and became Tareja's lover.

But life did not turn out all wine and roses for Tareja. After several wars with her half sister, she was finally besieged and captured and only through a coordinated brokerage between the archbishops of Braga and Santiago de Compostela was Tareja freed. The treaty saved the government of Portugale, but the price for her freedom meant the Portuguese county was once again held as a fief of Castilla e León.

It was bad enough that the Portuguese nobles should continue tolerating life as vassals to a foreign court, but things got uglier for Tareja herself when she foolishly awarded her paramour the governorship of the cities of Porto and Coimbra. Fernán Péres de Traba developed delusions of his own grandeur, his character changing for the megalomaniac, beginning with the assumption that her assets now belonged to him, to the point where he even considered himself Lord of Portugale. He effectively placed important Portuguese cities under the control of Galicians, who were allowed to infiltrate every aspect of Portuguese society. The situation deteriorated further after the death of Urraca, when Tareja moved to form an alliance with the new king of Castilla e León, who also happened to be her nephew. It seemed as though the Portuguese county would never be free of outside interference. Even worse, Tareja, under Fernán's lover's charm, sought to usurp the sovereignty of Portugale from her own son and merge the county with Galicia and Castilla e León.

One person who certainly had had enough was her headstrong son, Afonso Henriques, who even as an adolescent teenager was mature enough to comprehend political intrigue and the repercussions of the ongoing travesty between *that* Galician and his mother. Perhaps Viriato's fighting spirit was speaking through his genes; Afonso shared the same birthplace in Viseu with the great Lusitanian warrior whose tactics once stonewalled the Roman takeover of his kingdom. As far as Afonso was concerned it was not simply a matter of foreigners laying claim to his territory; his own mother also was gambling with lands he would inherit on his fourteenth birthday, the legal age when he would be considered ruler of the county.

Kids certainly grew up very fast in those days. They had to.

Finding little in common with his mother, young Afonso developed a close bond with his principal mentor, Payo Mendes. Payo was a native of the nearby town of Leça, where he had been involved with a number of property transactions on behalf of the Knights Hospitaller,[1] including the hospital he received from that brotherhood in Braga, which he promptly transferred to the Order of the Temple shortly before Afonso's father passed away.[2]

In 1118 Payo Mendes was appointed archbishop of Braga, coincidentally at the same time Baudoin II was proclaiming the Knights Templar in Jerusalem. Although not a learned man—even the clergy in those days were required to take up arms in favor of books—Payo was prudent and resolute, stubborn, and a keen defender of individual rights.[3] His ethics had made him friends with Afonso's father, and indeed it was

Payo who resumed the construction of the cathedral begun by Count Dom Henrique. Actually, his enthusiasm got the better of him and he transformed it into a major architectural work, possibly in homage to the Knights Templar, seeing as building work resumed as soon as the Order was officially announced in Jerusalem.[4]

No doubt Payo also adopted the continuation of his former sovereign's ideals when he became councilor to the impressionable Afonso, whose view of the world and of Portugale already differed greatly from that of his mother, so much so that it made both men foes of the queen.

It was probably this close bond that incited the suspicious Tareja to have the archbishop imprisoned, even though, with humorous irony, it meant she was also imprisoning her own councilor!

The man of the cloth was released soon enough on written orders from the pope, who also informed Tareja that such conduct toward a member of the clergy was unacceptable. So Tareja resolved the delicate impasse by exiling him instead. As for her son, rather than do the disciplinary-motherly thing and have him sent to his room in the tower, she exiled him too. The fact that Afonso was fast reaching his legal age may have played into her calculations.

If Tareja was under any illusions that she would usurp control of Portugale from her son, circumstances would soon deny her. Afonso may have been a mere thirteen years of age, but even so he had already gained allies among the nobility of Portugale;[5] for one thing, they too had had enough of Tareja, Fernán, Galicia, Castilla, León, and the steady erosion of the administrative power of Portugale to incoming Galicians. Plus, Afonso was nephew to Duke Odo I of Burgundy, and many of the Portuguese nobles maintained family ties with said duchy.

Even Archbishop Mendes lost his patience with the Galicians, specifically his counterpart Diego Gelmírez, the Benedictine archbishop of Santiago de Compostela, whom he saw as an impostor making dubious claims of the discovery of relics of Saint James, conveniently in his hometown, by which he hoped to turn the Galician city into a major pilgrimage center and suck authority from all other cathedrals in the Iberian

Peninsula. And as a by-product, receive a fatter purse from the pope.

Payo had a good point. The spit between the Diocese of Braga and Santiago de Compostela centered on the stealing of the former's holy relics by Diego Gelmírez himself during a visit to Braga. They were the most valued items in the old metropolitan city and symbols of her tradition and prestige; some of those relics even signified past religious glories. They were much loved by the people, yet despite protests by the Portuguese, even the Galicians, the relics did not budge from Compostela and remain there to this day.[6] It can be validly argued, therefore, that the international status enjoyed by Santiago de Compostela is due to stolen goods.

But we digress. If there had been a dream since the days of Count Dom Henrique to create an independent nation, backed by his Burgundian and Templar connections, the opportunity was rapidly approaching with Afonso's coming of age. Under Payo Mendes's guidance, Afonso Henriques sailed with the archbishop up the river Douro in the direction of the holy town of Zamora, where, prior to

The holy city of Zamora.

his imprisonment, Mendes had spent a mysteriously long time, making his absence from his diocese in Braga arouse the neurosis of Countess Tareja. Mendes had long been suspected of working with the Knights Templar, and a paper trail of property transactions established this; the Hermitage of Saint Mark in Braga, as well as a hospital, was donated to the Order of the Temple by a man called Pelagius, the name by which Payo Mendes signed his documents.[7]

If Mendes's job was to protect and groom the future king, the placid sail upriver would have seen Afonso briefed on his place in the bigger scheme of things.

The two men were a remarkably good fit. Like Afonso, Payo was an independent and headstrong fellow with little tolerance for the arrogance and corruption of power. Soon after his rise to archbishop he was in contempt of the privilege of the Roman Church when he presumed to consecrate the successor of the deceased bishop of Coimbra, even though the See of Coimbra was subject to that of Compostela—and Payo's nemesis, Diego Gelmírez. Mendes's actions incurred a curt letter from the pope, stating that "it had been the pleasure" of the Roman pontiff to honor Diego and give him power over Coimbra, to which Payo responded by consecrating yet another bishop. Two further letters from Rome went unanswered.[8] And so the continuing love of all things Roman and Spanish and Galician were shared between mentor and prince.

They navigated the truculent waters around the steep and curvaceous Douro valley. The view of the numerous steeples of Zamora around the river bend must have seemed like déjà vu for Mendes.

Zamora was referred to as the "eye of the river Douro," the place of numerous military entanglements between Muslims and Christians, but also a fabulously holy city boasting the greatest number of Romanesque churches in Europe, a city of pious kings. It was also the city where "Queen" Tareja and Queen Urraca had once agreed to a rare—and brief—pact of peace. Clearly the location in which to exalt Afonso's manhood could not have been better chosen.

Afonso's presence on this strategic military and ecclesiastical hill declared his intentions to the region. It sent a defiant message and a provocative middle finger to the enforced bonds and fiefs between Portugale, Galicia, and Castilla e León. As he strode widely into the cathedral of Zamora, it was remarked how Afonso was unusually tall, a giant of a man-child, possessed of qualities that led him to be described as the "Christian Viriato."[9] And so on May 25, 1125, Afonso Henriques was celebrated with an official knighting ceremony, a ritual heavy with significance and symbolism, representing as it did his passage into full adulthood and, more importantly, all the rights of inheritance.[10] The new leader of the new Lusitanians took the ceremonial cloth and the sword and arose a knight.

A number of accounts and traditions declare that he "took the order of knighthood" and the "order of the militia," giving rise to speculation that he was ordained not as an ordinary knight but as a Templar knight.[11] Be that as it may, it was around the time of the ceremony that many knights belonging to the Order of the Temple requested to join Afonso in raising an army, just as they had offered his father before him.[12] The prince took them up on their generous proposal and, suitably empowered, set forth reclaiming his rightful lands from his mother and her rich Galician count.

Payo Mendes assisted by offering several more homes in the city of Braga to members of the Knights Templar to use as their base. And well he should, for in addition to playing the role of Afonso's mentor, Payo Mendes was also a Procurator of the Knights Hospitaller[13] and, later, their third prior, a title equivalent to that of Templar Master.[14]

There comes a point in every people's history when circumstances force a defining moment, when some button is pressed just deep enough to turn on a light within their collective will. In Portugale it happened in 1125.[15] Tajera's tiresome dealings with the Galicians were one thing, but now Castilla e León had a new king in Affonso VII, and he was under the illusion that the entire Iberian Peninsula should be one kingdom.

His.

And to leave no doubt as to his intentions, Castillian armies began carving away chunks of Portuguese territory.

So just to make sure cousin Affonso VII also got the message, Afonso Henriques's ceremony in Zamora took place exactly on the same day the king of Castilla e León had himself been granted the same ceremony in the cathedral of Compostela.[16]

14

1126.
CLAIRVAUX. A VERY, VERY,
VERY MODEST ABBEY IN
CHAMPAGNE . . .

It was early autumn when the relatively new monastery of Clairvaux received two bearded visitors clad in anonymous old clothing,[1] yet beneath their couture there could not have been two more distinguished men: Brother Gondemare and André de Montbard, two Knights Templar.

André was uncle to the man they had traveled all the way from Jerusalem to see, Bernard de Clairvaux, head of the Cistercian Order and the most influential and respected figurehead in all Christendom. Bernard had not seen his uncle for a good decade, and for this alone the visit was joyous enough.

Still, there was other good news, particularly with regard to the burgeoning Templar fraternity. The brotherhood had been diligently following God's work on Temple Mount, and just the previous year King Baudoin II had acknowledged Hugues de Payns as the Grand Master of the Knights Templar, citing him as *magister Templi* on a grant of privileges to the Venetians.[2]

The two Templars came bearing a letter from the king to Bernard. It read:

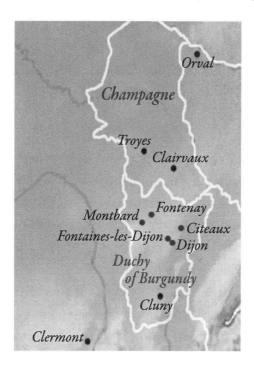

The Templar brothers . . . desire to receive apostolic approval and also their own Rule. . . . Since we know well the weight of your intercession with God and also with His Pontiff [the Pope] and with the other princes in Europe, we give into your care this two-fold mission, whose success will be very welcome to us. Let the constitution of the Templars be such as is suitable for men who live in the clash and tumult of war, and yet of a kind which will be acceptable to the Christian princes, of whom they have been the valuable auxiliaries. So far as in you lies and if God pleases, strive to bring this matter to a speedy and successful issue.[3]

That the Templars had come with a "two-fold mission" was not entirely accurate. Baudoin II's letter was opportunistic; he sought to expand his campaign against the Arabs, and for that he needed men and arms and money. A papal decree would free up these requirements just as surely as it had done for the First Crusade, and Bernard was in a position to champion his cause to the pope.

But this had nothing to do with the Templars' principal motive for their dispatch to Champagne. Their leader Hugues de Payns was not a fief of Baudoin II, nor did the knight owe him any favors; nor did the two bearers, neither of whom were in Baudoin's employ but in the Grand Master's.

The central purpose of the meeting was, first of all, that Hugues de Payns was seeking a Rule for the Templars from an ecclesiastical figure of high repute that incoming members could follow, especially those knights concerned with temporal matters that inevitably brought them into close contact with the tumult that was life in the Holy Land. These were insecure times, and boys will be boys, away in a foreign land, tempted by the growing opportunities around them, with the power of a sword at the hip. It would be the first of several pleas from Hugues, who was clearly struggling to maintain discipline in the ranks, and one of his letters to the Templars stationed in Jerusalem illustrates the fragility of the situation.

> Dearest brothers, the more the devil stays awake to deceive and sub-vert us, the more we, through the zeal of our circumspection, ought to be particularly on our guard not only against evil but also while doing good. The first task of the devil is to draw us into sin; the second is to corrupt our intentions in good deeds; the third is that as if with the appearance of helping he should divert us from our intended act of virtue and make us falter. To guard us from the first error the Scriptures say, "Son, take care never to consent to sin." To avoid the second error they say elsewhere, "Do good well"; for he does not do good well who seeks in the good work his own glory and not that of God. For the third error they state in yet another place, "Stay in your place"; as though he who is always diverted from that which he is obliged and duty-bound to do other things because of the lack of constancy in his mind and the capriciousness of his desires, does not want to stay in his place. . . .

If all the members of the body had one and the same function the whole body could not survive. . . . The humblest are often the most useful. The foot touches the ground but supports the whole body. Do not deceive yourselves; each one shall receive his reward according to his work. The roofs of houses receive the rain and the hail and the wind, but if there were no roofs, what would happen to the painted galleries?[4]

Many of Hugues de Payns's discourses to the Templars indicate an interest in following a monastic life rather than involvement in military activities. He was concerned that the knights' core purpose had been weakened by pride and ambition—the devil inside—which must be tempered with humility, duty, perseverance, and patience if a man is to stay the course; in all cases, the religious aim must supersede the temptation to fight lest it becomes an obstacle to inner contemplation.[5] If the words of the Templar Grand Master were not enough to guard men against temptation, a rule establishing a code of conduct from a renowned spiritual figurehead, such as Bernard, would present the best possible management tool.

This was the first aim of the Templar envoy to Clairvaux.

It has been suggested that Bernard and Hugues de Payns had known each other for many years, least of all because when Hugues resided at Chateau Payns in Champagne the two men were practically neighbors.[6] In truth they were much closer: Hugues de Payns was the uncle of Bernard de Clairvaux.[7]

The second aim of the envoy was a signal to Bernard that whatever the Templars had been up to on Temple Mount—which had been conducted with the utmost secrecy—had been accomplished, and preparations were now necessary to pave the way for its implementation. This plan most likely involved Brother Gondemare, as he was an alleged member of the Ordre de Sion[8] and, more tellingly, the son of a Portugale family.[9] Certainly, this was no casual meeting between the three men at Clairvaux. When the Knights Templar swore an oath of obedience it was not to a king or a pope or even their own Grand Master, but to this Cistercian abbot. Thus, to understand the motivation behind the Order of the Temple it is necessary to first understand their primary benefactor.

Bernard was born in Fontaines-les-Dijon, within sight of Count Dom Henrique's original family estate. Likewise, he was a descendent of the dukes of Burgundy,[10] son to a Burgundy lord, and member of a family who belonged to the military nobility typical of the era, in which the binds of family and land were strong. Slightly built, with a sparse brown beard and tonsured head, he looked frail for his young years due to physical weakness from a gastric disorder.

His mother Aleth had dreamed she would give birth to a healer, someone who would refresh the direction of the Catholic Church and become its watchdog. If the dream had meant to be prophetic, Bernard grew up to fulfill it, and then some, for in his lifetime he was famed as a thaumaturge.

Bernard de Clairvaux.

As for Aleth, she was the sister of Templar knight André de Montbard, one of the two men presently sitting beside her son bearing news from the Holy Land.

From an early age Bernard sought a direct, mystical experience of God, and began by persuading a small group of friends and relatives to establish a monastic community in his parental home—at the age of twenty-two! Then he learned about the Cistercian Order, its unique brand of asceticism, and its abbey at Citeaux founded by rogue monks who wished to break with Benedictine tradition and opt for an even stricter, more ascetic way of life.

Citeaux's own story begins with Robert, a teenage noble of Champagne who renounced his wealth, became a monk, and founded a monastery at Molesme in Burgundy. In 1075 he was sought out by Albéric de Cîteaux and his group of hermits, who emerged from deep in the woods and asked Robert to erect a new monastery. The initial structure consisted of nothing more than a smattering of huts made of branches surrounding a chapel dedicated to the Holy Trinity. Nevertheless, it grew in popularity, so much so that when new and unsuitable monks joined this burgeoning group of Benedictines the brothers became disturbed by the growing lack of asceticism. Inevitably, Robert de Molesme left, along with Albéric and a third monk, the Englishman Stephen Harding, to found the abbey of Cîteaux deep inside a dense forest in a desolate valley, with the full support of the Duke of Burgundy.

Citeaux became the cornerstone for the new Cistercian Order. But the monks may have taken the idea of asceticism a tad too far because within a brief period of time the extreme austerity drove out so many brothers that the abbey almost ceased to function. By the time Bernard de Clairvaux and his small band of followers requested to join, the Cistercian Order was on its knees, literally, but the newcomers' influence and business acumen quickly revitalized its fortunes.

Cistercian ideals were far removed from the Vatican's. They pertained to education, agriculture, and the sacred arts, and the timing could not have been more fortuitous. The twelfth century was witnessing a move toward settlement, agriculture, and continuous growth of a market and monetary economy. Cathedral schools became established in several towns—particularly in Lorraine, Champagne, and Burgundy—and were heavily attended by sons of nobles who took up study in favor of militarism. People training to be monks, particularly those joining the Cistercian Order, "knew more of the outside world than previously had been the case. This trend also caused a change in the understanding and portrayal of the love toward God, which now more closely reflected the love between men and women."[11] Such an expanded view allowed for a healthier relationship between monasteries and the nobility, who in those days were also the military elite.

The Cistercians capitalized on this trend toward religious renewal and the shift to husbandry of the land. Even so, Bernard soon became unhappy with the lack of asceticism practiced at Citeaux and began to look for a new location where to build himself an abbey to develop his own brand of piety and austerity.

The news reached the ear of the Count of Troyes, better known as Comte Hugh de Champagne, who was more than happy to donate a goodly parcel of land to his relative, since he happened to own this part of Europe.[12] He was, after all, one of the wealthiest lords, and in his time he had already made a number of important donations to abbeys and cathedrals in and around his seat in Troyes,[13] even founding the Abbey of Cheminon.[14]

Comte Hugh understood Bernard's vision only too well. In 1104 he had met in conclave with a close-knit group of lords, some of whom had just returned from Jerusalem.[15] Whatever was conveyed at the meeting compelled him to sail immediately to Jerusalem with his cousin and vassal, Hugues de Payns,[16] who had requested his patronage in support of a new Order of knights. While in Jerusalem, Comte Hugh would have been introduced to his illustrious Flemish neighbor, King Baudoin I, and a Burgundian knight by the name of Dom Henrique of Portugale, who, like himself, had traveled a great distance.

Comte Hugh returned a second time in 1114—coincidentally at the time of Dom Henrique's death—but the stay was not only mysteriously brief, he also appears to have been privy to something of great importance, for "he announced a more serious project, he thought he should stay in these faraway lands for the rest of his life, and be part at the birth of the new militia."[17] Whatever vision the comte experienced, he returned in haste to Champagne less than a year later to renounce his worldly goods. But not before walking Bernard around his fields at Clairvaux and acquainting him with a tract of land he had chosen as the most suitable building site for the monk's future abbey.

Bernard looked around the fertile land beaming with potency under the warm June air, graciously thanked him, and declined. True to his ideals, the monk instead requested an adjacent site in the Vale d'Absinthe, one of most inferior quality, in a dismal part of the forest that required extensive clearing. Slightly bewildered, Comte Hugh reflected on Bernard's choice and granted his wish, and on the feast day of John the Baptist, in a valley possessed of a most notorious reputation as a haven of thieves and robbers, a new temple was founded in a place abundant in poverty of spirit.

In the decades that followed, the choice of locations for new Cistercian abbeys under Bernard's leadership regularly deviated from the Rule originally set by the mother abbey of Citeaux, sometimes even relocating the site altogether.[18] Indeed, after the founding of Clairvaux, Citeaux and its satellite monasteries would adapt Bernard's methods and codes of conduct.

By his twenty-fifth birthday Bernard had not only become abbot of Clairvaux, his will also had completely revitalized the Cistercian Order. During his abbacy the Order grew to 345 monasteries and 167 filiations, with Clairvaux enjoying exceptional status. For good measure, Bernard also rebuilt the ruined chapel on the Scottish island of Iona into a Cistercian abbey, thereby rescuing the failing Celtic church.[19]

Clairvaux was admitting monks at such a rate that, within three years, sister abbeys needed to be founded, at which point Bernard's cousin Godefroy came to his aid. One of the original members of Bernard's troupe of monks, Godefroy de la Roche had been given a hermitage on the outskirts of the town of Montbard, and the grounds on which it stood proved suitable for the building of a larger abbey. The de la Roche family made financial contributions toward the construction, and at their insistence, Bernard founded the abbey of Fontenay in 1118. Godefroy de la Roche would in time become its abbot, and a decade later, prior of Clairvaux.[20] Interestingly, religion played an important part in the de la Roche family: Godefroy's sister was the first abbess of the sacred well of Orbe, and more importantly, members of the family had once moved to Portugale and one had given birth to a boy, Pedro Arnaldo da Rocha. Thus, Godefroy's cousin Bernard de Clairvaux was also related to the man who became prior of the Ordre de Sion.

Life under Bernard at Clairvaux was just as you would expect from a man of passionate devotion. The monks slept on leaves and straw in unheated dormitories without blankets. Their diet consisted of wild berries, roots, and leaves; on extravagant days the menu's pièce de résistance consisted of boiled vegetables. Bernard himself led an even more ascetic lifestyle than his peers, sleeping in a kind of hovel, a space under the stairs leading to the dormitory. But at least he enjoyed some privileges: the brethren at Clairvaux gave Bernard ample space to allow "his mystical contemplation of the blessings of Paradise that the saints may taste in their ascent to God."[21]

Given his principles, it is understandable that Bernard should speak out against the corruption of bishops and priests within the church, for which he had little tolerance, evidenced by no less than seven letters to four consecutive popes requesting the removal of the archbishop of York, William FitzHerbert, because the Englishman acquired his position through bribery. In his treatise *De Consideratione,* Bernard is clearly disapproving of men of the cloth lobbying the pope in order to gain influence for their sole ends. He saw the overtly decadent and comfortable lifestyle of Benedictine monks in Cluny and other abbeys as a path to oblivion. These people drank the finest wines, ate the rarest of foods, and spent much of the year in luxury homes in Paris, all paid for with jewels, land, money, even works of art solicited by abbots through the advertising slogan, "Nothing can be too good for God."

Writing in his *Apology,* Bernard broaches the extravagances of religious orders and the pomp and circumstance in which abbots indulged.

> I will overlook the immense heights of the places of prayer, their immoderate lengths, their superfluous widths, the costly refinements, and the painstaking representations which deflect the attention while they are in them those who pray and thus hinder their devotion. To me they somehow represent the ancient rite of the Jews. But so be it, let these things be made for the honor of God. However, as a monk, I put to monks the same question that a pagan used to criticize other pagans. "Tell me, priest," he said, "what is gold doing in the holy place?" I, however, say, "Tell me, poor man, if indeed you are a poor man, what is gold doing in the holy place?"[22]

In the twelfth century Bernard was the focal point of Christianity, certainly in its purest form, for he saw in Christ an example of oneness and inner balance, and in his *Letter to the Rain* he describes the voluntary Cistercian lifestyle as closer to peasantry than other religious orders, thus showing solidarity with the common people.[23] His sermons and personal accounts offer an image of a visionary, a human being living on a foundation of love and compassion, and as far as he was concerned, anything a man did in life that was less than complete devotion to God was a waste of effort. But he also recognized the duality within man and preached austerity, poverty, and purity as a foundation for inner greatness.

He advocated the rights of the working classes, the poor, and the peasantry in opposition to the oppression of the class to which he was born. He outlawed slavery, had monks work alongside laborers, paid fair wages, provided free schools, fed and clothed the poor, and treated them in sickness. He forbade racial discrimination, promoted tolerance of Jews and women, and appears to have respected the codes of honor of different classes with whom he interacted: "He preached to all kinds of people, anxious as he was for the salvation of their souls. He adapted himself to each particular audience, on the basis of what he knew about their understanding, their customs and their interests."[24]

He practiced what he preached—a simple faith, complete surrender to God.

According to the abbot Guillerme de Saint-Thierry, Bernard was less concerned about the hardships he and his community endured than about the future blessings his example at Clairvaux would bring to the souls of mankind:

> His greatest desire was for the salvation of all mankind, and this has been the greatest passion of his heart from the first day of his life as a monk even to the day on which I am writing this, so that his longing to draw all men of God is like a mother's devoted care for her children. All the time there is the conflict in his heart between his great desire for souls and the desire to remain hidden from the attention of the world, for sometimes in his humility and low esteem of himself he confesses that he is not worthy to produce any fruitful increase in the Church, whilst at other times his desire knows no bounds and burns so strongly within him that it seems that nothing can satisfy it, but the salvation of mankind.[25]

In his sermon *In septuagesimo,* Bernard refers to Clairvaux as the city of Sion, the city of the eternal king, and warns of enemies who seek to destroy it from without, and traitors from within, particularly those who seek to soften spiritual discipline, wage war, and generally hurt the love toward others. He often compares his abbey to a fortress and repeatedly identifies it with the heavenly Jerusalem and an ideal state of peace—a metaphor of the eternal struggle between malice and injustice, and right action: "Clairvaux . . . is truly Jerusalem, united to the one in heaven by whole-hearted devotion, by conformity of life, and by a certain spiritual affinity. . . . [One] has chosen to dwell here, because here he has found, not yet, to be sure, the fullness of vision, but certainly the hope of that true peace, peace which surpasses all our thinking."[26]

For Bernard, Jerusalem was a like a mother who descends to Earth as a place of divinity and peace, and in this symbol lies an explanation behind the symbol of nine knights guarding the pilgrim trail. Their task was to protect the path to an ideal state, a kingdom of heaven. Metaphorically speaking, the Knights Templar assisted the pilgrim seeking a road to a better life. As for the popular concept of the Templars as "poor knights," this quite possibly arose from Bernard's description of Clairvaux as a community consisting of *paupers Christi*:[27] poor not insomuch as deficit in poverty, but humble, a desire to associate with the common man rather than people who covet material gain, for the person who is poor yet spiritually awake is permanently wealthy.

More than five hundred of Bernard's letters survive, and peering into them, as well as his prolific prose, offers a tremendous insight into the patron of the Knights Templar, and through him, the desire that motivated the Order of the Temple. Definitely it was not one of military might or of religious conversion by coercion. Bernard was, after all, a reformer of the Cistercian Order, whose practitioners renounced violence on pain of excommunication. Nor did they preach the word of God as missionaries; instead they sought the way of the Light through personal spiritual development and followed examples set by, among others, John the Baptist.

An example of this ideal lies in a letter Bernard wrote to Comte Hugh de Champagne following his donation of land for the building of Clairvaux, after which the comte set sail for Jerusalem to become a Templar knight:

> If, for God's work, you have changed yourself from count to knight
> and from rich to poor, I congratulate you on your just advancement,
> and I glorify God in you—however, it tries me sorely to be deprived

of your delightful presence by God's mysterious ways; but at least we might see you from time to time, if it is possible. How can we forget our old friendship you have shown to our house? And with what joy we would have cared for you, body, soul and spirit, had you come to live with us! But since it is not so, we pray constantly for the absent one whom we cannot have amongst us.

For a number of years Bernard also kept up correspondence with their mutual friend and relative Hugues de Payns, particularly around the early part of 1126, when the Templars grew noticeably active on Temple Mount and several members returned to Europe, as evidenced by the appearance at Clairvaux of André de Montbard and Brother Gondemare.

But they were by no means the only knights stirred into action by Hugues de Payns. In May of the previous year, the Templar Grand Master cosigned a document in which he and Prior Arnaldo established good relations between their respective Orders,[28] after which said prior also becomes noticeably absent from Mount Sion. Writing of this, the chronicler Lucas de Santa Catarina states, "The Grand Master soon dispatched several knights with powers to establish the Portuguese crown. Four of the Knights were Dom Guilherme, who supervised the others, Dom Hugo Martiniense, Dom Gualdino Paes, and Dom Pedro Arnaldo. They had the title and the power of Procurators of the Temple, which they exercised in due course, as many writers agree, while the Order sought to establish a home, and proceed as planned."[29]

Joining them on the clandestine voyage was a fifth Templar knight and Procurator, Raimund Bernard.

No doubt Brother Gondemare and André de Montbard shared this explosive piece of news with Bernard. And yet to the Cistercian abbot such a daring move would not have come as a surprise. Bernard may have been contemplating the idea of establishing a new kingdom of conscience for quite some time, a temporal New Jerusalem, a model

Abbey of Clairvaux.

nation-state that would come to represent the epitome of his ideals,[30] because seven years earlier, Bernard himself had dispatched a delegation of monks to that very same Portuguese county, domain of his late uncle, Count Dom Henrique.

And soon, Henrique's son, Afonso.

15

SEVEN YEARS EARLIER.
CLAIRVAUX. A SPECIAL MOMENT
ON JUNE 24 . . .

As if the young abbot did not already have enough on his plate, four years after founding Clairvaux, Bernard fostered a relationship with an even younger Afonso Henriques.

The Cistercian monastic chronicles record how, in a moment of meditation on the feast day of John the Baptist, Bernard de Clairvaux was shown another monastery that was to be founded in the westernmost part of the Iberian peninsula. After a few days of reflection he gathered eight monks—Boemund, Aldebert, Jean, Bernard, Alderic, Cisinand, Alano, and Brother Roland—and briefed them: "The purpose of your journey will be to found a monastery, to be inhabited by the laws of heaven, so that the inhabitants of the earth may be risen, and those who will inhabit its walls will find the right remedies for their souls, and in doing so they will be shown the road to glory."[1]

He told them they were to travel to where a sign from the heavens would present itself, then turned to Brother Gerald and asked the bursar of Clairvaux to organize the necessary provisions for their journey. Much crying was done by all at the time of farewell, for the trip would take them eight hundred miles away and beyond their known world.[2]

The itinerant monks followed one of the preferred pilgrimage routes

to Santiago de Compostela, finally reaching the town of Lamego, home
to the second oldest Visigothic chapel in Europe, forty miles to the
southwest of Braga. Their instructions were to meet with a colleague of
Bernard's, the hermit João Cirita, to whom they would hand a personal
letter from the abbot.

João's virtues and reputation were well known in the nearby
Portuguese court of Guimarães. After reading the letter, he and the
eight monks walked the 33 miles to the royal court and solicited permission to build a monastery from the heir to the Portuguese throne,
Afonso Henriques.

Upon reading the name on the letter, the eleven-year-old was so
overjoyed that he kissed the hems of the monks' habits; after all, this
was probably the first letter Afonso had received from his uncle Bernard
de Clairvaux.[3]

Attentively watching was Afonso's half brother Dom Pedro, who
"asked the monks many questions about France and Bernard, and as he
learned more about this distant family connection and how they shared
similar ideals, he took an interest in journeying to France one day to
discover the noble bloodline in whose footsteps he proceeded." When
Dom Pedro grew up he would do just so.[4]

Afonso promptly awarded the monks the property they sought and
put his name on the vellum deed, signed on his behalf on March 1, 1120,
by his then legal guardian, Countess Tareja.[5] The contented monks
were bid farewell and returned promptly to Lamego to built a hermitage
in a solitary valley at Tarouca,[6] exactly in accordance with Cistercian
principles of personal comfort in a *valle silvestri et horrida* (rough and
wild valley). Most likely it would have comprised a hut made of planks
of wood covered with the stalks of wild plants that passed for a church,
with no bed linen, nor any of the sweet things in life for the monks.[7]
When the building was gradually elevated in construction and status
to the monastery of John the Baptist, thirteen novices joined from the
Portuguese court.[8]

16

To put into place a plan as bold as "the establishment of a Portuguese crown,"[1] the Templars would require a domicile in a location already friendly to their cause and, ideally, accessible to the Portuguese court in Guimarães. Situated a mere nine miles to the northwest, Braga would suit the purpose well, as the fourth Templar Master in Portugal would later acknowledge: "the home of the Temple, which is in the city of Braga."[2] They already had a friend there in the form of the Procurator for the Knights Hospitaller, Archbishop Payo Mendes, who had earlier secured properties for the Templars in and around the Hospital for the Poor.[3]

When the five Templar Procurators from Jerusalem finally landed in the city of Porto (formerly Porto Cale), they were greeted at the quay by the typical damp, gloomy, gray weather that so characterizes the region in winter. Three of the men—Raimund Bernard, Guilherme Ricard, and Hugh Martin*—were of French origin; the fourth, a young man named Gualdino Paes, was born in Braga and was thus wholesomely Portuguese; and finally, Pedro Arnaldo da Rocha, Portuguese of Burgundian parentage.

---

*In Portuguese, Dom Guilherme Ricardo and Dom Hugo Martinense.

These men arrived armed with nothing more than a clear objective, no doubt minutely discussed with Hugues de Payns and the Templar inner circle, which would now call into play relationships and alliances that had lain dormant since the death of the Count of Portugale. Even during those early years, knights associated with the Order of the Temple had rendered him services: "It was well known and believed throughout the land that after D. Enrique engaged in war with the Moors, the Knights Templar had come to his aid, and asked to be admitted into his service."[4] As a gesture of gratitude Dom Henrique awarded them the castle of Souré in 1111,[5] coincidentally the same year he made a rapid and mysterious trip to France, presumably to his original home in Burgundy.[6]

This relationship would serve his son Afonso now that his star was rising in the east in the city of Zamora, his light spreading ever westward over his nascent kingdom, for just as they had once supported his father, so the Templars now rallied around his son against his ever more errant mother.

By the time Afonso Henriques arose a knight on his sixteenth birthday he was said to be "greatly obliged" to the Order of the Temple. How does a teenager acquire that much responsibility, and that to an elite group of knights over two thousand miles away? Could it be that Afonso Henriques was himself inducted into the Order in Zamora?[7] Given the bond between his father and the Knights Templar, it is realistic to assume the Order nurtured his offspring, taught him their method, then through fine grooming (and a touch of providence) Afonso would implement the vision of an independent nation-state begun by his father, assisted by the Templars and their co-dependent brotherhoods. We know the protective arm of the Templar fraternity always followed young Afonso because even after his father's death "they always came to his aid,"[8] especially at the time of his knighthood, when knights belonging to the Order openly offered him their allegiance.[9]

It was the confrontational Archbishop Payo Mendes who took up the role of mentor to the child Afonso following his father's death. In Mendes's grooming of Afonso for kingship we see an echo of the spiritual mentor/pupil relationship established between Peter the Hermit and Godefroi de Bouillon, who was also said to be "greatly obligated"—in his case to the Ordre de Sion—after being offered the throne of Jerusalem.

Likewise, we see an echo of Baudoin I and how he "owed his throne" to the Ordre de Sion, a fraternity with whom Hugues de Payns was well connected thanks to his friendship with Prior Arnaldo, now also a Templar Procurator in Braga, the diocese of Payo Mendes.

We are looking here at an extraordinarily intricate but well-developed web of connections, friendships, and family ties spanning three decades and three separate geographic regions!

One French source adamantly claims the Knights Templar was deeply rooted in Portugale by 1126,[10] given how the village of Ferreira was granted to the Order that June.[11] Templar involvement in Portugale accelerated around this period thanks to regional appointees (such as the Procurators), all of whom were invested with the power to make decisions and sign documents on behalf of the executive back in Jerusalem: "The highest Prelates, the first and principal heads of the Order in Portugal, sometimes were named preceptors, others ministers, and Provincial Masters, with regard to the Grand Master who resided in Palestine . . . they resided in homes, hospices, or small convents which the Order had in cities, towns or castles, so they could gather the fruits to raise the level of the people and agriculture."[12]

The Templar chronicler Bernardo da Costa not only concurred but also claimed their presence to be even earlier: "By the year of their confirmation the Order of the Temple was not only already accepted, but established in Portugal; and not only in that year but in preceding years, and shortly after the nine knights established the Order in Jerusalem."[13]

This is a remarkable assertion, so let us be very clear about it. The Order of the Temple was confirmed in 1117 by King Baudoin I, and the following year the knights relocated to Temple Mount and became known as the Knights Templar. Da Costa implies the Order was not only established in Portugale by this point, but it had been prior to this date, "shortly after the nine knights established the Order in Jerusalem." This would refer to the "brotherhood within a brotherhood" established in the Church of the Holy Sepulcher around 1104 when Hugues de Payns took up residence there. Those proto-Templars were still living there by 1114—the year Comte Hugh de Champagne sailed to Jerusalem to join this Militiae Christi. Clearly one of the richest men in Europe did not dispose of his entire wealth and embark on a perilous sea voyage to join a phantom organization, thus the Order of the Temple must have been a fully fledged group years before its official declaration.

The same argument holds true in Portugale. A land grant from Ejeuva Aires and sons is made out "to you Knights of the Temple of Jerusalem, Pelagio Gontimiris and Martino Pelagii," a property owned by the family in the city of Braga, "around the well of the hospital."[14] The transaction could not have been made to any other organization because one of the recipients is Pelagio Gontimiris. Pelagio typically denotes a member of the clergy, and Gontimiris is the Latinized form of Gondemare. This Brother Gondemare is none other than one of the original Templars, the very same person who met with Bernard de Clairvaux, and he would have had good cause to do so because Brother Gondemare was himself a Cistercian monk.[15]

But the plot thickens because Brother Gondemare was also the son of a Portugale family[16] and, if the source documents are correct, a member of Ordre de Sion.[17] This makes him not only a direct link between the Templars, the Cistercians, and the Ordre de Sion, it also proves that one of the founding Templars lived in Portugale right from the very beginning.

Of all the original knights, Gondemare stands out in that he is one of only two original knights not named after his place of origin, a deviation from the standard practice of the age (i.e., Hugues *de Payns*, André *de Montbard*, etc.). Or is he? A few miles from where the Knights Hospitaller owned their first chapter house at Leça, there existed at that time another monastery in the town of Gondemare. To all intents and purposes, if Godemare was not in fact the knight's name but his domicile, it means all that was required of the Cistercian monk to accept the aforementioned property transaction in Braga on behalf of the "Knights of the Temple of Jerusalem" was a brief twenty-eight-mile horse ride.

There is another revelation in the chronicles of Bernardo da Costa concerning the Templars' presence in Portugale, and it is equally riveting. It states, "After the death of Conde D. Henrique, due to his son D. Afonso Henriques being a minor, governorship of the Kingdom was taken up by Queen Tereza . . . . Already by this time the Order of the Temple was accepted and established in this Kingdom, and in the government of Queen Tereza, as the original documents in the Archive of the Convent of Tomar prove . . . the same Queen had made another title deed to the Order of the Temple, without a date, but it can be shown this deed was made before those in 1128."[18]

Da Costa is unequivocal about the Templars and their regional representatives being embedded within the Portugale court from a very early date. The deed without a date refers to a substantial property donation for a small town in the vicinity of both Gondemare and Braga. It reads, "I, Queen D. Tereja give to God and the Knights of the Temple of Solomon the village called Fonte Arcada, in the land beside Penafiel, with all its terms and benefits, for the good of my soul."

It is accepted by and signed, "I, Guilherme, Procurator of the Temple in this territory, receive this document."[19] The aged parchment goes on to mention no less than seventeen additional land grants by local families.[20]

The ancient village and its arched sacred spring (known as Fonte Archatus by the seventh century) is the first documented location where the Knights Templar developed a convent.[21] The original title deed still exists,* signed by Tareja with the highly imaginative title "independent sovereign of all of Portugale." Indeed, it bears no date, so a little sleuthing is required here.

By law, Afonso Henriques should have ascended to the throne on his fourteenth birthday in July 1123, becoming de facto ruler of Portugale and thus administrator of the affairs of state and signatory of legal documents. Until then his mother acted as regent with sole authority to sign official documents on his behalf. Since the grant of Fonte Arcada bears her signature there are two possibilities: either it was made before July 1123, or before 1128, when her historical—and questionable—status as sovereign ceased altogether.

Between these dates Afonso was in exile and at war with his mother, literally, thus he had little or no access to government offices. It is plausible that Tareja's need to assert herself as a ruler meant she started signing away property that technically was not hers to give away, what

---

*The document, formerly in Tomar, is now in Torre do Tombo.

amounted to a usurpation of power. Whether this was the case or not, the accepting signatory on the donation of Fonte Arcada holds the key to the dating of the document: Guilhermus P. Templi, *P* standing for Procurator, a person with the power and authority to conduct transactions on behalf of the Grand Master of the Knights Templar. Guilherme Ricard was one of the five Procurators arriving in the autumn of 1125 to "establish the Portuguese crown."[22]

Early in 1126 he was elevated to first Master of the Knights Templar in Portugale,[23] his new title again reflected on a follow-up land grant for half the estate of Villa-nova, donated by Affonso Annes "to God, and the brotherhood of the Knights Templar,"[24] which he signed Magister Donus Ricardus (names in those days were written in different languages and spellings). So the most likely date for the donation of Fonte Arcada—when he was still a mere Procurator—would be the fallow days of 1125.

It is worth bearing in mind that a property transaction is a complicated and time-consuming process; both the paperwork and legal framework do not appear overnight but over the course of months, sometimes longer. And in those days of pen, ink, and vellum, the process would have been equally laborious, if not more, meaning that the preparations to transfer such a considerable property must have been on Countess Tareja's mind for quite some time. If so, the Portuguese court must have known in advance of the impending arrival of five Templar Procurators from Jerusalem.

Tareja was an extremely insecure individual to begin with, and as acting head of state she would hardly have awarded a large property like Fonte Arcada to complete strangers of unknown provenance. Furthermore, in twelfth-century Europe nothing moved without papal blessing, and since in 1125 the Templars had yet to be recognized by the pontiff, officially speaking the Knights Templar did not yet exist. So the Order of the Temple must have established quite a solid reputation within Portugale during Tareja's tenure. If her late husband trusted them, in theory so did she.

Which may explain why later that year a small Templar army quietly disembarked along the Portuguese coast, at the estuary of the river Mondego,[25] twenty-six miles from the administrative city of Coimbra, to take possession of the town of Souré, the exchange being made to the captain of the army.[26]

17

1127. AUTUMN.
ABOARD A GALLEY IN
THE MEDITERRANEAN . . .

ugues de Payns was born in Chateau Mahun near Annonay in the Ardèche,[1] into a family branch of the dynasty of the Counts of Champagne.[2] He married Catherine de Chappes,[3] whose relative, Henri de Saint Clair, crusaded with Godefroi de Bouillon.[4]

His grandfather, being Moorish, would have instilled in young Hugues an appreciation of the benefits of cross-cultural pollination, particularly with the Islamic world, which at the time was light-years ahead in education in Europe thanks to its knowledge of mathematics, astronomy, and medicine, learned from the Egyptians via their impressive library at Alexandria, one of the great academic wonders of the world—at least before a fanatical mob of Christian fundamentalists burned it down. As such, he would have been exposed to Islam's esoteric branch, Sufism.

Around his 33rd birthday Hugues spent much of his time traveling throughout Asia Minor, possibly to widen his wisdom, probably to find a deeper purpose in life. By the time of his second voyage to Jerusalem around 1114, he had already counseled with kings, received counts from Europe, lived in not just one but two of the world's most famous religious temples, created a new order of warrior monks from

Hugues de Payns.

scratch, and on May 2, 1125—the Celtic fertility feast of Beltane—he had become their Grand Master.[5] Not bad for a minor noble from an otherwise obscure town who gave up his riches to become poor of pocket but rich in spirit.

This much may have been sailing through his mind as he stood on the deck of the wooden galley, watching the harbor at Jaffa diminish in the distance, replaced by a wide expanse of blue Mediterranean, finally substituted for the limestone shore of southern Italy. The work the Templars had been secretly pursuing on Temple Mount was complete, and now they were on their way back to Europe to set events in motion. Accompanying Hugues on this voyage were at least five Templar brothers.[6]

Two years earlier he had dispatched another group of knights to Portugale, including his colleague Arnaldo da Rocha,[7] but not before the two leaders cosigned a document affirming the continuing relationship between their respective Orders.

There was much to do and his mind should be clear: first, he would travel to Rome and meet Pope Honorius II,[8] who was on good terms with the Cistercians, least of all because he too did not see much *bene* in the behavior of the Benedictines. To the pope, he would put forward a strong case for receiving a blessing for his "new" knighthood. Like it or not, few favors were granted in twelfth-century Europe without a nod of approval from Rome, and even as Buddhists well preached, with your arms wrapped around your enemy, he cannot fight you.

Hugues also ensured the Cistercians were kept abreast of the progress on Temple Mount. Only last year he had sent his Templar brothers André de Montbard and Brother Gondemare as envoys to brief Bernard de Clairvaux.[9]

Once his affairs were completed in Rome, he'd journey north, through Burgundy to Champagne, and meet with Bernard—longtime friend, relative, spiritual compass, benefactor—before presenting himself at an ecumenical council, which no doubt would be convened after the pope heard what he'd come to say.

18

t was both a busy and confusing month for Raimund Bernard. On April 19, the longtime French resident of Braga took possession of yet another residence in the city.[1] He handled the translucent vellum bearing the deed and signed it, in Latin, "in manu D. Raimundi Bernardi."[2]

Not only did the French knight own and acquire property, he'd done so as a Templar Procurator ever since the day he arrived from Jerusalem with four other members of the brotherhood. Obviously, Hugues de Payns was pleased with his work because three years after his arrival he was elevated to Templar Master in Portugale. "Master Raimundo Bernardo lived there, a Frenchman, and always a foreigner . . . in the year 1128 he occupied this ministerial post, since his Order had already established residence in Braga."[3] For some reason, the Templars developed a sudden thirst for property in this region, and in Dom Raimundo Bernardo—as he was known locally—they had a reliable man looking out for the burgeoning interests of the Order.

Indeed, Master Raimundo's signature seemed to be in great demand of late. Earlier in the month he had accepted a special deed on behalf of the Templars, a castle from Countess Tareja, who, for some bizarre reason, donated the same property again less than two weeks later. The first donation of the castle of Souré was made on April 4, and her name appears on the document. Ten days later the transaction is replaced by an expanded donation, with the entire town of Souré thrown in.[4] The signatories on the second deed differ greatly—and suspiciously— from the first, the most notable being the addition of her nephew Affonso VII, now king of Castilla e León, plus that of her lover, Fernán Péres de Traba, along with a new clause stressing that the land and the castle about to be donated had previously been granted to Fernán by Tareja. Regardless, both documents were signed and graciously accepted by Raimundo Bernardo, Templar Master and Procurator.[5]

And so concludes a confusing transaction. But this being twelfth-century Portugale, the story could not possibly end there.

The town of Souré had for quite some time marked the southern frontier between the Portuguese and the invading Moors and changed hands accordingly; back in 1111 its castle was donated to the Order of the Knights of the Temple by Count Dom Henrique.[6] Which makes one wonder, if it already belonged to the Order, why should it be regranted to the same people seventeen years later by his widow? It would appear Tareja was either suffering from a loss of memory or she was keen to ingratiate herself with the Templars at whatever cost and quickly. One historical account sheds some light on the circumstances: "With the permission of her husband, said Queen [Tareja] made a donation to the Order of the Temple of the Castle of Souré. . . . Another donation was made by the Queen to the same Order of the deserted lands between [the towns of] Coimbra and Leiria."[7]

The first thing we learn is that Fernán Péres de Traba has been elevated to the status of husband. This tragic event allegedly took place in Coimbra in 1125, where Tareja was indulging her lover. In her defense she accepted his proposal while suffering from a protracted fever and illness, which presumably excuses her actions.[8]

The second thing is that the donation was made with Fernán's permission, not Tareja's, indicating how the Galician lord had deluded himself into believing he was ruler of Portugale. He was not, so the addition of his name along with the king of Castilla e León's indicates Tareja was being strong-armed. Her actions read like an act of desperation. But the pressure was not so much coming from within as from without, applied by her exiled son Afonso Henriques, whose three-year campaign against his mother, Galicia, and his cousin Affonso VII was having far more destructive impact than anticipated.

Afonso Henriques, the rightful owner of the county of Portugale, was receiving logistical support from the Templar knights, just like his father before him.[9] Their military numbers were further bolstered by the Knights Hospitallers, whose charitable mandate had since been expanded by the pope to include military activities.*

It is quite possible none of the incumbents in the Portuguese court were fully aware of the strength of the bond between the Templars and the heir to the Portuguese throne, but certainly they were aware of the Templars' military arm and its prowess on the battlefield. In their calculations, breaking that bond made perfect strategic sense, and a sizeable donation of a castle, a town, plus the surrounding, albeit useless territory would do just that. Should the Templars take the bribe they would in effect become a buffer between Tareja, Fernán, Affonso VII, and the truculent Moors. It would also put an end to Afonso Henriques's campaign.

But the plan went askew when the ever-scheming Tareja conveniently forgot she was married and that she had previously awarded the castle to her new husband; she hoped the Templars, too, had forgotten the donation of 1111—and for that matter, that their military arm had been stationed in Souré itself for the past three years, making the donation redundant![10] Perhaps she may have entertained, for a brief moment, a vision of the Templars siding with her own army, thereby giving her the tactical advantage to run everyone out of Portugale. With their patronage the kingdom would be protected, and it would be hers. Perhaps.

---

*The change to the charter took place in 1113. It is documented that the Hospitallers were very hostile to this.

Perhaps the same motive lay behind her previous donation of Fonte Arcada. In any event, it appears Tareja's move was unmasked. Or circumstances forced her to sweeten the deal the second time around: after her half sister Queen Urraca passed away, the ambitious Alfonso VII demanded Tareja's loyalty. Having discovered the benefits of independence for herself, she refused. But with the Spanish king's armies carving away her territory on one front and those of her son waging war on another, and rightly so, Tareja's best course of action was to make an ally of the king of Castilla e León and tempt the Templars to change sides. So the donation of Souré was expanded, with the "gang of three" added as joint partners, hoping the Templars could be turned like mercenaries to break allegiance with her son.

There was one major point in their favor, a powerful figure with whom they were on excellent terms: Pope Honorius. News had just arrived from Champagne that Hugues de Payns had approached the pontiff with a request for papal approval of his Templars. Should the pope agree, he would no doubt instruct the knights to side with his favored Spanish and Galician brethren.

It was an excellent plan. Except for the one tiny glitch: the Knights Templar never swore allegiance to the pope.

19

hatever Pope Honorius II heard from the lips of Hugues de Payns moved him to convene an ecumenical council for January 13, the feast day of Saint Hilarius.[1] It would take place not in Rome but in the town of Troyes.

The city was named after its famous Trojan predecessor as a distant reminder of the Sicambrians, the descendents of the Trojans who settled nearby. By the twelfth century Troyes had become a center of commerce and hub of intellectual activity where an academy of esoteric studies and a Jewish Kabalist school flourished, founded by the famous medieval Rabbi Rashi; one of the school's most illustrious alumni was Chrétien de Troyes, soon-to-be composer of a medieval Grail romance.

The choice of Troyes appears premeditated and predisposed to the key figures involved with the Knights Templar and the Cistercian Order, the city being eight miles from Hugues de Payns's hometown,[2] and fifty from André de Montbard's, the uncle of Bernard de Clairvaux, whose own abbey stood 33 miles to the east on land granted by Hugues de Payns's cousin, Comte Hugh de Champagne, in whose territory all these places sat; conveniently, Hugh was also the Count of Troyes and, for a number of years now, a Templar knight.

"It would be difficult to tell them all," wrote Jean Michel, the scribe in charge of covering the convening multitude of dignitaries steadily filling the vacuum of the cathedral. Over one hundred lords, archbishops, and kings arrived from French and Germanic kingdoms, warm bodies wrapped in silks and furs mingling about on a stone floor made colder by the January frost. Although the council had been convened by Pope Honorius II, the pontiff was absent; instead it would be presided over by Cardinal Matthew, and yet no one in the building would argue that Bernard de Clairvaux was the man in charge, such was his ambassadorial reputation, one augmented by a number of outstanding manuscripts on spiritual conduct he had recently published.

Respect was accorded.

There were several items on the agenda. First up was Baudoin II's request for military and logistical support in Jerusalem, even though the king had already sent delegates to Rome the previous year to petition the pope for an identical appeal.[3] Couldn't this item have been dealt with in Rome?

The second main reason for summoning the council was to give a ruling on the quarrel between Louis VI and Bishop Stephen of Paris.[4]

Then came the third, an opportunity for the church to publicly endorse the Knights Templar, most of whose original members presently sat throughout the nave: Hugues de Payns, Godefroi de Saint-Omer, Payen de Mont-Didier, Archambaud de Saint-Aignan, Godefroi Bisol, and Brother Roland.

It has often been posited that the council was set up by the pope as an attempt by the Catholic Church to muscle in on whatever the Templars and the Cistercians were concocting between them. The Templars had been beavering away under Temple Mount for nine years now, and rumors were rife that they had discovered a treasure of some unspecified nature or stumbled upon documents of enormous import. There may be grounds for this. The fortuitous geographic location for the council and the extraordinary turnout of Europe's finest nobles and clerics makes the conclave seem all too designed to find favor with a group of humble men.

Perhaps we will never know for certain, but we do know that Bernard did not see a need to sit in on the event. His reticence was on account of the pope insisting he preach a sermon soliciting new recruits to the Knights Templar to fight the Muslims—much like the one Urban II once preached at Clermont to draw a vast body of men into the Crusade. Bernard refused on humanitarian grounds, citing how "every human being is your neighbor. To kill your neighbor, even though he be a Muslim, is against the laws of Jesus Christ," and as far as he was aware neither Christ nor the apostles had ever preached for a holy war. Neither did Bernard see warfare as the mission of the Templars, so much so that he excused himself from attending, adding, "Your reason for invading my peace is on account of matters that are either easy or difficult. If easy, my assistance is not necessary. If difficult, I am not in a state to attend to them—at least, I cannot do anything that is impossible to other men."[5]

The pope did not acquiesce to his request and insisted that Bernard preside over the council, a shrewd move given Bernard's diplomatic track record with clerics all over Europe. Bernard again declined on the grounds of illness, which indeed was true, he was suffering from a high fever.[6] So the pope sent a litter and bearers to Clairvaux and had Bernard carried the 33 miles to Troyes.

Bernard de Clairvaux was a visionary of his time, a man of great literacy, scrupulous in the face of opposition, and a figure of great influence on the religious beliefs and orders of the day. So in his discourse to the council he drew a comparison between secular soldiery and the soldiery of Christ. His proselytizing illustrated just how different in the eyes of God are the bloodshed and slaughter perpetrated by the secular militarist and the actions of the knight pursuing a noble ideal: "Among you, indeed, nought provoketh war or awakeneth strife, but either an irrational impulse of anger, or an insane lust of glory, or the covetous desire of possessing another man's lands and possessions. In such causes it is neither safe to slay nor to be slain." He followed by stating how the "soldiery of God and the soldiery of the world differ from one another," and how the perfect knight is "careful to preserve the unity of the spirit in the bond of peace."[7]

He reached for a decanter of water and continued with renewed vigor. "There is no doubt that murder is always evil, and I would forbid you to slay these pagans if another means can be found to prevent them from oppressing the faithful. But as things stand, it is better to fight them with arms than to allow them to prevail over the just, for fear that the righteous be delivered into iniquity."[8]

Bernard was hardly naïve; he knew that in his time war was sometimes necessary to remove lands from people who had little regard or respect for others, even life itself. People needed to fight in self-defense or in circumstances where property or people had been wrongfully taken—such as the case with the city of Lisbon and its inhabitants, who were all seized by the Moors and held for over three-and-a-half centuries.[9] The Middle Ages were violent times, often bordering on the barbaric, and violence would inevitably come knocking, even on the doors of monks, and often it did. Bernard's point was that if knights took up arms not to cause harm but to defend a just cause, they had nothing to fear, and he reiterated the point by making a distinction between spiritual and secular knights—the latter being empty and violent, the animalistic condition of the baser human being.

Nevertheless, enormous pressure was put upon Bernard by various members of the council. The ailing abbot capitulated and reluctantly endorsed the church's plan. Perhaps the final item on the agenda was worth a small compromise.

Hugues de Payns was invited to present his case to the council. The Templar Grand Master stood up and walked to the center of the delegation. He was oddly dressed for a knight; there were no coats of arms, no silks, no furs; instead, Hugues appeared to be a kind of old hermit, tattered garments and all. Nevertheless, he was eloquent in his speech, outlining the creation of the Knights Templar, their aims, and the difficulties of doing their work in Jerusalem. "Often," he said, "I hear 'Why do you labor in vain? Why do you expand so much effort to no purpose? Those men whom you serve acknowledge you as partners in labor but are unwilling to share in brotherhood. When do the benefactions of the faithful come to the Templars by the faithful throughout the whole world?'"[10]

His request was straightforward: to continue its work the brotherhood required logistical support, the blessing and recognition of the church (a prerequisite in those days), and a moral code to guide and govern the new members of the growing Order. And this would suffice.

Hugues and the Templars received the papal approval they sought, and a Latin Rule was drafted among the ecclesiasts and seculars present, some of whom were illiterate. The code of conduct was seventy-two articles long, labored, stringent, rigorous, and austere, a fine stereotype of design-by-committee. It requested, among many things, stringent devotional exercises, fasting, prayer, submissiveness, and gentleness, even the observance of what food should be eaten on Fridays. For example:

Rule VI: We have it that . . . when you hear the divine service you stay standing for too long. We do not advise this; in fact we condemn it. We command that everyone, strong and weak alike, should sit down when the psalm . . . is finished, as well as the invitation and the hymn, so as to avoid scandal.

Rule X: In general, brothers should eat in pairs so that one may look after the other with care lest the harshness of life or secret abstemiousness become part of the communal meal.

Rule XXXVIII: No brother should presume to exchange his belongings with another brother nor ask him for anything, without the permission of the master, and even then it should be small, trifling and unimportant.

Rule XLVII: We specially command and direct every professed brother that he venture not to shoot in the woods either with a long-bow or a cross-bow; and for the same reason, that he venture not to accompany another who shall do the like, except it be for the purpose of protecting him from the perfidious infidel.

Et cetera. Some articles at least bear Bernard's fingerprint, such as the attention to "the consummation of the divine mysteries." Also:

Rule VIII: . . . in emulation of the psalmist, who says, I have set a watch upon my mouth; that is, I have communed with myself that I may not offend, that is, with my tongue; that is, I have guarded my mouth, that I may not speak evil.

Rule XX: To all the professed knights . . . white garments, that those who have cast behind them a dark life may know that they are to commend themselves to the Creator by a pure and white life.

Rule XXXVII: We will not that gold or silver, which is the mark of private wealth, should ever be seen on your bodies.

Since the Rule also made distinctions between different members of the Knights Templar—knights, sergeants, priests, and clerks for religious services, and servants and artisans—it demonstrates how the Order had expanded well beyond the original nine (or eleven) men.[11] Although the Rule was overwhelmingly religious in nature, several clauses were added pertaining to the military duties of the Templars, although clearly this was not an Order whose core members had been

The Knights Templar are sanctified at the Council of Troyes.

doing much fighting, if any at all. The long-winded document was drafted, then edited by Bernard, and penned by "the humble scribe of these present pages," Jean Michel.[12]

And yet for all its worth the Latin Rule may well have been nothing more than an academic exercise. Despite the laborious craft, its final paragraph states that the Rules should be left to the discretion of the Grand Master, and thus of no real official value; over the next 140 years successive Grand Masters would subtly amend the Rule with more than six hundred additional clauses.

Regardless, of greater value was that by January 14, 1128, the Order of the Knights Templar gained official recognition from Rome.

1128.
BACK IN CLAIRVAUX.
UPON THE CONCLUSION OF
THE CONCLAVE . . .

is business at the Council of Troyes concluded, Hugues de Payns reminded Bernard to compose another kind of Rule: a sermon of encouragement for the Knights Templar, an affirmation of the validity of the Templars' lifestyle, and a spiritual compass for the members of the Order. Bernard noted, "Once, twice, three times, dearest Hugues, you have asked me to write a work of exhortation to yourself and your fellow knights."[1] In time, the perpetually traveling-writing-preaching Bernard would grant his request.

Thirteen chapters long—apparently the Cistercian rule of asceticism did not apply to words—*Book to the Soldiers of the Temple: In Praise of the New Militia* is a work more closely suited to Templar and Cistercian ideals; it even analyzes the spiritual significance of holy sites that were now the Templar's role to protect.[2] In his tract Bernard again makes clear the distinction between *militia* and *malicia*—between a knighthood engaged in true Christian virtues and one of worldly knights engaged in malevolence. Those who engaged in war for war's sake gained nothing, for if they died they lost their life, and if they won they lost their soul. Bernard regarded the latter as murderers who coveted riches, vanity, and personal glory. The real battle lay in the conquering of spirit over base human faults; thus a warrior monk placed ideals above barbarism, he allowed for the fight against "sinners" so they would cease menacing the "just."

The motivation behind the Knights Templar on Temple Mount and the abrupt return to Europe of its inner brotherhood and affiliates is laid bare in the preliminaries to the Rule that Bernard was drafting, in which he reveals, "Well has Damedieu [mother of God or Notre Dame] wrought with us and our savior Jesus Christ; who has set his friends of the Holy City of Jerusalem on march through France and Burgundy. . . . The work has been accomplished with our help. And the knights have been sent on the journey through Champagne under the protection, as we shall see, of the Count de Champagne, where all precautions can be taken against all interference by public or ecclesiastical authority; where at this time one can best make sure of a secret, a watch, a hiding place."[3]

What kind of work had they accomplished?

Why should it require preventive measures against church interference?

What secret did they bring back to Champagne?

The passage points to the Templars having undertaken a predetermined mission in Jerusalem, and their return to Champagne being arranged with the full knowledge of Bernard de Clairvaux. With their mission completed, the Cistercians and Templars adopted the beehive as their symbol, suggesting they had been collecting "pollen" to be brought back to the "hive" in Champagne.[4]

The symbolism is revealing. Ancient Middle Eastern and Egyptian cultures regarded the bee as a bridge between the living and the Otherworld,[5] and this divine association was adopted by the Merovingians, who used the bee as the symbol of immortality and resurrection. This is the very same lineage into which Bernard de Clairvaux and Godefroi de Bouillon were born.*[6]

---

*Godefroi de Bouillon was a scion of illustrious ancestry whose family claimed descent from King Charlemagne.

Whatever they were up to, the Templars had been putting a lot of energy into a new domicile far from ecclesiastical interference. Portugale was as distant from Rome as was possible, and its inhabitants had a history of paying lip service to papal authority. Obviously, Bernard and his Cistercian Order were involved in this plan, and his previous meeting in 1126 with the Templars André de Montbard and Brother Gondemare had been no casual get-together, especially as all three, plus the remaining Templars—Bisol de Saint-Omer, Archambaud de Saint-Aignan, Nivard de Mont-Didier, and Brother Roland, along with Hugues de Payns and Comte Hugh de Champagne—are all listed as members of the Ordre de Sion.[7]

Their secret was given safe passage through the substantial territory in central Europe owned by Comte Hugh de Champagne, one of the first sponsors and patrons of the Cistercians, whose donation of land allowed the abbey of Clairvaux to be built; later, he donated to them the abbey of Orval, the building originally erected by the monks addressing themselves as the Ordre de Sion.

Could this secret, then, involve the creation of an ideal state, a temporal mirror of the heavenly Jerusalem so idolized by Bernard de Clairvaux? After all, why would a group of men from central Europe travel all the way to Jerusalem, only to then expend all their energy settling a territory bordering the Atlantic thousands of miles to the west? There are no simple answers, and yet when Bernard drafted *In Praise to the New Militia* and various church leaders and sovereigns requested he establish a Cistercian abbey in Jerusalem, he declined, as though the holy city no longer played a role in the Order he had just publicly endorsed. Even in a letter to the pope, Bernard voiced opposition to the establishment of a Cistercian presence in Jerusalem by the abbot of the Cistercian House of Moribund, on the grounds that "he wishes to propagate the observances of our Order in that land, and for that reason to lead a multitude with him, who cannot see that the necessities are fighting knights not singing and wailing monks."[8] It seems the protection of the Holy Sepulcher or the expansion of Christianity was no longer the central aim of a holy order of knights, perhaps because it never was, and the ultimate purpose of the Templar-Cistercian alliance lay elsewhere.

Bernard de Clairvaux often meditated on the concept of a model Christian nation where the ideals of the kingdom of heaven could be experienced right here on Earth.[9] Such a vision of utopia must have felt delightful amid the dissonance of the twelfth century, and a look at the bare facts indicates Portugale was high on Bernard's inner radar.

The Cistercians had long ago established a relationship with Count Dom Henrique, whose close friends—the former Archbishop of Braga and the Bishop of Coimbra—had both come from the monastery at Cluny, from which a group of monks had left to form the Cistercian Order at Citeaux.[10] When he journeyed to the Holy Land, it was a Cistercian monk living in the Hermitage of Saint Julian in Alcobaça who "served Conde D. Henrique of Portugal in the wars, who was with the Moors, and the journey to Jerusalem."[11] Furthermore, Dom Henrique and Bernard de Clairvaux shared the same Burgundian lineage and ideals, and both their families' estates back in Dijon were practically within shouting distance of each other.

The three brotherhoods of knights—the Hospitallers, the Knights of the Holy Sepulcher, and now the Knights Templar—had gradually established themselves in Portugale since 1104; working among them were high-ranking members of the Ordre de Sion, notably Brother Gondemare (also a Cistercian monk) and Prior Arnaldo da Rocha (a relative of Bernard); even at that very moment the Templars were assisting Afonso Henriques in reestablishing his claim over the territory usurped by his mother and a Galician interloper.

If Bernard sought a new territory to implement his vision, the portents for a favorable outcome in Portugale looked good, especially since the abbot had fostered a relationship with his young nephew Afonso Henriques as early as 1119, after he had sent a delegation of monks to request land for a monastery. As an adult, Afonso fulfilled his duties as a kind of vassal to Clairvaux by gifting said abbey fifty pieces of gold.* The payment was made every year on the spring equinox "to Abbot Dom Bernardo [Bernard de Clairvaux] and his successors" and delivered on Afonso's behalf by a Procurator of the Knights Templar in Portugale. Subsequent Portuguese kings maintained this inviolable promise and were still doing so two and one-half centuries later.[12]

Suffice it to say, both the Cistercian and Templar Orders were by now deeply invested in Portugale.

The Knights Templar, in turn, did more than pledge allegiance to the Cistercian code established and expounded in Bernard's ode *In Praise of the New Militia*,[13] they were bound by the Cistercian Order, as proved in a document (in the Cistercian monastery of Alcobaça) describing the oath by which every new Templar Master or Procurator in Portugale should conduct himself:

> I [name], Knight of the Temple, newly elected master of the Knights that are in Portugal, promise . . . to defend the Mysteries of the Faith, along with the seven Sacraments, the fourteen Articles of Faith, the Symbol of the Apostles . . . and of the Virgin Mary . . . and the bloodline of King David. After this I grant sovereignty and obedience to Grand Master of the Order, according to the statutes of our father Bernard . . . and never to deny help to the religious, through words, arms and good deeds, in particular the pious of the Order of Cister and its abbots, for they are our brothers and companions.[14]

Thus the Knights Templar was predominantly a secular extension of the Cistercian ideals of Bernard de Clairvaux, and it was still being asserted as such four centuries later by Cistercian chroniclers such as Brito.[15] In a later deposition to the Holy Inquisition, Brother Aymery of Limoges made a defense on behalf of the Templars imprisoned in the abbey of Saint Geneviève, in the form of a prayer to God, in which he reveals the Templars' sponsor: "Your order, the Temple, was founded

---

*He signed the original promise in the cathedral of Lamego.

in general council for the honor of the holy and glorious Virgin Mary, your Mother, by the Blessed Bernard, your holy confessor. . . . It was he who, along with other overseers briefed and gave them their mission." He then addresses the divine Virgin, "Mary, Mother of God . . . defend your order which was founded by your holy and dear confessor, Blessed Bernard."[16]

Not only were many of the key figures of the Knights Templar connected through family ties to the Cistercian Order, most of them also were handpicked by Bernard de Clairvaux himself.[17] It is feasible, then, that if the Templars swore a vow of obedience to Bernard, their tour to Jerusalem was a mission *entrusted* to them, not of their own making. Thus, Bernard's discourses on the Templars and their public approval by him at the Council of Troyes had been mere window dressing, a public gesture, which to some degree explains his reluctance to publicly endorse the Templar Order at the council. It was a fait accompli.

There is another part to this equation, and it involves the Templars' sister fraternity, the Knights Hospitaller; they even shared the same emblem, the red cross—the Templar version defined by its sinuous semicircular pattern in contrast to the Hospitallers' hard, angular lines and edges.[18] Relatively speaking, both Orders had a presence as old as each other's in Portugale, but, just as in Jerusalem, they fulfilled very different roles.[19] The Hospitallers' first conventual house and primary chapter in Portugale was in Leça in 1112;[20] the property was expanded ten years later to include a monastery and its four houses eight miles away in Gondomare.[21]

The first significant thing about these places is their geographic proximity: Gondomare lies eight miles from Fonte Arcada—the Templar's major donation of 1125—which in turn lies 33 miles west of Tarouca, the first monastery founded by Cistercian monks. The second significant thing concerns one of the monks sent by Bernard to found said monastery, Brother Roland, whom locals described as "an expert of the deeds of France."[22] Could this man be the same Brother Roland, one of the original Knights Templar handpicked by Bernard de Clairvaux?

If so, it places *two* of the founding Templars (three, if we accept the assertions about Prior Arnaldo da Rocha) in Portugale many years before the Council of Troyes—Brother Roland at Tarouca in 1119, and Brother Gondemare at the monastery of his namesake Portuguese town, who took possession of a nearby property on behalf of the Order of the Temple in 1114.[23]

And while Brother Roland moved to Portugale from Champagne, the itinerant Brother Gondemare journeyed from Portugale to Jerusalem to join the other original Templars; then in 1126, he boarded a galley bound for Champagne to deliver news of the knights' discoveries to Bernard de Clairvaux.

It appears all the comings and goings between Clairvaux, Portugale, and Jerusalem were by design, and the groundwork laid in Portugale by Cistercians, Templars, and members of the Ordre de Sion was one long, patient enterprise undertaken long before the pope placed his stamp of approval upon Hugues de Payns and his knights.

21

1128. APRIL.
A CHAMBER IN THE
ROYAL RESIDENCE OF
GUIMARÃES . . .

ccording to the account by a Spanish historian, the conversation between Afonso Henriques, his mother, and her husband, Count Fernán Péres de Traba, went something like this:

Fernán: "Prince, let us not tire ourselves anymore over this contest, but fight me in battle one day, me and you, whenever you want, and either you will leave this kingdom, or I."

Afonso: "It would not please God very much if your wish is to kick me out of the lands that my father inherited."

Tareja: "It is *my* land, my father gave it to *me,* and allowed *me* to inherit it."

Fernán (to his wife): "Let's end this discussion or I will drag you back to Galiza; or leave the lands to your son, if it makes us more powerful."[1]

This cordial family scene could only mean one thing: Afonso Henriques had fully returned from the exile his mother had imposed, and, judging by his boldness to show his face at court, his war so far was proving very successful. On his way to Guimarães he took the opportunity to seize the castles of Faria and Neiva, overran other nearby battlements, reclaimed towns around Braga for good measure, and a quick glance beyond the windows of the palace would have shown that his troops were now in plain view of the royal seat. And now that we know just what a manipulative and dysfunctional family he had, one sympathizes.

Afonso Henriques's confidence as a knight was ascendant, no doubt bolstered by the good news that had just reached him from Troyes of the Knights Templar securing formal papal approval.

His relationship with the Order, not to mention the military advantage they presented, was becoming ever more obvious with the string of battles already won. Clearly the opposition's gamble to buy the Templars' affection with the donation of Souré had not paid off.

If the fortune of the gods favored the just, the time to strike for an independent kingdom was now. Afonso picked a location for a showdown with his mother and Fernán Péres de Traba on the fields of São Mamede, just beyond the walls of Guimarães.

He kneeled to his God and prayed for guidance. The confrontation would take place on the feast day of John the Baptist.

Castle of Guimarães.

22

1128.
MEANWHILE IN
CHAMPAGNE . . .

o sooner had the Council of Troyes adjourned than the Knights Templar received the first of hundreds of donations, this one from Raoul the Fat and his wife, of all their possessions near the city;[1] as expected, Hugues de Payns himself donated his own lands to the Order of the Temple.

Hugues and Bernard de Clairvaux bid each other a fond adieu. The knight's exhaustive European tour to secure diplomatic ties and raise funds and recruits was about to get underway.

Hugues left first for Anjou to meet Comte Fulk d'Anjou, who had himself been ordained into the Knights Templar and in time would succeed Baudoin II as King of Jerusalem.

By April he appeared in Le Mans, then ventured south to Roussillon, on the French side of the Pyrenees, to meet with Raimund Bernard, Templar Master of Portugale.[2] Indeed, the two men were glad to be reunited for the first time in three years, following Raimund's dispatch by the Grand Master from Jerusalem in the winter of 1125.[3]

Since taking up residence in Braga, the Burgundian knight had been every bit as productive as Hugues, and only weeks prior to the meeting he had secured the donation of the castle and lands of

Souré—twice.[4] He then acquired either the fastest horse or hitched a ride on the fastest galley to rendezvous with Hugues. Surrounded by the fragrant air of a Mediterranean spring, Master Dom Raimundo would have delighted the ears of his Grand Master on the excellent forward progress currently taking place in Portugale, how its young prince was living up to all expectations, and with Templar assistance, the declaration of an independent Portugale was now just a matter of time; Dom Guilherme Ricard—the other Templar Master in Portugale—also sent his best regards.

As did Archbishop Payo Mendes, who was adding five chapels to Braga's cathedral—essentially fitting a crown on the body—in honor of the sanctioning of the Knights Templar, the moment the Order itself was symbolically "crowned."

The esoteric implications are notable, for in the number of chapels lies a reference to the pentagram, the five-pointed geometric form associated with *sophis* (wisdom) and Isis, the divine virgin whose temple served as the foundation for the cathedral.

Business concluded, Dom Raimundo shook hands with Hugues and returned posthaste to assist Afonso Henriques and the affairs of a new nation in the making.

Talk about devotion to duty.

Satisfied, Hugues returned to northern France, soliciting help along the way. In June, he met with Henry I of England in Normandie. "The king received him with great honour and gave him great treasures, consisting of gold and silver; and then he sent him to England and there he was received by all good men and they all gave him treasure, and in Scotland also, and sent by him to Jerusalem great Property entirely in gold and silver."[5]

He then boarded a boat with the Templar brother Payen de Mont-Didier, soon-to-be Templar Master of England, for the short crossing to England. During his visit he raised extraordinary amounts of money and men, and a preceptory at High Holborn in London on the site of a former Roman temple.

Hugues de Payns's connections in Jerusalem no doubt opened the doors for what would, in hindsight, prove to be a crucial trip to Scotland, following the late Godefroi de Bouillon's brother Eustace III's marriage to Mary of Scotland.[6] There, Hugues found great favor with King David I, who obviously liked what he heard because he granted Hugues the lands and village of Balantrodoch (later to become Temple), where he set up a preceptory and church. King David was himself very taken with the Templar Order, for he "entrusted himself entirely to the guidance of religious [monks], retaining beside him the most noble brethren of the distinguished military order of the Temple of Jerusalem, he made them both by day and night custodians of his morals."[7]

The indefatigable Hugues was back in France by September 1128 to meet with his longtime cofounder Godefroi de Saint-Omer, no doubt to exchange notes and catch their breath and marvel at the speed in which their proposal was winning everyone they encountered. Whatever the Knights Templar were selling, everyone was buying. Houses and estates and hundreds of donations were received within the year throughout France.

All the while their networks were activated to enable the foundation of a secure land base in the west of Europe,[8] where relationships had been nurtured for some twenty-four years and donations were being received by the Order of the Temple at a faster pace than elsewhere in Europe,[9] probably as a result of Afonso Henriques's efforts on a battlefield near Guimarães.

Indeed, everything seemed on course to manifest Hugues de Payns's first Templar nation and Bernard de Clairvaux's temporal New Jerusalem.

On one side stood the combined armies of Fernán Péres de Traba (representing Galicia), Archbishop Diego Gelmírez (representing the Diocese of Compostela), and some Portuguese troops loyal to Countess Tareja. On the opposing side, the forces commanded by Afonso Henriques, troops loyal to Archbishop Payo Mendes of Braga, and just about every other person capable of bearing arms and representing all the lords of Portugale.

Not one to stand by her own son, Tareja turned to her husband and declared, "I want to go into battle by your side, because you have more reason to do things for my love, and however hard I have worked to imprison my son, the two of us together are more powerful than him."[1]

Which, as it turns out, was not exactly an accurate assessment of the situation. Not only had Afonso acquired the unanimous support of the nobles—a substantial number of whom, like him, were of Burgundian descent—a charter dated May 27 also placed the rights of the churches of Braga in Afonso's service, meaning that the prince secured the ecclesiastical support of the bishopric of Braga, the most influential church of the region.[2] The charter was signed by an impressive list of local dignitaries, including his mentor Payo Mendes as well as the indefatigable Templar Master Dom Raimundo Bernardo, barely returned from his meeting with Hugues de Payns in the south of France.[3]

The net result was that the forces commanded by Afonso Henriques ultimately prevailed on the battlefield of São Mamede. Both his mother and Fernán were imprisoned, yet despite having Tareja clapped in irons she still managed to send word to her nephew Affonso VII to come rescue her. Which he did, along with the combined armies of Castilla e León, Aragon e Galicia, and, like his aunt, he too was vanquished in battle.

Afonso finally banished his mother to a convent in Galicia, although not before she put a curse on him as a parting gift; as for her husband, he was released back into the wilds of Galicia and disappeared into obscurity. Some say he went abroad.

And so on June 24, 1128, the battle of São Mamede established the de facto independence of Portugal. The ancient lands bordered by the rivers Minho and Mondego, once known as Lusitania, are finally united and no longer subordinate to anyone—all of this a mere five months after the Council of Troyes, where the Knights Templar were formally recognized as a sovereign organization.

A jubilant Afonso Henriques entered Guimarães as de facto prince of Portugal and reissued the city's charter, effectively reestablishing the rights and concessions made earlier by his late father, while amplifying the rights of its dwellers in acknowledgment of the support they gave him.[4]

Afonso has been described as a shrewd diplomat, erudite of speech, prudent in his deeds, tenacious, and prepared to defend his country against all threats, and the wording on the charter of Guimarães is an indication of such qualities. Not only is the document a declaration of independence from the yoke of Spanish influence, but also, scribed upon its caramel parchment are unmistakable signals as to who was behind the events that remolded Portugale from a county into an independent state. In its wording, Afonso claims his authority extends throughout his territory *ab omni pressura alienus* (free from any outside interference), an echo of the words employed by his uncle Bernard de Clairvaux in describing the protection afforded the Templars on their return to Champagne with their secret.[5] It is perhaps the most overt statement acknowledging the invisible hand played by the head of the Cistercian Order in paving the way for a new, model Christian kingdom and an indication that whatever secret the Templars had been working with in Jerusalem was equally at play in Portugal.

But Afonso's passionate words are subordinate to the symbol around which they wrap and to which the eye is indubitably drawn: the unmistakable cross of the Knights Templar. It dominates the vellum, a seal of approval by the Order, implemented by one of its own brothers. After all, to all ends and purposes, Afonso Henriques had been the administrator of the Knights Templar in Portugal.[6]

Charter of Guimarães.

ccording to the historical account, "Knowing of this donation [Souré], and intending himself to be the landlord of this property, so as not to let down the members of the Order (to whom he was greatly obligated) by rescinding the donation, he thus granted the donation of said castle, but this time in his own name."[1]

Afonso Henriques nullified the previous donation of Souré and within the year replaced it with an expanded donation in his own name, without the restrictions imposed in the original document.[2]

Afonso's wording on the reconstituted charter to the Knights Templar evokes the passion of a young, focused man, referring to his new position as "only by the mercy of God, Prince of the Portuguese," but also unequivocally reveals why he was so "greatly obligated" to the Order of the Temple: "I make this donation, not by force or by persuasion, but for the love of God, and for the good of my soul, and of my parents, and by the cordial love that I have for you, and because within your Brotherhood and in all your works I am a Brother."[3]

It was not unusual for the inner members of the Order of the Temple to address each other informally as "brothers"; the highest-ranking member himself is addressed as such in the Rule, "Master,

Brother Hugues de Payens."[4] Thus, Afonso Henriques reveals that at the age of twenty he is a fully fledged member of the brotherhood of the Knights Templar, and probably had been since his knighting ceremony in Zamora, as suspected.

Beside his name on the vellum document is inscribed the unmistakable Templar logo.

Afonso Henriques.

1139.
OURIQUE.
PREPARING TO BATTLE
THE MOORS . . .

mid his new duties as head of an independent state, Afonso never forgot the importance of the role played by his mentor, the Templar sympathizer Payo Mendes. A month after taking up residence in Guimarães, the ebullient prince made a generous property donation to his friend in anticipation of the day "when I have acquired the land of Portugal."[1]

If Afonso was under any illusion that the day he would own the remaining Portuguese territory would come easily or soon, it was quickly dispelled. Although the threat from the armies of Castilla e León in the north was temporarily in check, the Moors had reoccupied Portuguese lands south to the river Tejo once liberated by his father, including the city of Lisbon. A definitive blow had to be delivered to the Arabs, and that day arrived eleven years later on the plains of Ourique.

The Moors obviously viewed the impending skirmish as a potentially defining moment in Portuguese solidarity, given how they mustered the combined forces of no less than five caliphs. In the decade since the Portuguese had taken the city of Guimarães, the Arabs painfully watched the successful southward reconquest of territory, so much so that Afonso Henriques was able to move the seat of power eighty miles south to Coimbra, a historic city abutting the frontier territory currently under Arab dominion. The move gave Afonso room for a fresh start, a break with the old politics of the established territories of the north and the dense intricacies of aristocratic privilege that hampered forward progress in building a nation-state.[2]

No sooner had he settled into his new abode when, contrary to military preparedness, his first major activity in the city was to attend to the founding of the monastery of the Holy Cross for a community of regular canons of Saint Augustine, which would feature as a major urban property along the city's walls. By conventional military terms this was an odd endeavor in a time of war, and war there was aplenty, starting with the thousands of gathering Moorish forces whose swelling ranks gradually masked the contours of the rolling plains around Ourique.

The Portuguese army began preparations around July 22, the feast day of Mary Magdalene. Three days later, the tall figure of Afonso Henriques walked pensively toward the head of his army, his mind oscillating between the demands of military preparation and the prophetic dream he had experienced the previous night, in which he was convinced his armies would prevail on the battlefield. His reverie was interrupted by a contingent of nobles and knights approaching him, among them Guilherme Ricard, the first Templar Master of Portugale, who took the prince by surprise with an unexpected proposition. Following a secret meeting of the gathered lords, it was their unanimous

Battle of Ourique.

wish that Afonso be declared king of Portugal before the commence-
ment of hostilities.[3] Afonso was startled: "My brothers, it is my honor
to be your lord, and I feel well served and protected by you, and because
I am satisfied with this I do not wish to be called "king," nor to be one,
but as your brother and friend I will help you with my body to defeat
these enemies of the faith."[4]

But the knights insisted. Not only was it their desire, but given the
insurmountable odds faced by the Portuguese troops against a vastly
superior Arab army, the men would doubtless be encouraged at the
prospect of marching into battle behind a monarch.

Afonso reluctantly accepted the honor, like an echo of his predecessor Godefroi de Bouillon when he too was offered the title of king
of Jerusalem without his solicitation and during the same time span of
July 22 to 25.* Following a brief ceremony on the battlefield, Afonso's
horse was brought forward, covered with his customary white man-
tles; his knights rode left and right and took charge of their respective
flanks, and the battle to rout the Moors commenced.

Hostilities raged for three hours beyond midday in the stifling heat
of July, both sides made indistinguishable by the orange dust propelled
skyward by hands and feet engaged in fevered combat. Against all odds,
the Moors were vanquished.

By July 25, the triumph was complete. Afonso commemorated the
event by amending the shield of Portugale he carried with him, an
inheritance from his late father—the blue cross over a field of white—
to incorporate thirty silver bezants, a reminder of the symbolic entry
requirement into the Templar Order.[5]

Three days after the cessation of hostilities, Afonso returned to
Coimbra and the monastery of the Holy Cross, where he met with its
prior, Dom Telo, for advice on the issue regarding prisoners of war,
not to mention the scores of Arab citizens who in a twist of fortune

---

*Godefroi de Bouillon was offered the throne within days of the council convening to
discuss the matter on July 22, 1100. The decision was made between July 23 and 25.

suddenly found themselves under Portuguese domain. The aged prior suggested to the victorious king the honorable course of action would be to take the high ground: show mercy, for even the Cistercians would acknowledge that to fight a war for war's sake defeated the purpose of the spiritual warrior. By setting an example, in time one's enemies may become friends.

The new king listened. A pardon was announced and Muslim prisoners were released.[6]

Afonso then rode north to gather the first assembly of the estates-general, and in a cathedral ceremony at Lamego—a stone's throw from the first Cistercian monastery he once helped a group of monks from Clairvaux to found in Portugale—Afonso Henriques was officially crowned King of Portugal by none other than Payo Mendes.

When he arises, he does so not just as head of an independent country but also as king of Europe's first nation-state.[7]

26

1139.
CLAIRVAUX. EARLY DAWN,
OUTSIDE THE CHAPEL . . .

ernard was in the middle of conducting *matins* when the crunching sound of horse hooves on gravel announced the arrival of two excited, albeit tired knights—Afonso's half brother Dom Pedro and one of the original Knights Templar, Brother Roland, who had rushed from Portugal bearing a letter announcing the success at the battle at Ourique, the crowning of a king, and the birth of a nation.[1]

Bernard sat down and opened the letter bearing good news, in which Afonso addressed him as his close relative.[2] Uncle Bernard would have been equally pleased to learn that despite his nephew's rise as leader of a nation, Afonso had not succumbed to the lust of power; he had honored his vows, and no sooner was he awarded the crown of Portugal than he demonstrated his gratitude to his supporters by donating yet more properties to the Knights Templar, the Knights of the Holy Sepulcher, and the Cistercian Order.[3]

The Templars were equally pleased. Their devotion to this bold young man had paid off, as did their decades of patience in this geopolitical enterprise. However, their involvement in the battle of Ourique came at a heavy price: the first Templar Master, Dom Guilherme Ricard, fell in battle defending his Templar brother and king. Afonso ensured continuity by appointing the next Templar Master, Hugh Martin. He additionally ordained several knights into the Templar Order while on the battlefield, including Gualdino Paes, one of the five Preceptors sent by Hugues de Payns to "establish the Portuguese crown."[4] Only a man who was already a high-ranking member within the Knights Templar would have had the power and authority to make such appointments.

A year after the battle, another figure who helped steer the course of events from the onset, the indefatigable archbishop Payo Mendes, was also laid to rest,* but true to his style, not before making his nemesis, Archbishop Diego Gelmírez of Compostela, recognize the new Portuguese bishop of Porto and relinquish the Galician church's influence over this, the most Portuguese of all cities. Ironically, the new bishop would replace Payo a year later, upon his autumn funeral, almost as if Payo had had a premonition of his own passing.

Payo also bequeathed his estate to the Knights Templar.

Another illustrious figure who did not live to see the manifestation of a temporal New Jerusalem was the Templar Grand Master Hugues de Payns, who passed away in Jerusalem in 1136.[5]

Nevertheless, 1139 proved to be a watershed for the Templars. In France, the Order received one of its most important donations, one that would play a pivotal role in the efficient movement of resources—and ultimately their treasure—the port of La Rochelle, "entirely free and quit of all custom," donated by a most enlightened woman of the period, Eleanor of Aquitaine. Meanwhile in Rome, the long fight for the recently vacant papal throne was finally won by the painstaking diplomatic efforts of Bernard de Clairvaux, whose protégé Innocent II was elevated to the status of pope. Given that Innocent had been a former monk at Clairvaux, it will come as no surprise that no sooner had he ascended the highest chair in Christendom than he issued *Omne datum optimum,* a papal bull underwriting the Knights Templar's privileges.

---

*Some accounts give this as 1138, but if Payo crowned Afonso in Lamego in 1139 he could not possibly have been dead.

The bull asserted the knights owe no allegiance to any secular order or ecclesiastical authority other than the pope himself, and since the pope was a Cistercian, the decree may as well have stated the Templars owed allegiance only to Clairvaux. Their power would now be totally independent from kings and prelates and free of interference from political or religious authorities. To all intents and purposes, the Order was now an autonomous international corporation. In time, the Templars would collectively become the richest order in Europe, surpassing even the incalculable coffers of the church, and yet paradoxically, its first generation of knights renounced all wealth and lived in austere conditions.

They were, however, rich in real estate, for one of their brotherhood was now king of a entire nation-state.

In just three decades the tiny kingdom of Portugal grew into a formidable social, political, economical, religious, and military Templar territory. In fact, the fortunes of Portugal, the Templars, and the Cistercians were intertwined, all entities rising in tandem. Still, the campaign to oust the Arab colonizers fully from Portuguese territory would occupy Afonso Henriques for a decade, even with generous assistance from both the Templars and the Knights Hospitaller, not to mention colorful infidels such as Geraldo the Fearless, who was renowned for scaling Moorish battlements unseen and hiding among the enemy at night, then just before dawn making such a frightful racket that made the townspeople believe a whole regiment was attacking. He would then raise the portcullis of the drawbridge and allow Afonso's troops to enter while he returned to camp with a sack full of booty.

Curiously, during these consolidating years the core Templars generally detached themselves from military affairs and instead devoted an enormous effort exclusively to one aim: the creation of a territory within Portugal where the Order would flourish based on Cistercian ideals and the knowledge gleaned from their secret work in Jerusalem. At first, the center of operations remained in and around Braga, as a document from 1151 states: "Your brothers of the Temple S. Petro Gratial & Martino Pelais, who live in Braga under the command of Dom Ugo."[6] Two years later, the Templar Order was sold a property on the river Aliste in the nearby town of Villar, followed by the sale of a property in Feira for twenty-three pieces of gold.[7] "This is the charter of sale, which I wish to make to you Master Ugo, and to your brothers of the Temple, voluntarily and in peace."[8]

The eighteenth-century Franciscan historian Viterbo elegantly summarizes the importance of the events at hand: "How useful it would have been to have an entire monarchy available, founded from the dissolution of lands formerly under Spanish control."[9] For that was precisely what transpired with the independence of Portugal in 1128, followed by its sovereignty eleven years later. Except it all had not been a matter of convenience, but of patient design. The Knights Templar, in association with the Cistercians and the Ordre de Sion, achieved their objective, the creation of a prototype Christian state, and yet what they would create there would be as impressive as it was mysterious.

The question is, why Portugal, why so far from the Templars' point of origin? The answer would begin in the municipality of Ceras, in a dilapidated church on the edge of a ramshackle town beneath a limestone promontory bearing a passing resemblance to Mount Sion.

INTERMEZZO

et us recap the story so far. Toward the end of the eleventh century the duchies of Lorraine, Champagne, and Burgundy form a nucleus of European enlightenment. Their noble households are connected by an intricate web of lineages and marriages, the most prominent being the Merovingian bloodline, which is said to represent a tradition of enlightened priest-kings dating back to the time of Troy and Sumeria.

At this time, a group of monks addressing themselves as the Ordre de Sion arrive at Orval and grooms a young knight named Godefroi de Bouillon, who, thanks to the convenient timing of a Crusade, journeys to "free the church of the Holy Sepulcher." With the Ordre's assistance he becomes princeps of the holy city. In return, he installs the monks in the dilapidated abbey on Mount Sion, where their roots allegedly began around the time of John the Baptist.

Meanwhile, a noble named Henri of Burgundy receives the county of Portucale as a dowry and becomes its governor. As Count Dom Henrique, he journeys to Jerusalem at the time of its reconquest; with him is Pedro Arnaldo da Rocha, a Portuguese-born man of Burgundian heritage whose family has close ties with the Cistercian Order. The two men form bonds with a number of kinfolk in the holy city, including Godefroi de Bouillon, future Templar Grand Master Hugues de Payns, and Comte Hugh de Champagne, an early benefactor of both the Templars and the Cistercians.

Under the protection of Count Dom Henrique, the proto-Templars, the Knights Hospitaller, and the Knights of the Holy Sepulcher all establish a presence in Portucale as early as 1104. As do the Cistercians, whose abbot, Bernard de Clairvaux, sends a delegation of monks in 1119 to request the founding of a monastery from the young Afonso Henriques—Bernard's nephew and future king of Portugal. One of the monks, Brother Roland, a founder Templar knight, acts as emissary between Portugale and Clairvaux. A second monk, Brother Gondomare—also an original Templar and alleged member of the Ordre de Sion—is revealed to be Portuguese. He accepts a property donation in the city of Braga on behalf of the Order of the Temple as early as 1114.

Even though Count Dom Henrique succeeds in reconquering Portuguese lands all the way south to Lisbon, his untimely death puts a temporary hold on plans discussed with the proto-Templars until such time as his young son, Afonso, is old enough to rule. In the meantime, the prince's mentoring is undertaken by Payo Mendes, archbishop of Braga and prior of the Knights Hospitaller.

$$\mathcal{Q}$$

Back in Jerusalem the proto-Templars move on to Temple Mount in 1118 and become the Knights Templar. Hugues de Payns develops a close relationship with Arnaldo da Rocha, who has become the abbot of the Ordre de Sion; Cistercian chroniclers claim him to be a previously unknown founder Templar knight.

In 1125 the Templars discover something on Temple Mount. Hugues de Payns sends five Templar Procurators—three French, two Portuguese—to establish a Portuguese crown. Thanks to long-standing connections within Portugale, the Templars set up permanent residence in and around the city of Braga and nominate a regional Master, Guilherme Ricard. Three years before they receive official acknowledgment by the pope at the Council of Troyes, the Templars receive strategic properties in Portugal and continue to do so there at a faster rate than anywhere else in Europe.

Afonso Henriques comes of age and is secretly ordained into the Order of the Temple shortly before engaging in a war against his mother to regain control of his rightful territory, with open support from the Knights Templar.

Five months after their official proclamation in Troyes, the Knights Templar assist Afonso Henriques in securing the country's independence; eleven years later, following Afonso's victory at the battle of Ourique, they are instrumental in establishing Portugal as Europe's first independent nation-state.

These are the facts so far.

The big question is, why would a group of knights and monks venture all the way from the Frankish and Flemish duchies to Jerusalem, only to establish a new territory 2,500 miles to the west?

Did the Templars and the Cistercians really believe they could build a temporal New Jerusalem in a remote corner of Europe?

Why would they constantly reference John the Baptist, Mary Magdalene, Isis, ancient places of veneration, and pagan feast days?

Were their motives related to the secret they uncovered in Jerusalem, a secret that required special protection from the church and one that the knights would rather die than reveal?

And if so, did they deposit this secret in Portugal?

1867.
JAFFA. A MULE TRAIN
HEADING TOWARD
JERUSALEM . . .

On the afternoon of February 15, a team of British excavators landed at the pier despite the convulsions of the waters of the Mediterranean. After unpacking various crates filled with spades, handspikes, crowbars, theodolites, and sextants, they headed east on the dirt road to Jerusalem at 4 a.m. to the accompaniment of a piercing cold wind that at times was forceful enough to blow over the laden mules. Corporals Birtles, Phillips, and Hancock, together with Captains Warren and Wilson, were seasoned to such inclement weather. What they were not prepared for was the creeping pace of their party, which accomplished the 33-mile journey in an unreasonable thirteen hours.

Upon finally reaching Jerusalem, Captain Wilson presented himself to the British consul, and together they called on Governor Izzet Pacha, who regretted to inform the captain that a necessary letter had not arrived, and that pending its appearance he would be happy to grant Wilson authority to dig anywhere except inside al-Haram ash-Sharif— the Noble Sanctuary, the Dome of the Rock. The Moslems were jittery about the engineers digging on Temple Mount to begin with, especially es Sakhra (Sacred Rock), for it was tradition that beneath this foundation stone all the rivers of the earth's energy sprang, and prying into

Digging beneath Jerusalem.

this holy site could bring calamity upon the country. The world, even.

Nevertheless, the letter requesting archaeological approval finally arrived, asking that the men be afforded "the necessary facilities in respect of the object of the mission, and permission and all possible facilities to dig and inspect places after satisfying the owners . . . with the exception of the Noble Sanctuary and the various Moslem and Christian shrines."[1]

The digging was slow, cumbersome, uncomfortable, and dragged on for years. It consisted mostly of square shafts sunk into runny shingle and hard limestone and layers of debris of ancient cities piled one on top of the other. Sometimes the Royal Engineers encountered ancient sewage that would fester any blister on the digger's hands. The working trenches were sometimes no more than two feet wide and in soil so loose it would widen into holes large enough to swallow an ox.

Warren and his team found encouragement whenever they broke through unexpected galleries and chambers. And there were many.

Some had formed by the natural force of water acting on the porous limestone, yet others were clearly shaped by men from a bygone era. Who had been deranged enough to dig tunnels under Temple Mount in air so vitiated that even candles found it difficult to breathe?

Their tenacity was rewarded as they came across halls and vaults and archways flanking the subterranean foundations bearing the sanctuary's walls. Arches were supported by more arches beneath, creating a labyrinth of chambers. This was easily the oldest masonry in Jerusalem, or under it, some overlaid with later Saracenic architecture.

One chamber above all stood out from the rest and merited Warren to be lowered by rope into its rectangular form, thirty feet by twenty-three, the walls built of square stones and joined without mortar, each corner marked with a pillar topped by a capital; in the center arose a column. One such room adjacent to the Temple of Solomon itself was once described in the Talmud as a secret chamber reserved for special ceremonies.

Then the engineers came across tunnels cut centuries earlier in which were found artifacts belonging to the Knights Templar: a cross and sword as well as a spur and remnants of a lance.

The artifacts made their way to a Templar archivist in Edinburgh, the grandson of a friend of Captain Parker, one of the Royal Engineers who'd assisted Warren in the digs; he was also given a letter written by Parker explaining that during one of the excavations beneath Herod's Temple he discovered a secret room beneath Temple Mount with a passageway leading to a wall. When he broke through the stonework he found himself briefly inside the Mosque of Omar, in the south courtyard of the Church of the Holy Sepulcher. His astonishment was curt, however, as he was immediately chased by an angry mob of devout Muslims praying inside the mosque.[2]

Among the many findings by the Royal Engineers was one of the shafts sunk by the Templars beneath Temple Mount, eighty feet in depth through solid rock before branching out horizontally in a series of laborious radial tunnels. Like the British, the Templars before them had obviously dug surreptitiously to avoid a confrontation with the Muslims, who continued to be granted access to their sacred sites even after their defeat in 1100.

Almost a century elapsed before the next significant excavations were conducted by a group of Israeli archaeologists, who also stumbled upon a tunnel dug by the Knights Templar:

> The tunnel leads inward for a distance of about thirty metres from the southern wall before being blocked by pieces of stone and debris. We know that it continues further, but we had made it a hard-and-fast rule not to excavate within the bounds of the Temple Mount, which is currently under Moslem jurisdiction, without first acquiring the permission of the appropriate Moslem authorities. In this case they permitted us only to measure and photograph the exposed section of the tunnel, not to conduct an excavation of any kind. Upon concluding this work . . . we sealed up the tunnel's exit with stones.[3]

Tunnels beneath Temple Mount.

Without question, the Templars had dug their way to the most sacred parts of Jerusalem—the Church of the Holy Sepulcher, the es Sakhra of the Muslims, the Shetiyya of the Jews—the very foundation stone of the sacred mount where Solomon's Temple had once stood. But what specifically had they been looking for, and how had the Templars known where to dig?

28

1146.

COIMBRA. AT HOME WITH
AFONSO AND HIS NEW BRIDE . . .

Afonso Henriques must have paused for breath because he suddenly became aware he was thirty-seven years of age and single. Maybe he was finally letting down his guard after the pope's emissary convinced him that to engage in further hostilities with his brutish northern neighbor Affonso VII of Castilla e León—whom Afonso defeated in Guimarães but who'd since regained his fighting spunk—only benefited their common enemy, the Moors. And so the two sparring cousins, Afonso and Affonso, finally shook hands in peace, ironically back in the holy city of Zamora, where the Portuguese king was knighted.

Now here he was, in the prime of his life, monarch, Templar brother, creator of Europe's first independent nation-state, surely a magnet for any number of eligible noble women wandering the European circuit seeking good aristocratic stock. His lineage from the dukes of Burgundy probably had some part to play in his decision to stiffen his resolve and propose to Mafalda, a cousin of the Duke of Burgundy, who gladly accepted, and the two distant blood relatives were joined in matrimony.

The newlyweds enjoyed a relatively brief moment of conjugal bliss because on March 10, 1147, upon receiving a letter from Clairvaux, Afonso marched his troops out of Coimbra without giving them the

vaguest idea where they were headed. They stopped in Souré to pick
up its resident Templar militia, and four days later, in the middle of the
night, a select group of 120 knights sneaked into the Moorish-held city
of Santarém.[1] By sunrise, the well-fortified city was taken with the min-
imum of resistance.[2] Removing Santarém from the hands of the Moors
was sweet recompense for the Templars' defeat at Souré three years earlier at the hands of Santarém's Arab governor, Abu-Zakaria, who leveled
the town and brought half its population back with him as slaves.

On the charter issued to the city, Afonso made a solemn promise
to the Templars.

> When I began that journey to that castle which is called Santarém, I
> made a proposition in my heart, and I took a vow, that if God in his
> mercy should permit me, I would give all the ecclesiastical posses-
> sions to God and to the military brothers of the Temple of Solomon,
> established in Jerusalem for the defense of the Holy Sepulcher, part

of which [Order] was established with me in the same country. And since God made such honor to me and well fulfilled my wish, I Afonso, above-named king, together with wife, Mafalda, make the charter to the above-mentioned knights of Christ for every church in Santa Irene [Santarém], that they and all their successors might have and possess in perpetual right, so that no cleric or layman can question this. But if by chance it happens that at any time God, in his mercy, gives to me that city which is called Lisbon, they are to agree with the bishop on my advice. Should anyone attempt to annul my gift, he may not do so on any condition, and should anyone want to contest it may he be removed from the fellowship of the Holy Church, and may he not share the joys of Jerusalem.[3]

The document was corroborated and accepted by the current Templar Master of Portugal, Hugh Martin (Hugo Martiniens, as the Portuguese knew him),[4] and with Santarém secured, the Templars moved their base of operations out of Braga.

Oddly, despite Santarém being of prime strategic importance—the bulwark of the frontier of the burgeoning Portuguese kingdom and the doorstep to the great city of Lisbon—the Templars showed little interest in guarding their new ecclesiastical seat against retaliation by the Moors. Their singular focus centered on the city's ecclesiastical holdings, specifically the main church the king granted them. They moved into the mosque, dedicated it to John the Baptist,[5] then put the greatest effort into building a new temple in the form of the church of Our Lady of Alcaçova, founded by no lesser a figure than the mysterious Arnaldo da Rocha.[6] A dedication stone above the main door of the church reads, "This church was founded in honor of the Virgin Mary . . . by the soldiers of the Temple of Jerusalem, by order of Master Ugonis, this edifice under the care of Petrus Arnaldo."*[7] It would have been a fitting tribute to Prior Arnaldo given that this city was his birthplace.[8]

---

*The stone is posthumous and goes on to state, "May their souls rest in peace."

It is strikingly odd that Afonso Henriques, new king of a new nation, having expended resources and personal effort in both conquering and defending it from the Moors, should persistently and effortlessly donate enormous tracts of land, churches, and strategic castles to the Templars. Such actions only make sense when one considers he was the administrator of the Templar Order in Portugal and without doubt the leader of its military arm.[9] Still, it makes one wonder why the Templars should require so much territory. The inheritances were vast and certainly beyond their capacity to both administer or protect. Writing in the eighteenth century, the chronicler Bernardo da Costa described the enormous quantity of donations made to the Knights Templar in Portugal at this time and how "copying all of them down would make this story too large." Obviously, he had access to far more contemporary documents than are now available, because a devastating fire in Viseu destroyed the Cistercian central archive in 1841.

Even more bizarre, the Templars showed extraordinary indifference to the rights they were awarded, nor did they take advantage of the exceptional property they were given, as though they were executing a preconceived plan or pursuing something of far greater value, something intangible and nonmaterial.

Afonso was equally kind to his uncle Bernard de Clairvaux, with whom he maintained a healthy correspondence.[10] The Cistercians received extensive donations of land from the Portuguese king, such as the forty-four thousand hectares on the mountain of Candeeiros;[11] the hermit João Cirita (who had once petitioned a young Afonso, along with the group of monks from Clairvaux) visited the now grown-up king to request another monastery, at Alafões, for which Afonso gladly issued a new charter in 1146; and when the See of Porto once again became vacant, it was offered to a Cistercian monk named Pedro.[12] Thanks to these and further donations in the area around the king's birthplace of Viseu,[13] the Cistercians thrived in his new Portugal and contributed to the profound change in agricultural and educational fortunes, the two central tenets of Cistercian philosophy.[14]

Perhaps the biggest surprise to Bernard de Clairvaux was the day when a messenger arrived at his abbey with a letter from Afonso requesting the aging abbot send monks to take charge of a present to which Bernard replied, "May you in perpetuity receive infallible signs from heaven for the use of your kingdom," and thanking him for the gift of land for a new monastery.[15] He immediately dispatched five monks from Clairvaux to Portugal armed with lengths of rope marking the measurements of various rooms, so they could reproduce on the virgin parcel of land an accurate outline of said abbey. Located at the confluence of two rivers, the land was thickly wooded and impenetrable and horrible. Just the way the Cistercians liked it. But it would herald one of Europe's most magnificent Cistercian monasteries, the elegance of its architecture surpassing even that of the Order's mother abbey at Fontenay.[16]

Named after Al Cobaxa, the Arabic name describing the shape of the surrounding hills, the monastery of Alcobaça would be Afonso's greatest gift of affection to his uncle, not to mention the late Count Dom Henrique, because in choosing the site beside the old hermitage of Saint Julian, Afonso honored the monk who once lived there and accompanied his father on his first voyage to Jerusalem.

Alcobaça was founded on February 2, the pagan and Celtic feast day of Imbolc (the Christianized Candlemas), symbolizing light emerging from the dark of midwinter, when fertility is once more restored to the land. One of the first people to join the monastery was Afonso's brother, Dom Pedro.[17]

The architecture of the building mirrors the Cistercian Rule. It is stone stripped, shaped, and arranged to the bare essentials of balance, rhythm, light, and shade, creating an environment where God is sought and the ego denied. This small insistence was sufficient to restore stability to the life of a mortal individual. Bernard was not keen on opulent churches and championed the importance of focusing on divine things without distraction, as he once reminded the lavish Benedictines, "I say naught of the vast height of your churches, their immoderate length, their superfluous width, the costly polishings, the curious carvings and

Monastery of Alcobaça.

paintings which attract the worshipper's gaze and hinder his attention to God."[18]

Like the association between the Knights Templar and the founding of Portugal, the relationship between Portugal and the Cistercians runs even deeper, occurring as it does with the arrival of Count Dom Henrique, as one Cistercian chronicler clearly states:

> The beginning of the reign of Portugal and the Cistercian Order occurred at the same time. . . . [To the Cistercian Order] the reign of Portugal is greatly obligated because, besides being gifted with the holiness of its monks, as recorded in its beginning years . . . [the Order] reached out to it with spiritual and material assistance, such as the conquests of Santarém, Lisbon . . . and other successes, for which assistance was provided by the intervention of Bernard and his contacts: this is proof of the material assistance . . . [Bernard] placed within reach of Afonso Henriques in the instigation of his reign, for which the king placed his reign under the [Rules] of Clairvaux.[19]

Thus, the Cistercian Order and the Portuguese shire were temporally and spiritually intertwined, born as they were simultaneously, as Bernard de Clairvaux himself declared. "And so we have here presented a mystery, for heaven ordered that the reign of Portugal and our Cistercian Order should be born at the same time. In 1098 Robert [de Molesme, one of the founders] instituted the sacred reformation of Cister, and in the same year . . . Count D. Henrique was given the state of Portugale as a dowry."[20] The connection becomes even clearer on account of the family relationship between Bernard de Clairvaux and Dom Henrique.[21]

That the relationship proved advantageous in the development of the Cistercian ideal is an understatement. The Order made its greatest impression in Portugal by raising the largest concentration of monasteries anywhere in Europe.[22] Within a few years of settling at Alcobaça,

Cistercian monks.

the monks were already trading a surplus with Lisbon. In half a decade their extensive knowledge of plant varieties and agronomy made a formerly destitute region bloom. They organized mining, the smelting of iron, planted extensive orchards, organized boat building and fisheries and the drying and salting of cod (creating that most national of Portuguese dishes, *bacalhau*). Their recipes for preserves and cured hams and sausages would not only become staples of the Portuguese diet, they also would survive into the twenty-first century, along with their hand-blown Atlantis crystal, still to this day a product of international repute.

*Panel in Alcobaça showing monks arriving from Clairvaux,
marking the site with rope, in the shape of the constellation of
Virgo, the divine virgin.*

The foundation of the Cistercians' success was firmly supported on a humane platform that must have seemed totally alien in medieval Europe. They outlawed slavery, paid fair wages to laborers and toiled beside them in the fields, opened free schools, fed the hungry, sheltered the dispossessed, educated the young, and cared for the elderly. They also honored the divine feminine and granted equality to women. The Muslim theologian and mystic Al Ghazahli compares the doctrine of the Cistercians to that of Islam's own esoteric brotherhood, the Sufi: "Their science has for its object the uprooting from the soul of all passions, the extirpation from it of vicious desires and evil qualities, so that the heart may be detached from all that is not God, and give itself for its only occupation, meditation on the Divine Being."[23]

But the story of how the Cistercians and the Knights Templar came to be so instrumental in the foundation of Europe's first independent nation-state is not complete without highlighting the involvement of the third part in this holy trinity—the Ordre de Sion, particularly the figure who was perhaps the most influential in carrying out this great work, a man whose footprint is so large yet paradoxically so little is written of him, possibly because he preferred it that way and probably because his involvement in something as sensitive as nation-building was designed to remain low-key: the mysterious Prior Arnaldo da Rocha.

29

1147. APRIL.
BRAGA. THE MYSTERIOUS
PRIOR ARNALDO IN HIS
NEW ABODE . . .

he bill of sale for a riverside house outside the city, on the slopes of Mount Ferrocan, is from Dona Sancha Viegas and sons, given to "Petrus Arnaldo, a Friar of the Temple."[1] No one earned this bucolic setting more than he.

Born in Santarém to the de la Roche family of Burgundy,[2] Arnaldo da Rocha sailed to Jerusalem with Count Dom Henrique to rendezvous with Godefroi de Bouillon, became prior of the Abbey de Notre Dame du Mont Sion, and continued as such well into the mid-1120s.[3] He is credited as one of the founders of the Knights Templar in Jerusalem and with introducing them into Portugale.[4]

His name appears on two documents cosigned with Hugues de Payns expressing continuing cooperation between their respective organizations.[5] At the express orders of the Grand Master himself, he returns to Portugale in 1125 bearing the additional title of Procurator,[6] and together with four other Templar knights he is instructed to create a home for the Order and "establish a Portuguese crown."[7] This coincided with the Templars discovering something of monumental importance, which concluded their digs inside Temple Mount.

He is present at the start of the drive toward Portuguese independence, arranging properties and accepting donations on behalf of the Templars. Then, for the best part of thirty years, this man of obvious high rank and reputation takes a humble back seat to three successive Templar Masters in Portugal yet continues to work behind the scenes. Why should such an extraordinary individual remain virtually incognito during a nation's formative years?

Frustratingly little documentation survives concerning this most influential of figures. Whenever Prior Arnaldo steps into the limelight he does so fleetingly, as though engaging in subtle diplomacy. Given how he presided over an equally mysterious and close-knit group secreted behind a fortified basilica on Mount Sion, perhaps it is hardly surprising he should have conducted his work in the same manner upon returning to his native country, the timing of which coincides with the knighting of Afonso Henriques at Zamora. (Was he present at the ceremony?)

Were Countess Tareja's frantic renegotiations in granting the property of Souré to the Templars a mark of his influence? Paranoid sovereigns did not hand over territory and strategic castles unless they implicitly trusted the people with whom they were dealing, and Arnaldo, with established family ties in and around the Portuguese court, confidante of her late husband and relative of Bernard de Clairvaux, clearly was a man of unimpeachable reputation. If ever there was a diplomat so centrally placed between so many factions, Prior Arnaldo was the prime candidate, the central pillar of the entire operation.

There is a further point. The Templars were obviously involved in a geopolitical design, and as such, they would hardly publicize it openly. The influence of a foreign organization on sovereign soil, let alone the idea of nation-building, is a subtle affair; it is an exercise in forging friendships and invisible alliances. That French knights, Procurators, and Masters moved into Braga is one thing (given the Burgundian heritage of the Count of Portugale, this would hardly have raised eyebrows), but Arnaldo was Portuguese from a Burgundian family and a clergyman. The late Templar researcher André Paraschi was succinct on this hypothesis: "The installation in the country of the Order of the

Templars needed to be a subtle affair, for it would have been a difficult task to achieve by anyone already invested with obvious authority such as a regional Master."[8]

Paraschi goes on to suggest that Prior Arnaldo was the undocumented Templar Master in Portugal ever since their domicile was established in Braga, shortly after his return from Mount Sion in 1125: "He was the mastermind of the Order's expansion and consolidation in the Peninsula . . . work which had to be done with patience and secrecy, far from the eyes of the profane world."[9]

Arnaldo's governance assumes a mysterious, transcendental cohesion not unfamiliar to anyone involved with esoteric movements.[10] To all intents and purposes the figures he surrounded himself with were engaged in a theocratic democracy; even the actions of people recruited into the Templar Order suggests the brotherhood was guided as though by a ministerial college.

Shortly after Afonso Henriques donates the ecclesiastic properties of Santarém to the Templars, Arnaldo da Rocha once again comes back into the limelight and, acting as a Procurator of the Order, accepting and supervising large donations in this territory.[11] Then in 1157, upon the death of the Templar Master Hugh Martin, he finally—and it would seem, reluctantly—accepts the title of Master.[12]

But his tenure as the fourth Master of the Knights Templar in Portugal is brief, less than a year in fact, and he spends much of it grooming his successor, a knight he had known as a young man in Braga and who'd shared his adventures in Jerusalem—Gualdino Paes—as though the prior of Sion was steering this young knight on an important course of action.

30

1119.
TEMPLE MOUNT. A TUNNEL,
EIGHTY FEET BENEATH . . .

ven for a knight it was hard work picking away at the limestone and debris of a thousand years of accumulated civilizations beneath es Sakhra, the sacred rock over which so much blood had been spilled, all in the name of a formless deity. Twice did Hugues de Payns journey to Jerusalem to assess the probability of locating an object relating to this cause, but now the Knights Templar were more than convinced they were on the right course of action.

Even common sense dictates that the story of nine knights patrolling 33 miles of road between Jaffa and Jerusalem to protect thousands of pilgrims from brigands, thieves, Saracens, and mountain lions is a preposterous idea. One giant medieval smoke screen. Even Fulk de Chartres, the king of Jerusalem's chronicler, never portrayed the Knights Templar acting as policemen for pilgrims, probably because security was already performed by the Knights Hospitaller.[1]

The Hospitaller's initial duty was to defend and care for visiting pilgrims. Upon being granted official status in 1113 by papal bull, their name also expanded to the Order of the Hospital of Saint John of Jerusalem—named not for John the Baptist, as one would assume, but

The landscape around es Sakhra on Temple Mount.

in memory of Jean l'Aumônier,* a Cypriot noble who, after his wife's death, gave away all his worldly goods to the poor, rose to the rank of bishop of Alexandria, and became a model of exemplary charity.[2] Thus, the Knights Hospitaller adopted as their patron saint a man who devoted his life to helping others.[3]

Their association with John the Baptist stems from their hostelry having been built on the ruins of his former church.

A Rule of conduct was drawn up by their Grand Master, the knight Raymond De Puy, which did not include military aims, but by the mid-twelfth century, by order of the pope, the military spirit superseded their original charitable function, much to the chagrin of the members.[†4]

---

*Jean l'Aumônier lived in 610 AD.
†Under the guardianship of Gilbert d'Assalit, the Knights Hospitallers planned an invasion of Egypt and requested assistance from the Knights Templar, who refused. "It

Rather than ministering to the pilgrims of the Holy Land, the core members of the Knights Templar spent their first seven years sequestered away in Solomon's stables armed with picks and shovels, stubbornly refusing admission to the site to anyone outside their inner brotherhood.[5] But in 1121, something changed that led one of the founding Templars, Godefroi de Saint-Omer, to return to Flanders armed with scrolls.

(cont. from p. 170) appeared a hard matter to the Templars to wage war without cause, in defiance of treaties, and against all honour and conscience, upon a friendly nation, preserving faith with us, and relying on our own faith." The chronicle goes on to state that the Hospitallers attempted to arm themselves as a great military society "in imitation of the Templars." Supposedly, the senior Hospitallers reminded Gilbert that they were a religious, not a military order and that "the church had not put arms into their hands to make conquests." Inevitably, they were swayed by the younger and more foolish within the Order, and money was procured from Florentine and Genoese merchants, who introduced mercenaries into the Order and organized the Hospitallers into a military unit. See William of Tyre, *History of Deeds*. The Knights Hospitaller would transform into the Order of Acre, the Order of Rhodes, and the Order of Malta.

elagius built a certain house, a dwelling-place for pilgrims, as a remedy for his soul and those of his parents, in Braga, to the sustenance of which house he brought with his generous hand, vines, landed property, many benefits and many incomes. After his death, however, those wanting many of the perishable riches of this world . . . destroyed it, reducing it altogether to nothing. Afterwards I, Afonso, King of Portugal, saw the above-mentioned house to be so destroyed and diminished, and wishing to reform it for the better, established a charter of testament and stability for it, together with João, Archbishop of Braga, with God and the Knights of the Temple of Solomon. . . . I give and concede it to them, with all its appurtenances which now it has and used to have on the day of the death of Archbishop Pelagius, that they might have and possess it, and do whatever they wish with it in the service to the Temple.[1]

The letter by Afonso Henriques illustrates the enormous respect held by the king of Portugal for Pelagius, aka Payo Mendes. Afonso's decision to refurbish the former dwelling place for pilgrims and its hospital for the poor was opportune timing, for it would soon become the domicile of the Templars' next rising star, Gualdino Paes, following the knight's efforts in the recapture of the city of Santarém.[2]

Gualdino's life reads like a list of coincidences and ironies; in fact, it takes on a near mythological aspect. He was born on the outskirts of Braga, in the town of Marecos, in 1118, the same year the Knights Templar were established as an entity. By the same token, his death on the thirteenth day of October mirrors the infamous day when the Templars would be arrested throughout France and practically obliterated. He was descended from the first and highest nobility of northern Portugal, and his father, Paio Ramires, sided with Afonso Henriques against the prince's mother.

Gualdino traveled widely, honing his skills as man of the sword and adept of devotion, and by the then-mature age of twenty-one he fought alongside Afonso at the decisive battle of Ourique, the moment that defined Afonso as a king, Portugal as a nation, and Paes as a Templar Master-in-waiting.*

Like an echo of the simultaneous birth of Portucale and the Cistercian Order, the rise of Gualdino Paes goes hand in hand with the fortunes of the Templars, the Cistercians, and the golden age of both in Portugal.

In addition to his lifelong friendship with the future king (with whom he shared a singular vision of a kingdom accountable only to God), his family's noble status would inevitably have established bonds with another of Braga's most illustrious families, the la Roche, particularly Arnaldo da Rocha, and most likely it was the prior's exploits on Mount Sion that inspired Gualdino's parents to pack him off to Jerusalem. The young man obviously joined Arnaldo's inner circle, since he is named as one of the five Procurators dispatched to Portugal by Hugues de Payns. Which is an extraordinary concept, given that, back in 1125, Gualdino would have been a mere eight years of age!

It gets stranger. The following year (June 1126) this child Templar

---

*Gualdino was allegedly indoctrinated into the Knights Templar on the battlefield.

Procurator is named in the charter of the village of Ferreira by Countess Tareja.[3] An entry written alongside the document states, "This charter is an agreement and reaffirms that Master Gualdino and Arnaldo da Rocha take charge of our village of Ferreira." And as if the story could not become any more remarkable, one Cistercian chronicler categorically states that for the entire length of his life Gualdino Paes was a Templar Master,[4] "the principal knight in this kingdom, whom they were obedient to."[5]

What was so special about this child prodigy that required him to be groomed right from infanthood to be a Templar Master?

At the more sensible age of thirty he followed in the footsteps of so many illustrious, pious knights before him when he undertook the pilgrimage to Jerusalem, his second. After preparing his belongings, he hitched a ride on one of many fleets passing by the shores of Portugal from England, filled with crusaders, mercenaries, glory hounds, blood-hungry zealots, and all manner of fortune seekers hoping for a share of spoils in the Second Crusade then taking place in the Holy Land. It is unlikely that he was actually part of the crusading army, for Portugal was never a recruitment area, the reason being that all hands were either busy protecting their nascent nation-state or busy driving the remaining Moors south and back to North Africa.[6] One therefore has to ask, Why should Gualdino have been spared for this trip?

Once in Jerusalem, Gualdino joined other Templars and honed his skills as a knight for five years, taking part in the siege of Asqalân alongside one of the original Templars, André de Montbard.

A clue as to why he was sent to the Holy Land lies in his actions upon his return to the motherland. Along with his fellow Templars, he devotes precious little effort toward military goals or to upholding victories; instead, he dedicates himself to spiritual matters and, together with Arnaldo da Rocha, the pursuit and establishment of churches and their attached lands, even the erecting of new temples, and securing from Afonso Henriques guarantees of liberty from ecclesiastical interference and immunity from the state, which the king more than happily obliged.[7] Such actions are at odds with a man who went to the Holy Land to, presumably, spend his entire time engaged in warfare. It would seem that Paes's time was perhaps better spent doing exactly what Bernard de Clairvaux prescribed in his eulogy to the Templars: understanding the spiritual context of the land and visiting the sacred sites of the Near East.

Upon his return, Paes discovered a present waiting for him. During his absence, King Afonso awarded his friend the village of Sintra and its surrounding lands and made him Templar Commander of the entire municipality,[8] the implications of which reveal much about what the Templars learned in Jerusalem and what they were doing with it in Portugal. But we are getting ahead of ourselves . . .

If a man is to be judged by the company he keeps, then Paes's bond with a mystic named Dom Telo says much about his moral compass.

Dom Telo was the prior of Viseu, who, after returning from his own pilgrimage to Jerusalem, was offered the bishopric but turned it down on ethical grounds. Dom Telo was also an ally of the teenage Afonso Henriques against his mother and even vowed at one point to excommunicate Countess Tareja for her wayward behavior. Not surprising, then, that following Payo Mendes's death, it was Dom Telo who took up the mentorship of the now-grown king.

Dom Telo also made a second pilgrimage to Jerusalem, and upon his return in 1132 he met in Coimbra with Afonso Henriques, who had just moved the seat of Portugal there and was busy founding the monastery of Santa Cruz so that his recently returned mentor and eleven of his monks could live in brand-new premises. In return for this gesture of kindness, Prior Telo raised Santa Cruz into one of the most important monastic houses during Portugal's first dynasty; he in turn would be canonized as the first Portuguese saint (Saint Teotonio) in acknowledgment of his reformation of the corrupt habits of the Christian church in Portugal, and his example would spread worldwide via the Augustinian Order.

Telo's effort to reform a corrupt system is not unlike Bernard de Clairvaux's, so it is not surprising to learn that the two clergymen exchanged correspondence, in which they expressed "good relations are established between the monastery of Santa Cruz and the abbey of Clairvaux," a phrase strangely identical to the earlier accord signed between the Ordre de Sion and the Knights Templar.[9]

Needless to say, associating with such an exemplary figure as Dom Telo would leave an indelible mark on anyone. And no doubt it did on Gualdino Paes, because not only was the young knight raised in his monastery, but what he was taught there shaped his conduct in the Holy Land and thereafter.

Upon Paes's return from Jerusalem in 1156, he is awarded the title of Templar Commander.[10] He spends the next year in close contact with the newly appointed Templar Master Arnaldo da Rocha, who, on July 1157, confers that same title on Gualdino.[11]

(Interestingly, one of Arnaldo's later relatives, the Templar Master Aimery de la Roche, would himself initiate into the Order the most famous of all Templar Grand Masters, one Jacques de Molay.)[12]

After handing Gualdino the reins of the Templar brotherhood, Arnaldo returns to near anonymity, performing otherwise subordinate tasks. Two years later, after signing the charter of the town of Redinha as mere "Brother Arnaldo," the fourth Templar Master of Portugal, a true international man of mystery, gives his last breath unto God, humble to the very end.

This brief stewardship of Paes by the former head of the Ordre de Sion in the twilight years of his life appears as though Prior Arnaldo was instructing his young neighbor from Braga, adding to the speculation that Gualdino's path was meticulously planned with a certain end in mind. In hindsight, given the careful groundwork laid down by the Templars and their associates in Portugal right from the beginning, Paes's journeys to the Holy Land served as grooming for his future role, because it was under his tenure as Master that the Knights Templar came to establish a kingdom within a kingdom.

Gualdino Paes.

One of Master Gualdino's first duties was to preside over the apotheosis of a long-festering confrontation between Afonso Henriques and an Englishman named Gilbert of Hastings, a monk sailing with the Christian army who took part in the siege and conquest of Lisbon in 1147. After the fall of the city, Gilbert was appointed the diocese's bishop, following the convenient and likely premeditated murder of the incumbent Christian bishop and member of the Eastern Orthodox Church, which itself was involved in a decades-long spit with the Roman Catholics. Thus, his timely death conveniently prevented the Constantinople-based church from reclaiming the Diocese of Lisbon, and it was widely rumored that Gilbert, a Roman Catholic, was heavily involved in his predecessor's suspicious "removal."

Gilbert then took it badly that the king awarded the Templars

properties in recently reconquered Santarém because its diocese came
under the jurisdiction of Lisbon. The Englishman made enormous—
and ludicrous—demands (such as a new church actually built by the
Templars), maneuvering hard to acquire the benefits enjoyed by the
knights by writing a petulant letter to Rome outlining the manner in
which he was being disrespected. The situation was a delicate one, not
least for Afonso Henriques, who'd secured Lisbon thanks to the convenient timing of an armada of 164 ships sailing along the coast on
its way to the Second Crusade. But how did Afonso come to possess
knowledge of this armada?

As the ships made landfall on June 16 in Porto to take on food,
water, and provisions, they found Bishop Pedro Pitões waiting for them
at the quay.[13] In the Cistercian's cloak was a letter from the king: "To
Pedro, Bishop of Porto, greetings. If perchance the ships of the Franks
should come to you, take care to receive them with all possible friendli-
ness and courtesy; and, in accordance with the agreement which you
may conclude with them to stop with me, offer yourself and whoever
else they may desire with you as security for its absolute inviolability;
and so you may come with them to me at Lisbon. Farewell."[14]

Essentially, the king commandeered the fleet and was instructing
it to make an unscheduled stop in Lisbon. The proposition would be
tempting to the soldiers, especially for the manner in which the region
around Lisbon was described by Raol, the armada's chaplain:

> . . . second to none, rich in products of the soil, whether you are
> looking for the fruit of the trees or the vines. It abounds in every-
> thing, both costly articles of luxury and necessary articles of con-
> sumption. It also contains gold and silver and is never wanting in
> iron mines. The olive flourishes. There is nothing unproductive or
> sterile or which refuses to return a harvest. They do not boil their
> salt but dig it. Figs are so abundant that we can hardly eat a fraction
> of them . . . the air is healthful. In its pastures the mares breed with
> a wonderful fecundity.[15]

Beside the city flowed the mighty Tejo, at the time so bounteous it was said to consist of two parts water and one part fish and shellfish. Afonso reasoned that this western Eden would tempt the men to stay awhile. And while there they might as well help expel the Moors from the magnificently fortified city and complete the task his father had attempted forty years earlier.

How had Afonso known an armada was arriving in Porto? There exists a cryptic letter written at the time of the ensuing skirmish from Bernard de Clairvaux to his nephew Afonso, alluding to the king having sent an emissary to Clairvaux requesting help in removing the Moors then entrenched in Lisbon: "I have received Your Highness' letter with great pleasure. . . . What I have done in the matter will be evident from the outcome, as you will see for yourself. You will see with what promptitude I have complied with your request and the exigencies of the matter. Pedro, the brother of your Highness, and a prince worthy of all honour, has acquainted me with your wishes. . . . My son Roland will bring you documents which set forth the liberality of the Holy See."[16]

Clearly, Bernard used his influence in Rome in persuading the Holy See to divert a contingent of men scheduled for the Holy Land by cunningly suggesting they remove infidels from the western flank of Europe en route, the natural consequence of which would help his illustrious nephew consolidate the Cistercian-Templar plan to secure a new territory where their New Jerusalem could flourish. A later Cistercian chronicler made this very clear: "[The Cistercian Order] reached out to [Portugal] with spiritual and material assistance, such as the conquests of Santarém, Lisbon . . . and other successes, for which assistance was provided by the intervention of Bernard and his contacts: this is proof of the material assistance our saint [Bernard] placed within reach of Afonso Henriques in the instigation of his reign, for which the king placed his reign under the [Rules] of Clairvaux."*[17]

---

*The Cistercian Rule came into affect at the Council of Coimbra in 1162, at which time the affiliated Templar Order of the Knights of São Bento de Avis was also created. Its center was in Évora. Its Grand Master was Pedro, brother of Afonso Henriques.

In shrewdness, both uncle and nephew were alike.

As Bishop Pitões opened negotiations in Porto on the king's behalf, the Norman and English knights sailing with the fleet at first refused to attack unless the king gave them the right to plunder everything inside Lisbon's city walls, without sharing as much as a brick with the Portuguese army. Back at his camp to the north of Lisbon, Afonso debated the situation: "Having been constantly harassed by the Muslims, it surely has not been our destiny to accumulate material wealth," he said, and with that he conceded the terms, with the caveat that "myself and all my men shall have absolutely no share in them."[18] The Crusading soldiers not only stripped Lisbon of its wealth, they also reneged on the provision for the peaceful terms of surrender, forcing Afonso to intervene in stopping the ensuing atrocities.

So Afonso won the city on the back of the Crusades, but since the army was under orders from the pope, technically he owed Rome a small favor. And Rome wished that Bishop Gilbert would be given what he wanted. It was a bittersweet position for Afonso, for the king was no friend of the antics of the Roman Church, and proved so when he promoted a black monk to the post of Bishop of Coimbra with the power to conduct mass. This symbolism of a monk conducting mass— let alone an African—was an affront to the Holy See, who had complete dominion over the anointing of bishops.[19]

Afonso dug his heels in, and the dispute with Gilbert smoldered for twelve years.

Then suddenly, around 1158, as though Afonso had been waiting for the opportune moment, the king abruptly presented Gilbert with a tempting proposition: if the Templars relinquished their holdings in Santarém, would the bishop show good faith by exchanging them for a massive plot of less-than-prime agricultural land north of Lisbon presently belonging to his diocese, along with a dilapidated old town and its ruined castle?

By now, Afonso had become an acute reader of people, and his offer played to the bishop's greed and vanity: the cities of Lisbon and

Santarém for the bishop, a seemingly worthless tract of land for the Templars.

Greed and vanity triumphed. However, after Gilbert "gave up all his rights and those of his successors to all the churches already founded in that territory, in perpetuity,"[20] Afonso Henriques, as arbitrator, and probably in distaste of Gilbert's morals, withheld for the Templars the two main sites in Santarém demanded by the bishop—the church of Saint James and the temple of Our Lady of Alcáçova.

And so the Templars came away with the strategically poor and second-rate agricultural lands of the municipality of Ceras, a crumbling town, and its wreck of a castle.[21] The transaction was witnessed by Petrus Silva and accepted without one word of protest by Master Gualdino Paes on behalf of the Order of the Temple.

Why should the Templars negotiate such a ridiculous deal?

Afonso's abrupt change of heart coincides with a series of interrelated events. Following the taking of Santarém, Gualdino Paes and Arnaldo da Rocha each move to homes in Braga and spend the next six months making plans before returning south to assist the king in preparations for the liberation of Lisbon. After the battle, Paes makes his second journey to Jerusalem, where he teams up with André de Montbard to assist in the conquest of Asqalân.

For André it was a bittersweet time. Shortly before winning the city he learned of the passing of his uncle Bernard de Clairvaux. For Gualdino it was an opportune time and place, because two days later André is appointed Templar Grand Master.

The two knights spend the subsequent three years attending to business in the Holy Land until André himself passes away in January 1156, precipitating Gualdino's return to Portugal, whereupon he reconnects with Master Arnaldo. In essence, Paes benefited from five years of training under the supervision of not just two Templar Masters but two officials of the Ordre de Sion.[22]

It is at this point that Afonso Henriques makes his move and negotiates a massive swathe of territory from Bishop Gilbert and the church he represents, then transfers it to the Knights Templar and their recently appointed Master, Gualdino Paes. The timing suggests Paes returned to Portugal with some undisclosed instruction that required forward motion to take place.

Is it possible the vast and apparently worthless territory of Ceras played a part in this unrevealed plan?

The truth is that the territory awarded to the Templars may have been poor compensation for the rich ecclesiastical properties in and around Santarém—two of which the Templars kept anyway—but when combined with adjacent territory later donated by the king, the Templars were suddenly in possession of a massive chunk of land, one-third of Portugal to be exact, large enough to establish a kingdom within a kingdom. On top of this, the lands of Ceras were guaranteed "free from all ecclesiastical interference" from Rome, so when the charter was sanctioned by papal bull in June 1159, the Templars were effectively given the right to build without homage to the church.

Within a matter of weeks Gualdino and the Templars moved out of Santarém to their fifth and final base in Ceras, named for the goddess of agriculture, grain, and fertility of the land. In this lackluster domicile the golden age of the Knights Templar was about to begin, as though the entire exercise had been patiently premeditated.

32

1121.
SAINT-OMER. IN THE HOME
OF A CRYPTOGRAPHER NAMED
LAMBERT . . .

odefroi de Saint-Omer arrived back in his namesake town after three laborious years digging under Temple Mount with his fellow knights.

As the Flemish town was previously owned by the late Baudoin I, the scrolls secreted in the Templar co-leader's tunic would be assured safe passage and protection. The rest was up to a local human encyclopedia named Lambert de Saint-Omer, in whose warm study Godefroi now stood.

Lambert de Saint-Omer, retired canon and schoolteacher of the Chapter of Our Virgin, was not only a wise man (he compiled an

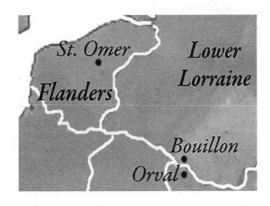

encyclopedia on human knowledge) but his personal friendship with Godefroi ensured that the deciphering of the scrolls about to be entrusted to him could be conducted in secret and the results kept in the family, so to speak.[1]

Whatever Godefroi and the Templars found, these scrolls were just the start. After years secreted on Temple Mount they would abruptly leave Jerusalem and within a historically expedient time frame build an enormous empire, amass an estimated £692 billion ($1.1 trillion)

Lambert de Saint-Omer.

in today's currency, and found Europe's first independent nation-state. Clearly they discovered something of great significance on the site of Solomon's Temple, and the speed at which donations of property were given to the Order meant it was of great benefit to counts, kings, and laypeople alike.

Assuming the knights numbered no more than a handful, it is safe to assume the donors had not handed over property by being threatened with violence.

What curious information did these scrolls contain? Vows made by incoming Templar recruits such as Arnold of Sournia, who joined the Order in 1142, unequivocally imply a promise of some considerable spiritual benefit: "I, wishing to come to the joys of Paradise, surrender my body and my soul to the Lord God and the Blessed Mary and the brothers of the knighthood of the Temple of Solomon in Jerusalem."[2]

One latter-day member of the Ordre de Sion equally describes the Templars' treasure as spiritual in nature, consisting in part of a secret that would facilitate a major social change.[3]

33

1947.
QUMRAN. TWO GOATHERDS,
IN A CAVE, BY THE DEAD SEA . . .

uhammed and Ahmed of the Ta'amireh tribe stumbled upon the weathered scrolls buried in one of the caves beside the ruins of a former community of mystics called Essenes, who existed around the time of John the Baptist. Until this fortuitous moment, the "treasure" of the Essenes was considered all but lost.

The crumbling parchments* revealed that in addition to a stockpile of gold bullion and silver ornaments hidden under Temple Mount from an advancing Roman army, "an indeterminable treasure" had also been secreted there.

Treasure typically implies one thing. Money. The sudden rise from rags to riches by the Order of the Temple indicates the brotherhood directed all its resources to find, dig, and spend a hoard of loot. And yet if they become overnight millionaires from this Essene heist, why should they need or even accept an unprecedented sum of donations from people all over Europe? Furthermore, the central caveat for joining the Templar Order was the renouncement of personal wealth; in fact, all knights had to honor a vow of chastity, obedience, and to hold

---

*This was the Qumran Scroll, deciphered at Manchester University in 1956.

all property in trust.* Clearly, money or the accumulation of personal wealth was not a prime motivation. Had the knights been looking for buried treasure there were far easier ways for noblemen to get rich than to become knights but work as miners laboring for years through solid rock in dangerous and hot and claustrophobic conditions! They could just as easily have held on to their inheritances.

A clue appears in the original rites of Royal Arch Freemasonry, in which the ritual of entry into the three degrees describes, allegorically, how the Templars found a secret buried chamber under Temple Mount. Access to this chamber is said to have involved the removal of a rectangular keystone with an iron ring. Once lowered inside they discovered an important scroll, but "being without light" they were unable to interpret the information it contained.[1] Once they had "received light," however, the men came to understand its knowledge.

The light they required did not come from a torch but its figurative interpretation: enlightenment. (In the Masonic ritual the initiate is blindfolded; then the blindfold is removed.) From that point the initiate undertakes an obligation to rebuild the former temple.[2] To all intents and purposes the ritual is a reenactment of a true event, and the scroll is nothing short of an archive containing spiritual laws, the Word of God.

The word *archive* derives from the Greek *arkheia* (magisterial residence), a very apt description for a place where God resides; its root

---

*The idea that they held a vow of poverty comes from an error in translation.

is *arkhe*. But there's more. Still assuming that the Templars were seeking nothing more than financial treasure, an examination of the etymological fingerprint of that word reveals otherwise. *Treasure* in Portuguese is *tesouro,* whose Greek root is *thesauros* (a storehouse, a treasure). Interestingly, in old Portuguese both words are interchangeable and synonymous with a treasure of learning, the latter often equated with books or a library.[3] So in a manner of speaking, the Templars did discover a treasure, but not so much a treasure of gold as a treasure of words.

But an ark containing a treasure of words? Are we dealing with a receptacle housing laws that, metaphorically speaking, descended from a very high source? Did the Templars recover the Ark of the Covenant, or perhaps some of its contents?

It is written that the temple of Solomon was built for the singular purpose of housing the Ark, and just before its Holy of Holies was breached by an encroaching Babylonian army, the sacred box was sealed in a secret room beneath Temple Mount.[4] It is also written that the Laws of God placed in this receptacle were important enough to merit that any stranger who approached the Ark without proper training was punished on pain of death. This seems rather a harsh attitude. But if by "stranger" the account actually refers to a non-initiate, this would be consistent with Egyptian Mysteries schools' principles in which only adepts and initiates of the temple could be entrusted with hermetic and gnostic secrets lest such knowledge be used irresponsibly.

The laws placed in the Ark of the Covenant should not be confused with the Ten Commandments, because those are hardly secret; even by Moses's time, around 1300 BC, they were commonplace. In fact, these Commandments—all forty-two of them—were already in vogue as the Utterances of the Pharaoh during the time of Thutmosis III, affirmations for the orderly conduct of one's personal life to ensure a favorable outcome when the soul finally departs the physical body for the afterlife.

In truth the Ark contained far more than Commandments. According to scripture, when God instructed Moses to come up to

Sinai, he said, "I will give thee tables of stone, and a law, and commandments which I have written, that thou mayest teach them."[5] That's *three*
separate items. In Exodus 34:27–28 it is made clear that the Tables of
Testimony were written by God, and the Ten Commandments were
written separately by Moses. The church has strategically ignored the
Tables and focused on the Commandments as the important issue.[6]

With regard to the Templars, it is the Tables of Law that are of
interest because they supposedly contain a kind of cosmic equation.
They are a precious instruction, an understanding of creative forces at
work in nature. Anyone in possession of such information has direct
access to how the universe functions and the very laws of cause and
effect. The power of the land is said to be derived from these instructions; thus, they are in themselves a means of power and certainly not
meant to be entrusted to the ignorant or the foolish.

Secrets of this magnitude deserved to be well protected. Any fool
determined to get past the heavily armed Levite guard faced an electri-
fied Ark, followed by a perimeter of unspecified defenses that proved
so effective that it gave the Philistines who approached it hemorrhoids.
Even if they survived these trials, the tablets containing the word of
God could only be read by a person initiated into the secret Mysteries—
such as Moses, who was an adept of the Egyptian Temple.[7]

Initiates, adepts, and Mysteries schools were not in short sup-
ply in the enlightened duchies of Burgundy and Champagne of the
eleventh century. Kabalistic schools may have existed there three centuries earlier when Jews were granted a kingdom within a kingdom
and insisted to have at its head a recognized descendent of the Royal
House of David. This took shape in Count Guilhelm de Toulouse, a
Merovingian, who acceded to the throne as king of Septimania, as the
region was then named.[8] Later, persecuted Jews found a new sanctuary
with the enlightened Counts of Troyes and Champagne, particularly
the Templar supporter Comte Hugh de Champagne, who sponsored an
influential school of Kaballah and other esoteric studies that flourished
in the town of Troyes around the year 1070. This Mysteries school

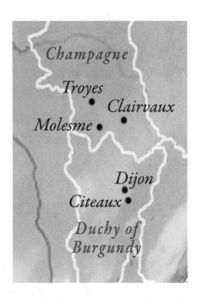

was founded by Rabbi Solomon ben Isaac, or as he was affectionately called, Rashi, a man of great intellectual repute with an obsession for procuring information on the Ark of the Covenant. And given that he resided in Troyes,[9] he was a frequent guest at the court of Comte Hugh de Champagne.

This Kabalist school, then, was well funded and placed and prepared for the continuing cryptic translation of documents found by the Templars under Temple Mount, especially as Lambert de Saint-Omer passed away shortly after receiving the first scrolls from the Templar knight Godefroi de Saint-Omer.[10] A scroll named *Seper Yatzirah* (Book of Formation) was given particular attention because it allegedly provided a guide to the creation of the universe. It was the most mathematical of all the scrolls, as though it were a formula or manual of manifestation or, in a manner of speaking, a kind of holy Graal.[11] Naturally, its esoteric contents were to be made accessible to no one but the pious and only then under certain conditions.

A second man who took a great interest in such Kabalistic studies was Stephen Harding, a clergyman who gave up a seat at Sherbourne Abbey in England to become a traveling scholar in France. En route to Molesme Abbey (a few miles south of Troyes), Stephen became

Solomon ben Isaac, known as Rashi.

acquainted with Rashi,[12] and no doubt his esoteric studies shaped his worldview when he became abbot of the Cistercian abbey at Citeaux.

In 1112 Stephen had the opportunity to share this passion for Kaballah's spiritual philosophy with a visitor to the abbey, a young monk by the name of Bernard de Clairvaux. When Bernard later created the abbey of Clairvaux, 33 miles southeast of Troyes he maintained the collaboration with the Kabalist school.

The knowledge transmitted at this school involved an understanding of sacred geometry, especially with regard to Solomon's Temple. Chief among Solomon's masons—the so-called Children of Solomon— was their master mason, Asaph, an architect skilled in the importance of geometric harmonics and the behavior of resonance, particularly as applied to sacred buildings. Such "masters of the craft" were denoted by degrees of knowledge and proficiency concerning universal laws. It is probable, then, that Bernard was taught to understand and apply the sacred geometry of Solomon's Temple contained in the scrolls, because when asked to describe God, Bernard cryptically replied, "He is length, width, height and depth."[13]

That God is geometry is something every Muslim knows, since the elaborate geometric tile work prominently featured in every mosque is said to depict the face of Allah; the same truth is encapsulated in every mandala, be it from a Buddhist monk or a Native American shaman, and it is claimed that working with such geometry induces an altered state of awareness.[14]

On one level, it would seem that the treasure rediscovered by the Templars during their digs was a thesaurus of cosmic laws that included the secrets of geometry and harmonics, knowledge sacred to architects of pyramids, temples, and other holy places. These savants were keenly aware that such harmonics are capable of inducing the kind of shamanic experiences that lead to a personal and mystical experience of God.[15] That the Templars applied this knowledge became obvious when the first Cistercian pope allowed them the unique right to build churches whose round form and octagonal geometry generate acoustics of such clarity they are capable of inducing trance-like states in the listener.[16] Even the pillars of the buildings produce a ringing tone.[17]

The understanding of the Templar and Cistercian architects was certainly advanced for medieval times (it is exceptional even by modern standards),[18] leading one contemporary eyewitness in Jerusalem to remark, "On the other side of the palace the Templars have built a new house, whose height, length and breadth, and all its cellars and refectories, staircase and roof, are far beyond the custom of this land. Indeed its roof is so high that, if I were to mention how high it is, those who listen would hardly believe me."[19]

Within six years of returning from Temple Mount they introduced this knowledge into Europe in the shape of Gothic architecture.

Gothic is derived from the Greek *goetia* (by magic force); its extension is *goeteuein* (to bewitch), a rather appropriate term given how the spatial relationship of the buildings generates frequencies that find their correspondence in the human body, particularly DNA,[20] not to mention the pineal gland,[21] as well as the area of the brain associated with mystical experiences, the amygdala.[22]

One of the first cathedrals to be erected in the Gothic style was Saint Denis in Paris, on the site of a previous structure founded by Dagobert I, a Merovingian king. In Portugal, the Gothic style appeared in 1153 when Afonso Henriques laid the foundation stone for the breathtaking Cistercian monastery of Alcobaça, a building of superlative acoustical properties built in honor of his uncle Bernard de Clairvaux. But perhaps the most bewitching of all Gothic buildings is the one that arose to the west of Troyes: Chartres cathedral.

Every facet of this temple reveals information, be it overt or coded, much like the Egyptians did with the Great Pyramid of Giza.[23] Bernard de Clairvaux himself held daily consultations with the builders,[24] and a careful look at the pillars framing the Door of the Initiates leaves no doubt as to where the knowledge came from. A relief carved in limestone depicts the Ark of the Covenant transported on a cart, its open lid revealing a tablet and an orb inscribed with the fleur-de-lys, symbol of the holy bloodline in France; beside it, a man conceals the wooden receptacle with his robe, flanked by four individuals who look as though they are ascending a stairway to heaven. On the pillar is inscribed the accompanying phrase, "Here, things take their course; you are to work through the Ark."[25]

It is as though the cathedral is a sermon by Bernard set in stone.

This was by no means the only craft known to Bernard de Clairvaux. He would sometimes let on that he was well versed in cryptography by using it playfully in his many works, particularly his sermons. The Latin text of the *Song of Songs*—referring to Bernard's experience of the divine—consists of exactly ninety-nine syllables. In Roman numerals this would be written IC, the initials of Iesus Christos.[26] Another

The Ark of the Covenant on the Door of Initiates at Chartres cathedral.

coded reference exists in the final quotation of sermon 74 of *Super Canticum,* which consists of exactly 159 syllables. In Roman numerals this is written CLIX. Since X was often interchanged and equated with S, the letters read CLIS, a common contraction for CLARAVALLIS, the Latin for Clairvaux. The abbot is suggesting his mystical experience of God is closely associated with his place of residence, an unusual choice of location for an abbey to begin with, where a person could live, move, and be in God. Such cryptic language suggests he knew the choice of location coupled with the spiritual practices conducted in a specifically shaped building were paramount to achieving the shortest route between the material world and another dimension.[27]

When they first arrived in Jerusalem in 1104, Hugues de Payns and Comte Hugh de Champagne carefully surveyed Temple Mount and ascertained the challenges involved in reaching their predetermined goal. They returned a decade later, perhaps a little wiser, because by then they knew where to dig and what to find when they got there. Since a number of the original Templars were also Cistercians (Brothers Roland and Gondemare, in particular[28]), if Bernard de Clairvaux was privy to knowledge gained from the Kabalistic school of Troyes, it is feasible he then transmitted it via these knights to the other Templars. He knew in advance that locked inside that sacred hill were documents holding the greatest of all treasures.

If the Templars found such documents outlining the process of initiation into the art of spiritual resurrection, it may explain why so many nobles and laypeople alike readily gave the Templars so much of their personal wealth, assistance, or protection. The Catholic Church was as loathed as it was corrupt, a symbol of oppression, and many monarchs merely paid lip service to its authority just to keep the peace or stay alive. What the Templars offered was a way out, a route for every candidate of the Mysteries to find self-empowerment through a direct experience of God—"the joys of Paradise," as Templar recruits claimed.

In a manner of speaking, Lambert de Saint-Omer was literally following the advice of Jesus a thousand years earlier, when he said to the apostles, "To you was given the Mysteries of the kingdom of Heaven. But others only see them through parables, so that when looking they do not see and hearing they do not understand."[29] Indeed, and when these Mysteries of initiation were recorded by the Essenes they were encrypted from profane eyes, their true meaning revealed only by those deemed worthy of receiving secret instruction.

To the east of Saint-Omer lies the library of Ghent University, where a twelfth-century work titled *Liber Floridus* survives. It is a copy of a diagram found in the Essene scrolls and depicts the heavenly

Lambert's decoded heavenly Jerusalem.

Jerusalem: a walled city with eight entrances inside a vesica piscis (the geometry depicting, with the Divine Feminine, the balance of opposites). Inside stand twelve towers, along with motifs of the square and compass, the prime emblem of Freemasonry. The foundation of this heavenly city is attributed to John the Baptist.[30] The picture is the work of Lambert de Saint-Omer. Obviously, he decoded what was concealed in the scrolls brought back from Jerusalem by Godefroi the Templar.*

It appears the Templars found the keys to the heavenly Jerusalem. And they may have undertaken an obligation to re-create it in a Portuguese municipality called Ceras, and specifically its dilapidated town, Thamara.

---

*The Templars erected a cathedral in Ghent in the thirteenth century, dedicated to Notre Dame.

34

1159.
CERAS. A PILE OF RUBBLE NEAR
A DILAPIDATED TOWN . . .

"Silence and perpetual remoteness from all secular turmoil that compels the mind to meditate upon celestial things." It was Bernard de Clairvaux's decree by which discipline is brought to a world governed by perpetual chaos. Amid an age of anarchy, his Buddhist ideal—New Age even—set a rare example of order.

The Cistercian model required a retirement from the sight of human habitation, insofar as it was possible. Thus, Cistercian properties tended to be located in some forgotten valley, a lonely hilltop, or some other empty, deserted environment. And in twelfth-century Portugal there was no better place than the depopulated territory around Ceras. This may partly explain why Bernard's monks and a group of affiliated Templar knights chose the furthermost corner of Europe to create afresh a country in which their utopia might be fully realized.

The Cistercians were masters of raising lands from the dead. "Give the Cistercians a desert and in a few years you will find a dignified abbey in the midst of smiling plenty," wrote the medieval chronicler Gerald de Barri. He was right. They drained marshes, tamed wild woods, and resuscitated the soil. The Templars who settled in Ceras would apply these principles to rebuild an entire functioning community within a

handful of years, while 33 miles away in Alcobaça, the Cistercians in their new monastery traded surplus food with local towns and cities. And between them they created a paradise.

When Master Gualdino Paes and the Templars first moved to the region all they had to work with was a tumbledown old church with grass growing out of its creviced façade. Nevertheless, they took refuge inside its sacred walls and used as beds the broken pews and the floor of damp flagstones. No doubt Bernard de Clairvaux would have nodded in approval from heaven.

From the church's position on a flood plain populated by oaks and elms and the clear waters of the river Nabão, they gazed up at a limestone hill and an acropolis in dire need of substantial rebuilding.[1] Below, the town of Thamara consisted of no more than ramshackle remains and rubble. It was quite a downgrade from their first home in Fonte Arcada back in 1125, or Braga, Souré, or Santarém for that matter,[2] but nevertheless they set about making plans for their fifth and final home in Portugal.

Whatever attracted the Templars to this place attracted others thousands of years earlier.[3] By 480 BC, a town had been founded by a tribe of Lusitanian Celts called the Turduli, who named it Nabancia, in honor of the goddess of sacred waters; two hundred years later, the Visigoths moved in and with them came a Benedictine monastery, which grew into two, along with a host of nearby sanctuaries. One

Benedictine monastery and statue of Saint Erea.

was a sacred cave by the river Nabão, a sanctuary where the virgin Erea practiced her orations.

Erea* was born into a wealthy family of Nabancia and joined the Benedictine monastery, where she became a very learned woman whose great intellect complemented her beauty. She used her knowledge to improve the lives of locals, and in time she was beloved by them. Particularly the local men. Needless to say, a woman of such magnitude inevitably attracted a foolish man vying for her affections. He came in the form of a youth named Britaldo, son of a noble family, whose unrequited love for Erea drove him to sickness that no remedy could cure.

---

*She was also known as Saint Irene.

The young man's family held her responsible for bewitching their son, and if that was not pressure enough, Erea's spiritual counsel also lusted after her, but upon learning he was one of many men with a bulge in his loins, he was overcome with jealousy and handed Erea a laced drink, giving the unsuspecting woman the outward signs of pregnancy. Predictably, she was expelled from the monastery.

She found her way to the cave by the river, and there she stayed awhile in contemplation and prayer until one of Britaldo's servants tracked her down and killed her in an act of revenge, stripping her of clothes as proof of his deed before dumping her naked body in the river.[4]

At this point, the story takes an extraordinary turn, particularly in relation to the Templars who had just moved upriver from Santarém to what used to be old Nabancia. The currents carrying Erea's body merged with those of the river Tejo, flowing south until the waters of the ancient river finally deposited her lifeless body gently upon a sandbar below the old city of Scallabis, 33 nautical miles from its point of origin. As is the case with legends of many holy people, her body remained incorruptible throughout the ages and a cult developed, so much so that the city where her body washed up was renamed in her honor to Sancta Irene, and finally Santarém—the birthplace of Prior Arnaldo da Rocha and the city that the Templars "lost" in favor of a seemingly useless territory and its decaying town of Thamara, whose patron saint is Erea.

So it would appear the Templars inherited a worthless plot of land just to follow in the footsteps of a local martyr. But to what end?

At some point after a Roman occupation, Nabancia was destroyed by a flash flood, and with it drained the fortunes of all who lived and prayed there. When the Arabs repopulated the area, they found the town in much the same condition the Templars did. They rebuilt it and renamed it Thamara* (also spelled Ta'amarah and Tamara),[5] meaning palm tree.[6] Since the local climate of that era was too cold to support such a variety of tree, it is an odd choice of name for a town.

---

*The locals were referred to as Tamarães.

The Arab lords were said to have been tolerant to the locals; they allowed them to cultivate their lands and continue their laws, and it was not unusual for mosques and Christian churches to be sited side by side.[7] When Afonso Henriques and the Templar army reached Thamara in March 1159, the town was guarded only by a token army of Moors, which was quickly dispatched thanks to the knights, who took the watchman by surprise.

The king then donated the town and its municipality of Ceras to the Order of the Temple under Gualdino Paes by way of a former promise, implying the Templars had earlier put in a request for this specific location.[8]

By the time they moved to Thamar (as the name was also spelled at the time), the Templars were already in possession of hundreds of properties throughout Portugal, all in far better shape than this one. Thamar was in tatters; it was situated on a plain prone to attack by Saracen and Moorish outlaws, only the seven gentle hills overlooking it from the west could be deemed a defensive position, and even that required a little imagination given that the fortification was also decrepit.*

Against standard military practice, not to mention common sense, Gualdino and the Templars ditched the safety of the hill in favor of the exposed old church on the river plain and took up residence there. Paes is said to have overseen its reconstruction take precedence over the fortifications, despite the two sites being within walking distance of each other, and for a whole year they mustered all resources to this exercise. They located the sacred spring feeding the river—the Fonte do Agroal—and honored its presiding menhir, in keeping with the local custom of touching the sacred monolith whenever approaching the spring. The stone had stood there since Neolithic times, like so many others in the vicinity, and now it had the Templar logo etched upon its granite face.[9]

What was so special about this ruined church? Sure, it stood on the

---

*It has been debated in Portuguese circles that the Templars first moved to the actual town of Ceras, a few miles to the north, but no evidence of a castle has been located there, so the current consensus is they actually moved directly to Thamar.

site of the former Benedictine monastery, and near where Saint Erea was martyred, "her sacred well still inside the monastery, site of many miracles,"[10] but beyond a gesture of respect their actions seem irrational, metaphysical even. Stubbornly, the group commenced no other projects until the church was complete.[11] Even the campaign to push the remaining Moors on Portuguese soil back to North Africa was wholly entrusted to Afonso Henriques.

The symbolism in the architecture of this building to which the Templars so devoted themselves reveals the reason for their apparent madness. Dedicated to Mary Magdalene,*[12] the church emerged as an exercise in purity, humility, and elegant simplicity, as though the architect were a Cistercian. An enormous twelve-pointed rosette dominated the austere Gothic façade, while the crown of the building featured an unusual apse consisting of seven chambers in a fan shape similar to the star emblem of the Egyptian goddess Seshat, the patron of sacred buildings. Inside, the

Sheshat and her seven rays.

---

*Now Santa Maria do Olival. The dedication to Mary or Notre Dame was always to Magdalene, not the mother of Jesus.

Santa Maria do Olival,
the "mother church of all Templar churches."

Symbol of Isis inside Santa Maria do Olival.

arch leading into the apse featured a smaller yet prominent circular window framing a carved limestone pentagram, the ancient Egyptian symbol of the divine virgin or Isis, but also Sophia, or *sophis,* the "wisdom" to which esoteric brotherhoods and gnostic sects are so dedicated.

That this building was of undisclosed importance is an understatement. In time, the church of Santa Maria do Olival would become the pantheon of the Templars, with all twenty-two future Portuguese Masters buried inside.[13] Interestingly, the biblical Mount Olivet (from which Olival derives its name) has long been prophesied as the place where the dead are brought to life;[14] it is the site where King Solomon first erected a number of altars,[15] not to mention where Jesus was betrayed for thirty pieces of silver, just as thirty silver coins became the token "price of admission" into the Templar Order. It is as though the Templars were making a point, and the humble church they erected became a focal point for a grand design when it was subsequently elected the "mother church of all Templar churches," including those in Africa, Asia, and the Americas, during the Portuguese period of Discoveries.[16]

Tellingly, this was the same title earlier awarded to the Essene church on Mount Sion; by Emperor Hadrian's time it was already referred to as the "Mother of all churches," built as it was over the tomb of King David and possibly an even older temple,[17] and the spot upon which Godefroi de Bouillon erected the eight-pillared circular Chamber of Mysteries.

After completing their church, the Templars finally took an interest in the adjacent limestone hill and moved to the next item on the agenda. According to legend, "Master Pais and some monks searched the site where Santa Maria do Olival now stands and found it had been built upon before . . . and launched spears three times, and three times they landed on that site and they agreed to build on that site."[18] Obviously, no human is capable of launching spears half a mile, let alone make them land three times on the same spot and on top of a hill, and yet the legend is not unusual. Identical stories exist in connection with the founding of sacred sites, one being the masterful English gothic cathedral of Salisbury, whose location was decided by the shot of an arrow from a nearby Neolithic sacred mound (also dedicated to fertility and the divine feminine) an even more preposterous two miles distant.

Paes would not have been familiar with that legend because it was still sixty years in the future, yet to someone inducted into the Mysteries the allegory is all too familiar. In ancient times, prior to erecting a sacred structure, an elite priesthood would be called to assess and locate a hotspot of favorable earth energy, which today would be called geomancy. This practice continued into Greek and Roman times via a priesthood called the College of the Augurs, whose name and purpose is still commemorated in the opening ceremony of important places, the in-augur-ation.[19] In Egypt the process included the act of "piercing the snake."[20] The snake represents the naturally occurring pathways of electromagnetism that flow through and along the Earth like invisible ribbons. This energy is a prerequisite for making the temple function like an electrical circuit, and every sacred site on Earth is located at the intersection of such telluric currents.[21] However, due to its meandering nature this energy must first be rooted to the spot by a kind of earth acupuncture, and all around the world there exist emblems depicting a god pinning down a serpent with a rod or a serpent wrapped around a tall needlelike stone.

*The serpent and the pillar, later known as the caduceus,
often depicted with a god.*

In medieval times the process acquired imagery recognizable to that period, such as the throwing of a spear or the shooting of an arrow. Gualdino Paes would have been familiar with such symbolism if during his second tour of the Holy Land he followed Bernard de Clairvaux's instruction to attend the sacred places and understand the spiritual context of the land. Evidence that he did just that comes from a eulogy inscribed on a white marble slab at the behest of Afonso Henriques in honor of his friend:* "Master Galdino blossomed, into a true noble, native of Braga, during the reign of the illustrious king of Portugal, abandoned the secular military, and shone as a bright star, because having become a knight of the Temple, he journeyed to Jerusalem and during five years did not put down his arms nor rested; together with the Master and his brothers he engaged in battle with the king of Egypt and Syria. After five years he returned to the one who educated and trained him a knight."

So, this knight not only "abandoned the secular military," he also "shone as a bright star"—not *like* a bright star but *as* one. This subtlety may seem trivial, but to anyone familiar with Egyptian mysticism the implications are immense.

---

*The original date of the stone is AD 1170. It was moved around 1208 from its original site in the castle of Almourol to Tomar and placed above the door of the sacristy.

A central component for initiates of the ancient Mysteries schools was a ritual in which the soul is awakened and the individual no longer associates solely with material forces. It would follow several years of observation of the candidate and instruction in esoteric arts. The metaphor associated with this rite is "raising the dead," whereupon the initiate becomes "as a star."[22] Paes spent five years in the Holy Land, long enough to come into contact with its sacred places, their spiritual practices, and the various esoteric sects teaching them, so it is highly likely

Interior of the church at Olival.

he was indoctrinated into the sacred arts. If so, he followed in the footsteps of Count Dom Henrique, for he too "venerated the Sacred Places" and was entrusted with holy relics in Jerusalem.[23] Certainly, upon his return from the Holy Land, Gualdino came armed only with the hand of Saint Gregory the Nazarene, which he later placed in the church he and the Templars dedicated a whole year to rebuild in Thamar, where its flesh remains "without corruption, just like his body in Rome, without corruption."[24]

In a metaphysical twist, the Templars' behavior in Thamar takes on a patina of ancient ritual.

Not only does the Templar Master appear to have been initiated into the Mysteries, he may even have excelled as a "master of the craft," because the three spears Gualdino figuratively launched correspond to the graphic mark carved by the master mason on the keystone of sacred buildings. This symbol at once resembles three spears or the three rays synonymous with the descent of the Holy Spirit. Such a mark exists on a keystone on the promontory above Thamar. Its date of March 1, 1160, marks the inauguration of a striking round church strangely reminiscent of the one in Jerusalem by the name of Holy Sepulcher.

35

68 AD.
MOUNT SION. MEN IN WHITE,
HIDING SCROLLS AND OTHER
IMPORTANT THINGS . . .

The Essenes were said to be "faithful even unto death" rather than give up the secrets of the Way, as though these mystics held some special covenant with God that embodied the spiritual aspirations of all peoples.[1] With the Romans advancing on Jerusalem, a decision was made to evacuate their church and synagogue on Mount Sion, but not before concealing several scrolls in a vault under the Holy of Holies on Temple Mount. Regardless of the outcome, the secrets would be preserved.

The mystical brotherhood escaped the Roman destruction of their temples by fleeing to Jordan and taking with them the remaining scrolls to be secreted in five other locations.[2]

Two years after the persecutions, the Essenes returned and rebuilt their sanctuary; after all, this had been the most important of Essene communities, located as it was on Mount Sion.* Leadership was provided by Simon Bar Kleopha, a descendent of the Davidic family.[3]

The Essene scrolls containing the sum of all their knowledge—their

---

*The new building plus the ritual baths and the Gate of the Essenes were validated during archaeological digs.

"treasure"—were considered all but lost for nearly two thousand years, when two goatherds stumbled upon them in a cave at Qumran. And thus, the world learned of the existence of secret books, rituals, and knowledge "revealed by God." One scroll made of copper even offered precise directions to no less than sixty-one different caches of goodies. More importantly, it revealed how the Knights Templar had known all along where to look under Temple Mount and how they came to follow and embody a mystical doctrine.

Many parallels exist between the Essenes and the Templars: both favored a monastic existence, wore white habits, disposed of their wealth one year after being ordained, believed in various levels of membership, and despite a broad outer group, only initiates were allowed into the inner sanctum of their temples.[4] Both undertook vows of obedience and absolute secrecy absolutely, to the point where initiates would take teachings to the grave. And no wonder, as both groups claimed to be in possession of very secret information offering nothing less than paradise itself.

Insofar as the Essenes and the Cistercians were concerned, both practiced a communal life dedicated to asceticism, piety, voluntary poverty, and abstinence from worldly pleasures. They devoted themselves to charity, forbade expressions of anger, and also studied the Mysteries and preserved their secrets.

All three were spiritual brotherhoods whose members practiced truth, righteousness, kindness, justice, universal benevolence, religious tolerance, honesty, and humility.

The Essenes also shared many traits with a contemporary gnostic sect called the Nasoreans, and sufficient evidence shows both groups were one and the same, to the degree that both names were combined as Naassennes.[5] The root *nasrani* means "a group of little fishes," hence their logo of two interlocking arcs resembling a fish. During his time, Jesus was seen as a member rather than an original leader of this sect.[6]

The Nasoreans survive today in southern Iraq as the Natzoraje, part of a Mandean sect. The Mandeans—whose name originates from *manda* (secret knowledge)—still follow an ancient form of gnosticism and conduct initiations leading to forms of ecstasy.[7] Interestingly, they trace their religious roots not to Jesus but to an individual named Yahia Yuhana, otherwise known as John the Baptist, and their texts state how their faith was once that of Egypt.[8] Like the Essenes in their time, the Mandeans' opinion of Jesus in the bigger scheme of things is quite low; they believe him to be a rebel who, in his rashness, betrayed secret doctrines entrusted to him.[9]

The thread connecting these sects is simple: they are all descendents of initiatory traditions—and antecedents of the Templar practices, which in turn were preserved in the rites of Scottish Freemasonry—that can be traced as far back as the fourteenth century BC and the time when Moses was privy to the same secret teachings of the pharaonic inner circle. Sufficient evidence suggests the reason for his hasty departure from Egypt while chased by an understandably angry pharaoh is that he absconded with secrets that should never have left the Holy of Holies of the temple. In the *Assumption of Moses*—an Essene work—Moses gives instruction to preserve these special books and the need to keep them hidden.[10] Like a forerunner of the Essenes' frantic efforts at concealment before the arrival of the Roman army, the books were to be placed "in earthen vessels in the place which He made from the beginning of the creation of the world."[11] Such places created by a deity at the beginning of time are known to indigenous cultures as primordial mounds or navels of the earth; they are sites of incalculable sanctity and, coincidentally, hotspots where the Earth's telluric currents meet and influence the human body to an extraordinary degree.[12] One such hotspot is Temple Mount in Jerusalem or, to be more specific, the rock beneath the Holy of Holies.

To be privy to the knowledge contained in such teachings, the individual was first indoctrinated into an esoteric or gnostic brotherhood. Upon successfully completing a period of observation the candidate was then admitted into an inner group, a brotherhood within a brotherhood, exactly like the Templars, and initiation into the fuller Mysteries

Under Temple Mount.

ensued. In ancient Egypt there is a recurring theme of members of the pharaoh's household being favored to join such an inner circle to "master secret things of the pharaoh." One individual who takes up initiation is led into a restricted chamber where he joyfully proclaims, "I found the way."[13] This expression, which can be traced to the Chinese practice of Dao (the Way) in 2800 BC, was adopted by the Essenes and by the Jerusalem Church of the early Christians, whose initiates were referred to as "those of the Way," as well as the "children of the light."

One of the unusual items unearthed in the caves at Qumran was the Copper Scroll, an engraved roll consisting of twenty-three items of inventory stamped across eight columns of copper, each sheet of metal riveted rather than sewn, and designed by the scribe to be handled as a normal parchment scroll, read from right to left and rolled from each end. It reads like a veritable treasure map: "In the Great Cistern which is in the Court of Peristyle, in the plaster of its floor, concealed in a hole in front of the upper opening: nine hundred talents. . . . In the cavity of

the Old House of Tribute, in the Platform of the Chain: sixty five bars of gold . . . nine cubits under the southern corner: gold and silver vessels for tithe, sprinkling basins, cups, sacrificial bowls, libation vessels, in all six hundred and nine."[14] In total, the Essenes concealed sixty-five gold bars, 1,280 gold talents, and more than 3,282 talents of silver.[15] That is in addition to the vessels.

Further along it is revealed that no less than two dozen of the locations are within the precinct of Temple Mount.[16] From these clues, and from cross-references in contemporary accounts by the historian Josephus, it became possible to identify the area under Herod's Temple where part of the treasure was sequestered, specifically in a roughly hewn chamber at the north end of the western cistern, later identified as the House of the Two Pools.[17] There, a copy of the Copper Scroll was secreted along with "scrolls amongst the jars," beneath the altar, in a cave capped with a marble block with a ring at its center.[18]

It was these other scrolls that were of interest to the Templars because, like those unearthed by the two goatherds at Qumran, they are concerned less with temporal matters and more with spiritual ones, in addition to works that not only precede but dramatically differ in content from the highly edited narrative put forward by the Catholic Church.[19] There were just two obstacles in reading the contents, then and now: one, they were written in a forgotten language, and two, parts of the scrolls were written in code.

One of the earliest researchers of these Dead Sea scrolls, Father J. T. Milik, noticed how certain scrolls used cryptic devices such as two parallel alphabets with randomly inserted symbols; in some cases the script ran in reverse. Then, a cipher discovered by the British Bible scholar and Nobel Peace Prize nominee Hugh Schonfield opened the way to illumination. Thanks to this Atbash Cipher, elements such as coded names hidden in the texts could now be revealed. For example, when applied to a character named Taxo (also spelled Tacho), who also appears in the *Assumption of Moses,* interesting details emerge. In the commentary, Taxo urges his sons to retire with him to a cave and undergo a symbolic death that ushers in a kingdom of heaven on Earth. An obviously allegorical tale, it describes an initiation of the enlightened through the resurrection of the soul that fosters a more ideal way of life. When filtered through the Atbash Cipher the name of this mysterious individual transliterates to Asaph, the name of the master mason who assisted Solomon in the building of his temple and the pseudonym adopted by the leader of the later Essene community.

At some point the name Taxo migrated westward to Spain and Portugal, where it is pronounced the same way but spelled Tajo and Tejo, the name of Portugal's principal river, whose origin is a mystery in itself.* But two things are certain: the river Tejo once defined the southernmost boundary of Count Dom Henriques's territory of Portugale, and it is the principal water route by which one reaches the Templars' final home at Thamar.

---

*It was also used as the pseudonym of the Templar Master in Spain.

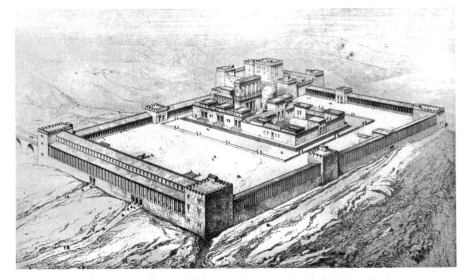

Temple of Solomon reconstructed.

The Atbash Cipher does not just work on the Essene Scrolls, it also works on Templar code words. For example, after the Templars were rounded up on October 13, 1307, the Inquisition accused them of worshiping a mysterious devil called Baphomet, yet when the cipher is applied the word simply transliterates as *sophis,* the Greek term for "wisdom."[20] So, not as sinister as the church has had us believe, in fact, quite the opposite.

The implications are clear: the Templars discovered a treasure of scrolls under Temple Mount *and* a monetary treasure, and they did it thanks to cryptographers who unraveled both the language and the cipher. With their newfound and carefully guarded knowledge they embarked on a journey of empowering people through enlightenment, using the finances at their disposal to build the finest medieval temples, the Gothic cathedrals, while resurrecting from the dead some of the most insensate parts of Europe. And they were loved for it.

This outstanding journey by a group of spiritual knights on a seemingly futile quest to recover a hard-to-get treasure bears all the hallmarks of a Grail quest.

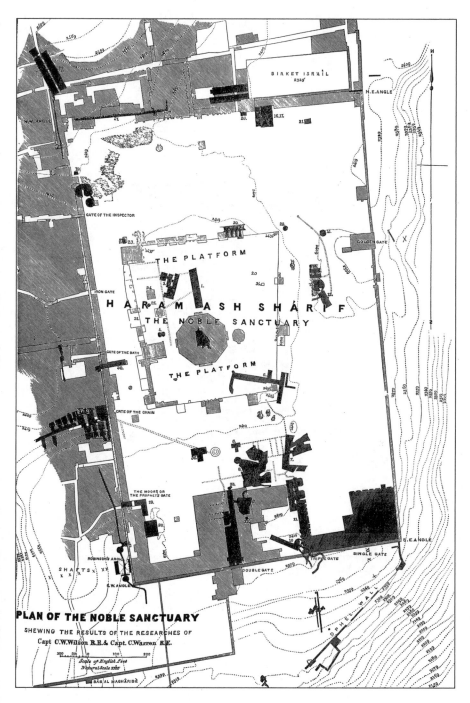

*Survey of Temple Mount by the British engineers
showing underground digs. 1884.*

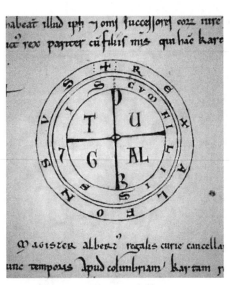

Seal of Afonso Henriques.
Charter of Ceras.

36

1159.
COIMBRA. THE KING OF
PORTUGAL'S DESK,
PART I . . .

"There exists in the Order a law so extraordinary on which such a secret should be kept, that any knight would prefer his head cut off rather than reveal it to anyone," revealed Gervais de Beauvais, a Templar Preceptor in France, during his interrogation by the Holy Inquisition.

The Order kept a book of statutes, much like a set of guidelines, but there also existed a secret book that could not be revealed beyond the inner brotherhood of trustees, along with an item in the general chapter of the Order that should anyone else read it, even if the king of France, the members would kill them.[1]

**1159.
COIMBRA. THE KING OF
PORTUGAL'S DESK,
PART II . . .**

The Iberian word for horse is *caballo,* and in Portuguese, *cavalo.* From *cavalo* comes *cavar,* "to dig below the surface," precisely what one must do to understand the secret knowledge contained in eso-teric teachings such as the Ka-Ba-Allah (spirit-body of God).

Every gnostic sect and secret society has promulgated its knowledge through the cunning use of allegory, metaphor, and symbol. In a world of corrupt clergymen and kings, it has proven to be the safest method of transmitting important concepts and for initiates to exchange signals with one another. In this respect the Templars were no different; they even developed a complex cipher in Latin.[1] In their monuments, seals, and talismans, a symbolic language lies encoded. It is a timeless language, and as such, it cannot be scoured by time. But to anyone immersed in the Mysteries it can be as easy to unravel as a nursery rhyme.

The most famous of Templar talismans is the symbol with which they are so readily identified: the two knights riding a horse. In mythol-ogy the horse is synonymous with knowledge, specifically sacred knowl-edge. Even in scripture, when God wishes to disclose information to humanity, It typically dispatches an archangel mounted on a horse.

The horse's counterpart in the Middle East is the sphinx, and legends

claim it sits protecting a hall of records, the repository of all knowledge. So when two Templar knights ride the one horse they personify not just the two levels of initiate within the Order, they also represent the complementary forces of light and dark, and it is the balance between the two that steers the knowledge on its intended and correct course.

The word *talisman* comes from the Arabic *tilsam* and means "complete religious rite," denoting an object or symbol that is imbued with magical properties. In order to understand the power of such magic it is important to first understand how the magic taught in esoteric schools is a science the cynical mind finds hard to accept because its roots have been corrupted through Victorian parlor trickery, the might of religion, the zealots of science, and of course, that Lucifer of the modern world, popular television. But it was not always so. Even in the seventeenth century, magic was administered every day in the form of medicine. Many accounts survive of notable figureheads being given amulets or prescribed remedies during illness or plague that today seem unpalatable. A ring given to Queen Elizabeth I by her physician to protect her from the plague, or the three spiders worn by Elias Ashmole to counteract the ague, or the hare foot worn by Samuel Pepys as a cure for colic all demonstrate how there was no distinction between natural remedies and symbolic magic. Yet when such remedies are analyzed from a chemist's point of view they reveal how natural elements in what appear to be unusual potions contain ingredients that prevent the types of illness for which the "remedies" were prescribed. Thus, "magic" was no more than a thorough understanding and application of natural laws.[2]

When enlightened kings and queens wished for their word or law to carry special favor they often would sprinkle herbs on the page prior to signing their names.[3] The herb may or may not have carried power in itself, but its properties would correspond with the intention of the message. In other words, the properties of the herb would help the monarch focus and amplify his or her intent on the written page.

Likewise, an accompanying seal would be designed using a specific geometry or cryptogram that was emblematic of the ruler's message or will.

This belief in the effective utility of any object, remedy, or geometry stemmed from ancient systems of observation and classification that noted the existence of correspondences and analogies occurring in all cycles of the natural world. Before industry and cold, hard logic separated human common sense from its god-given intuitive abilities, people observed and experienced life directly. Aboriginal cultures can still walk a barren desert by seeing or feeling the Earth's telluric currents and travel along them to reach an intended destination.[4] When one possesses such a degree of connection with his or her environment, it is possible to readily discern nature on a very subtle level, it is possible to deduce correspondences and interactions taking place all around. And armed with millennia of experience handed down orally or through tradition and teaching, it is possible to overcome problems on a physical level through the application of an alchemy based on natural forces.

This is magic. Only when a society loses the underlying understanding of a concept does one person's science and magic become another's ridicule and superstition.[5]

An important talisman for the Knights Templar was the octagon, the geometric blueprint behind their logo, their churches, and their temples.

For King Afonso Henriques it was also the design of the royal seal he was about to place on the charter of Ceras, for it would invest in Gualdino Paes the power to erect the mother church of the Templars, rebuild the town of Thamara, and consecrate an unusual round church above it.

38

1159.
COIMBRA. THE KING OF PORTUGAL'S DESK, PART III . . .

The Grail is variously described as a womb, a chalice, a bowl, a cauldron, a repository, a woman, a bloodline, an altar, an ark—and a salver, a tray made from a precious metal.

The Grail appears in medieval French literature as *Graal* and *Sangraal,* or *sang real,* and literally means "royal blood," referring to a bloodline of divine kingship. This bloodline is associated with a lineage of Merovingian priest-kings whose heritage stems from the female line of the Sicambrians circa 380 BC, but whose history extends further back in time to King David of Judah and his son Solomon, under whose direction an impressive temple was built on Temple Mount and inside whose Holy of Holies rested a wooden box said to contain the sum knowledge of God. The trail continues deeper into history with the Trojan royal family and the city of Troy, and before them, the priest-kings of Sumeria who followed the initiation tradition of the divine marriage and carried the title Sanga-lugal.

Solomon's kingly practices became the revered model for successive Merovingian monarchs just as his temple became the focus of attention for the Knights Templar—as did the Portuguese city of Braga, founded by Teukros, legendary archer of Greek and Trojan royal lineage. Which begs the question: Were the Templars pursuing this bloodline when they decided on Braga as their base?

The Merovingian tradition was not unlike that of the Druids, the Mandeans, or the brotherhood of ascetics living on Mount Sion, the Essenes. In their time the Merovingians were known as Newmage (New Covenant), ironically the same name adopted by the Essenes.[1] One of the Merovingians' primary concerns was the promulgation of secret esoteric knowledge, while their descendents—people such as Godefroi de Bouillon, Baudoin I, and ostensibly, Afonso Henriques— were committed to vows of obligation.

This royal bloodline includes Jesus and his consort, Mary Magdalene,[*2] whose union brought forth a daughter named Tamar.[3] This union was common knowledge throughout the Near East, even to gnostic Christians, but it was considered a huge threat to a new religion whose popes had come to anoint themselves as God's sole representatives on Earth. To preserve such a monopoly the Catholic Church made every attempt to deny the Davidic lineage, and for this reason, above all others, it exterminated hundreds of thousands—probably millions— in its effort to erase every trace of evidence that could destabilize its bogus claim to rule by hallowed appointment. It deemphasized Mary Magdalene's role as the continuation of the lineage by demonizing her as a slut, then subsequently suffocated the power of the feminine by demonizing women in general.

Bernard de Clairvaux, on the other hand, specified the importance of Mary Magdalene in the grand scheme of things, for in drafting the Latin Rule at the Council of Troyes he specifically stated how the knights should follow "the Obedience of Bethany, the castle of Mary and Martha," in other words, obedience to Mary of Bethany, known even to the medieval church as the Magdalene.[4] The knights would honor this oath by, among many acts, dedicating their cathedrals and countless churches to the divine virgin, Notre Dame, otherwise known

---

*The compiler of this bloodline was Fredegar, a seventh-century Burgundian scribe.

The divine virgin, Isis, with the infant Horus.

as the Magdalene,[5] while further amplifying the connection by locating the buildings on the sites of temples formerly dedicated to the original divine virgin, Isis, such as the cathedral of Braga. Even notable events in Templar history were conducted on her feast day, July 22.

The talismans of the Merovingians were the bee and the honeycomb, primarily because they so effortlessly characterize the manifestation of divine harmony in nature. The same is true of their priest-king predecessors, the Egyptian pharaohs, as well as priestesses honoring the cults of fertility, such as Ceres and Demeter, who were nicknamed *bees*.[6] As such, the construction of the honeycomb was associated with personal insight and wisdom, a concept immortalized in the Bible: "Jonathan . . . put forth the end of the rod that was in his hand, and dipped it in a honey comb, and put his hand to his mouth; and his eyes were enlightened."[7] And again, this time in the Book of Proverbs: "My son, eat thou honey, because it is good; and the honeycomb, which is sweet to thy taste: So shall the knowledge of wisdom be unto thy soul: when thou hast found it, then there shall be a reward, and thy expectation shall not be cut off."[8] Such talismans were later adopted by Bernard de Clairvaux, leading to speculation that, through his noble Burgundian parentage, he too descended from this bloodline.

The return of sang real is heralded as the restoration of fertility to a land that has become barren. It is the restoration of a divine order to territories reduced to rubble from protracted war, in other words, the resurgence of wisdom over barbarity. Whether such stories are interpreted literally or allegorically, the notion that the Templars, together with the Ordre de Sion, were engaged in a coup d'état against Rome to reestablish this spiritual bloodline is a plausible and tempting inquiry, especially since the "price of admission" into the Knights Templar was thirty pieces of silver, the sum for which the ministry of the Essenes/Nasoreans and their priests Jesus and John the Baptist were betrayed. It was a declaration, an inside joke, even, by the Order of the Temple of its aim to right an injustice that shut down a succession of rightful spiritual descendents and with it the negation of its most important initiation ritual, the "raising of the dead."

Bloodline is a recurring theme throughout the Templar story, as it is in the Ordre de Sion's, whose stated purpose was to reestablish the Merovingian bloodline in Jerusalem,[9] which it apparently did thanks to a fruitful relationship established by some of the Ordre's members—Peter the Hermit, in particular—with Godefroi de Bouillon, whom they subsequently placed on the throne of Jerusalem.

Given the prevalent intermarrying between the adjacent houses of Burgundy, Flanders, and Champagne, Godefroi would not have been the only offspring carrying sacred DNA. There would have been others; he was merely the most eligible and direct descendent of the Davidic bloodline.[10] Given the Burgundian lineage of the first king of Portugal and how he gained his throne due to the interrelationship between the Templars, the Cistercians, and the Ordre de Sion, it is tempting to consider that the Ordre de Sion may have quietly placed a second Merovingian on the throne, this time on the opposite flank of Europe. Certainly there are hints of this:

- The Ordre's central figure, Prior Arnaldo da Rocha, worked closely with Count Dom Henrique and the Portugale court to ensure the implementation of an independent nation-state following the count's untimely death, with his son as king.
- Afonso Henriques's family tree descended from the royal line of Frankish kings and includes Henri I and Hugo Capet.
- The king was nephew to both Bernard de Clairvaux and Duke Odo I of Burgundy, two alleged Merovingians.
- Like Godefroi de Bouillon, Afonso ascended to kingship indirectly—not as a direct son of a king, but of a count descended from a royal line.
- The proclamation of his kingship on the battlefield of Ourique coincides with the day Godefroi de Bouillon was himself offered the crown of Jerusalem.

Realistically, all this is circumstantial. Considerable obstacles stand in the way of definitive proof, since the Templars hid much of their written records during the organized persecution of the Order in 1307. What few records remained in Portugal were cleansed by the Inquisition and during the ominous period of reforms in the sixteenth century by the Jesuit priest Antonio de Lisboa,[11] who also vandalized all twenty-nine graves of the Templar Masters and knights buried in the mother church at Olival before scattering their remains. Brother Bernardo da Costa, chronicler of the Templar Order in Portugal, describes how numerous documents written prior to the reformation of the Templars vanished at this time, including the Order's famous diary. Lastly, a sizeable portion of the remaining Templar archive was lost when the National Archive in Lisbon burned down following a catastrophic earthquake in 1755.[12]

The idea of a sacred bloodline installed in Portugal would remain purely speculative were it not for a hint of a smoking gun. Between the twelfth and fifteenth centuries the monastery of Alcobaça amassed a large codex collection in its library. One surviving document held in the

Cistercian archives outlines the rites of succession of Templar Masters in Portugal, in which the swearing of allegiance by every new Master unambiguously declares obedience to the Order of Cister and a vow "to protect the bloodline of David."[13] Such a blatant line item would hardly be featured in the rite unless there was a bloodline to protect!

But there is another equally compelling angle to the interpretation of the Graal and it may help explain why the Knights Templar, the Cistercians, and the Ordre de Sion formed a complex pattern of allegiances that gave life to the kingdom of Portugal.

It is said that as a sacred vessel the Graal has the power to restore life to the dead. But since restoring a decayed organism back to life is a perversion of the laws of nature (not to mention olfactorily repugnant), it is very likely the phrase was intended symbolically. Every esoteric, hermetic, and gnostic society that ever existed always veiled its most important tenets in allegories and metaphors as a means to conceal important information from abuse or to protect its writers from torture, imprisonment, and certain death. Thus, to the casual reader, a myth or legend is accepted at face value, but to an initiate of the Mysteries, it reveals a deeper layer of information. Much like writing a message with lemon juice so that the ordinary eye sees nothing more than a blank piece of paper. Initiates of the Mysteries are a dab hand at masking material from the profane; Jesus himself was particularly good at it, as he once reminded the apostles, "To you was given the Mysteries of the kingdom of Heaven. But others only see them through parables, so that when looking they do not see and hearing they do not understand."[14]

One such parable concerns the "raising of the dead," an initiatory process as old as Egyptian pharaohs. The metaphor describes how the ordinary person walks through life as though asleep or unconscious (dead), but through initiation into the Mysteries and years of guided instruction (when they "drink from the cup of everlasting life") they become enlightened. Or to put it another way, they are "raised from the dead." Such practices were considered crucial to self-empowerment, so much so that the knowledge was withheld from the uninitiated lest it be abused by despots or ecclesiasts seeking control of an individual's direct experience of God. Adepts would rather die than reveal the secrets of the Mysteries. And many did, among them John the Baptist, who was deeply involved with the initiatory practices of the Essenes/Nazoreans.[15]

The Mysteries were essential components of esoteric sects who practiced and preached gnosis. *Gnosis* is Greek for knowledge, specifically "knowledge of spiritual mysteries." It is a knowing that comes not just from ancient teachings but also from a wider perception, much like the Buddhist who finds an expanded awareness from contemplating inner realms. The views held by these sects, including Christian gnostics, differed from those of fundamentalists in that they did not interpret the resurrection literally. They recognized the human condition for what it is, a spiritual death. For them, resurrection is the moment one discovers enlightenment, and the gnostic Gospel of Philip makes this distinction very clear: "Those who say they will die first and then rise are in error, they must receive the resurrection while they live." Gnostic Christians went so far as to call the literal view of Jesus's death "the faith of fools," and anyone believing this was confusing a spiritual truth with an actual event.*[16]

Philosophers such as Cicero, Plato, Pythagoras, and Voltaire unanimously claimed that immersion into the Mysteries provided the only bulwark against humanity falling into a state of depravity and brutality, and earlier Egyptian gnostics felt much the same way. For them, there was no such thing as formal religion, only *heka,* the nearest English equivalent being "magical power."[17] Derived from *heka* is the Hebrew *hekhal* (temple or sanctuary), its most energetic part being the Holy of Holies, equivalent to the altar, considered by virtually every culture as the dwelling place of a god. In other words, it is a space representing the closest possible simulation of the creative force here in the material world.

This is powerful stuff, hence why the secrets of the Mysteries schools

---

*This concept of a figurative death is still enshrined in the Masonic third degree, whose roots are traced to the practices of the Egyptian temple and the pharaoh Sequerente Tao around 1560 BC.

were well guarded and typically transmitted orally from generation to generation by wisdom keepers or priests of the highest moral integrity.

The Graal quest has always been associated with a close-knit group of savants privy to special knowledge who embark on a mission to find truth, enlightenment, and right action against injustice. The tales are packaged for the audience of the period, for example, Jason and the Argonauts, Arthur and the twelve knights, or Robin Hood and his merry men (the green-attired Robin representing the rejuvenating-resurrected nature gods Osiris, Pan, and the Green Man). During the years they spent digging under Temple Mount, if the Templars did rediscover Essene texts outlining the rites of living resurrection, then it is a simple logical leap to deduce this as the reason why everyone fell over themselves to hand over property and soul to the Templars, for it was they who could provide the keys to the kingdom of heaven, not the Catholic Church.

Personal salvation without a corrupt intermediary? Sheer paradise! As it happens, Templar resurrection ceremonies did come to light during questioning by the Inquisition in France, in which informants revealed ceremonies involving initiates being resurrected from a ritual grave.

Could this then be the central concept behind the Graal?

The Graal story appears in Europe in AD 717 as *Le Seynt Graal* via a hermit named Waleran following a vision of Jesus, who hands him a book and states, cryptically, "Here is the Book of thy Descent. Here begins the Book of the Sangréal." Nothing else is heard of it until 1128—a momentous year for the Templars—when the story resurfaces in the small town of Oxford, England.

Upon being awarded the title of Templar Master of England, Payen de Mont-Didier (one of the original Templars) bid Hugues de Payns *adieu* in London and set out on an impressive nationwide construction project, starting with a Templar preceptory in Oxford on land provided by Princess Matilda, wife to the grandson of Baudoin II, son of Count Fulk d'Anjou, who was himself an early financier of the Templars and later became a Templar knight and king of Jerusalem.

While in Oxford, Payen de Mont-Didier confided the story of the Templars and their purpose to a secular canon named Geoffrey of Monmouth, who published the account eight years later in a story titled *A Matter of Britain,* in which a kind of obscure messianic savior-king named Arthur Pendragon is carried westward to a magical land where his body is to rest until such time as he is resuscitated and the Light once again prevails across the kingdom. Geoffrey was adamant throughout his life that the events portrayed in the story were based on very ancient documents he'd been privy to in Oxford, yet was careful never to divulge their origin or whereabouts.[18]

Although Geoffrey's story stops short of introducing the Grail, a contemporary historian named William of Malmsbury did include it in his later version. William would not have been ignorant of Payen de Mont-Didier either, for the abbey in which he resided was but a half hour's horse ride from the Templar's other preceptory at Temple Guiting. And William, being a librarian, Preceptor, and chronicler of the church, would hardly have passed on the opportunity to meet this Flemish man engaged in a most unusual church-building program.[19]

After this the Graal reappears in France, in the work of the French poet and troubadour Chrétien de Troyes,[20] whose sponsor, Eleanor of Aquitaine, queen consort of France, donated the strategic port of La Rochelle to the Templars.[21] In 1160 her daughter, the comtesse Marie de Champagne, also became Chrétien's patroness, and he subsequently joined her court at Troyes. There, nestled in the heart of Templar and Cistercian territory, Chrétien wrote *Le Conte del Graal: Roman de Perceval,* in which a long and seemingly futile quest for a supreme object is carefully veiled in a veneer of acceptable Christian imagery so as to ward off charges of heresy by the church. It is an allegorical tale describing a pathway to spiritual transfiguration via an initiatory process in which the hero achieves an alchemical transmutation into "gold." At its most simplistic, the story's central character is a kind of hermit who leaves the woods to become a knight, trains with a spiritual mentor, then goes on a long quest and suitably returns with his eyes open, whereupon he meets a beautiful maiden and the two are wed. In other words, the hero is awakened to the greater mystery of life and walks a path to self-enlightenment.

And thus a "dead man" rises.

A significant moment occurs in Chrétien's story when the hero, Perceval, is witness to a procession in which a young woman carries the Graal on an elaborately decorated salver, and yet nowhere is there any mention of a cup, a chalice, or any association with a royal bloodline—in fact the attention is on that tray, and it is to this tray we shall return later.

What is riveting about Chrétien's allegorical work is that in reading between the lines one sees echoes of the lives of the personalities involved with the Templars as well as the various hermits and monks who played supporting roles, not to mention the central figures and events in the creation of Portugal. It is as though the author is transmitting an important historical yet deeply veiled account of the purpose behind the Sion-Cistercian-Templar alliance. That the story is synonymous with the Templar quest is revealed when Chrétien claimed his work to have been inspired by stories from Philippe d'Alsace, Count of Flanders, whose father was the cousin of the Templar Payen de Mont-Didier![22]

After writing nine thousand lines of text, Chrétien passed away, whereupon the story is continued by a translator named Wauchier de Danain, a name that implies an association with those mystical Celtic people, the Tuadhe d'Anu (or Tuatha Dé Danaan in Ireland), not to mention the predecessors of the Portuguese, the Lusitani.

A further piece of the Graal story was added in 1190 by an anonymous Templar, possibly one of the many poets encouraged to join the Order.[23] In this work titled *Perlesvaus,* the hero Perceval is received into a castle housing a conclave of initiates who are familiar with the Graal.

During a ceremony he meets 33 initiates "clad in white garments, and not one of them but had a red cross in the midst of his breast."[24] This time, emphasis is placed throughout the story on the importance of lineage, but what makes *Perlesvaus* stand apart is its focus on the initiates' understanding of alchemy and gnosticism, and how the Graal is intended to be an illuminating transcendental experience whereby one comes to see the world through very different eyes because the initiate symbolically "rises from the dead."

The esoteric leanings of the Graal are enlarged yet again in a follow-up by the contemporary Bavarian writer Wolfram von Eschenbach in his story *Parzival,* thanks to material transmitted to him by a troubadour monk named Guiot de Provence, who had worked as a spokesman for the Templars. Guiot himself may have received his knowledge from any number of Kabalist schools in Europe, from the Iberian city of Toledo, for example, which back then was run by both Arabic and Jewish scholars, or those of Montpellier or Gerona, or most likely the one in the Templar hometown of Troyes, which just happened to materialize around the same time a certain group of monks addressing themselves as the Ordre de Sion passed through town on their way to build a monastery in Orval.

In the story of Parzival the Templars are charged with protecting a castle, and behind the regular warrior monks there lies a more secretive order, a very spiritual group symbolized by a dove, who are guardians of the Graal. Wolfram describes how this brotherhood is fed by "a stone that fell from the sky." This purest of stones is said to resurrect a body, revitalize the ill, prolong life, and rebuild vigor and youth in the body. And it is referred to as the Graal.[25]

To the rational mind such a description seems ridiculous. Meteorites don't do such things. But to the esoteric mind, which reads such tales symbolically, this stone is akin to a library of information descended from an intelligent source (symbolized by the sky or heaven or God), much like the stone tablets given to Moses. In other words, this keystone embodies very ancient high wisdom, and properly applied, the knowledge it contains revitalizes and invigorates the individual, who in turn comes to embody its philosophy, so much so that the keystone becomes the spiritual foundation of the individual, even an entire philosophical movement.

The keystone is real enough: it is known in Jerusalem as the Rock of Sion and in Mecca as the Ka'Ba, and its tradition became embodied in the esoteric teachings of the Kaballah.

The imbibing of such wisdom would be liberating beyond belief, it would amount to a personal resurrection, and compared to the life you knew before, of course you would feel as though you had regained your youth. Such a transformation is comparable to an altered state of consciousness; it is Zen, a union with God. And besides being symbolic it is meant to be *experienced*.

And an experience of such magnitude would be something worth protecting with your life, it would be worth fighting for and, paradoxically, worth killing for.

It would seem, then, that the Graal is the embodiment of a protocol of initiation into the mysteries of life, a direct and mystical experience of God—the very credo of the Cistercian Order and its abbot, Bernard de Clairvaux.

Its roots lie in a Sumerian account from circa 2500 BC in which the *gra-al* is described as "the nectar of supreme essence" of the cup-bearing goddess Inanna, a queen of heaven akin to Isis, who takes for a bridegroom the initiate Dumuzi (also spelled Tammuz), and it is through this sacred marriage that this shepherd is resurrected as a god-man. Called *Song of Inanna*, it was the template upon which the Song of Solomon would later be modeled.

Inanna was a *hierodule* (sacred woman), a high priestess who presided over the highest and most secret aspect of initiation—epitomized by the union of the initiate with his divine bride—and was responsible for ensuring the initiate recovered from his or her out-of-body experience. Such priestesses were nicknamed "bees" and wore the red robe of *ritu* (truth), the origin of the word *ritual*.[26]

So in a manner of speaking, the Graal is synonymous with both a bloodline *and* a spiritual ideal, since it was up to a lineage of priest-kings, pharaohs, and initiates indoctrinated into the Mysteries to carry and transmit its knowledge, with the importance placed on the matriarchal line of women who perpetuated said lineage.

Like many perennial epics depicting the triumph of good over evil, the guardianship of the Graal asks of the invited to be warrior monks. During the quest, initiates seek to harmonize polar opposites: the needs of the soul and the obvious practicalities of the flesh, and in the twelfth century even monks had to think like soldiers just to survive. The mediation between the head in heaven and feet on the ground is the way in which the hero of the story remains faithful to the maiden he marries. This woman must have possessed exceptional qualities because he protects her at any cost.

Indeed, she is one radiant beauty, for she is repeatedly referred to as Sophia (wisdom).

This bride is the embodiment of the divine feminine in nature, knowledge of the very highest degree. She was the beautiful maiden to whom the Graal followers ultimately were wedded, and for whom they would willingly lay down their lives—and most Templars would one day do.

These principles were embraced by Bernard de Clairvaux. The Templars honored his oath to the divine virgin by following the "Obedience of Bethany, the castle of Mary and Martha" whenever and wherever they consecrated churches to Notre Dame or rededicated former temples to her Egyptian predecessor, Isis, just as Count Dom Henrique did in Braga when he honored the ruined temple of said goddess by erecting a new cathedral on its stones.

It is quite conceivable that one of the reasons the Templars invested so much effort in creating Europe's first independent nation-state was to conceal there such a secret, an object or a knowledge of such immense consequence that it required a territory as far away from Rome as possible, "free from all official and ecclesiastical interference."[27] In the original legend, the Graal is described as a gold object carried on a salver, a silver tray used in a formal ceremony. It is very similar to the Portuguese root word *salvar* (to save), from which arises the term *salvation*. And salvation through the Graal—this Sophia, this beautiful woman of knowledge—seems to be what the Templar quest was really about. Could this have been sufficient motivation to send a group of warrior monks on a quest from Lorraine, Champagne, and Burgundy to Jerusalem, then to assist in setting up a Portuguese crown on the opposite side of Europe, precisely as Hugues de Payns instructed?

The creation of a nation-state in twelfth-century Europe must have seemed like a Graal quest to the people involved, the undertaking of a perilous journey to achieve a seemingly impossible task. Even the event that established Portugal as a nation-state—the battle of Ourique—is itself shrouded in myth; the actual location has never been satisfactorily located. It is one of the great ironies of history that the defining moment of Portugal's history cannot be adequately pinpointed, like Iberia's own version of Perzival searching for the elusive Graal. The same is true of that other famous Graal knight, King Arthur, for his famous battle site at Mons Badonicus has not been adequately located either,[28] and battlefields of such historical import just do not disappear!

Descriptions of the terrain in the surviving accounts of Ourique suggest the conflict took place not far from the estuary of the mighty river Tejo, and in 1139 that area marked the nebulous frontier with the Moors. Right in the middle stood a village named Casal do Ouro, and exactly 33 miles to the north, the town of Ourém. Both places share the same root word with Ourique—*ouro* (gold)—and since gold is a metaphor for the Graal, is it possible the defining moment in Portuguese history may have taken place in the fields around Ourém? After all, the precise spelling of words and names in the twelfth century was a pretty nebulous affair in itself.

Positioned to the south of the castle of Souré, the hilltop village of Ourém was captured from the Moors by Afonso Henriques in 1136, three years before Ourique, but coincidentally on the same day, the feast day of John the Baptist. With territories being won, lost, and regained, and with records of this era being as sparse as they are contradictory, it is possible the two events are one and the same.

Two things make the idea rather compelling. First, of all the famous towns in his possession, Afonso Henriques granted the charter of this otherwise inconsequential village to a maiden of his own, his daughter Teresa (absolutely not to be confused with his mother). Second, a local legend claims that Ourém owes its name, of all things, to a love story between a Muslim and a Christian. An Arab princess named Fatima was captured by a knight named Gonçalo during the battle for the town, but later fell madly in love with him, converted to Christianity, and changed her name to Oureana, from which the town's name is derived.

For a chosen name, it is cunningly appropriate, for *ouro-ana* literally translates as "gold of ana," a clear reference to the goddess of the Lusitani as well as their Celtic cousins in central Europe, the Burgundii, the lineage of the king of Portugal.

Tragically, Fatima died while still a young woman. An understandably inconsolable Gonçalo joined the Cistercian Monastery in nearby Alcobaça as a remedy for his sorrow, and when its abbot built a small priory on a nearby hill, Brother Gonçalo took Fatima's remains to be interred there.[29] A town grew around the priory and over time became of the most Christian of pilgrimage sites, still remembered to this day as Fatima.

The story is hardly definitive proof that the battle of Ourique was in fact the battle of Ourém, but in reading between the lines of this seeming fairy tale—for the characters and events are real enough—this story representing the reconciliation of opposites, here represented by a Muslim and a Christian, would be in keeping with Cistercian and esoteric principles, the same principles that lie at the heart of the Graal quest, for it is precisely with a reconciliation that the quester finally discovers "gold."

The same reconciliation lies at the heart of the relationship between the Templars and enlightened Arabs, and the two worked much more closely than is often advertised. Afonso Henriques himself colluded with Sufi Master Ibn Qasi against the Almoravids who invaded Portugal; even the introduction of Gothic architecture was merely an extension of the Arab style. There was even mutual respect in their devotion to God, as the following account by a Muslim pilgrim to Jerusalem illustrates:

> When I visited Jerusalem I had the habit of walking to the al-Aqsa mosque, place of residence of my Templar friends. On one side there was a small oratory where the Franks placed a church. The Templars put this at my disposal for my prayer. One day I entered and said, "Allah Akbar," and as I commenced my prayer a man, a Franj [Crusader], ran up to me and turned me toward the east, and said, "This is how you pray!" Immediately some Templars came to my aid and moved him aside. I continued my prayer and again the man came at me, repeating, "This is how you pray." Again the Templars intervened and apologized: "He is a stranger, just arrived with the Crusades and never saw anyone pray without facing east." I replied that I had said my prayers, and left, stupefied by the behavior of that demon who was so aghast to see me pray in the direction of Mecca.[30]

Ultimately for Afonso, the Templars, and the Cistercians, the "gold" they nurtured was the birthing of a new nation, for in doing so they raised a kingdom of conscience out of a land long dead from decades of conflict.

It is worth pointing out two more extraordinary coincidences: one, Eleanor of Aquitaine—sponsor of Graal author Chrétien de Troyes—donated the strategic maritime port of La Rochelle to the Templars at the same time Portugal becomes a nation-state;[31] and two, Chrétien joins her daughter's court in Troyes and sits at his desk to write his Graal opus just as the Templars are laying the cornerstone to a round church in the town of Thamar.

Perhaps we shall never know how many of these thoughts about the Graal were going through Afonso Henriques's mind as he watched the ink of his royal seal dry into the vellum of the charter of Ceras. Secret societies love their symbols because, just like a parable, to the casual viewer they convey one message, while to the initiate of the Mysteries they conceal another.

To the casual viewer, the king's circular seal and its central quadrature of scrambled letters anagram the word PORTUGAL.

To the esoteric reader it reveals something altogether deeper: PORTUGRAL.

And to the initiate it reads, in Portuguese, POR TU, O GRAL— Through you, the Grail.

Could it be that the Templars deposited an aspect of the Graal in the town of Thamar, the namesake of the daughter of Jesus and Mary Magdalene?[32]

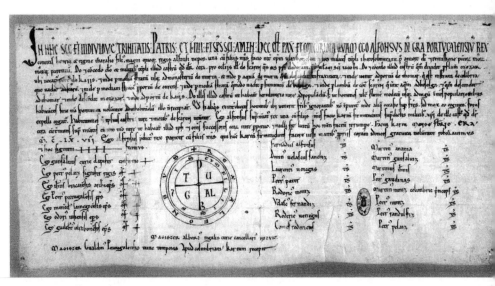

Charter of Ceras.

39

**1160. MARCH 1.
A DAWN CEREMONY
ON THE PROMONTORY
ABOVE THAMAR . . .**

aster Gualdino laid the cornerstone of the round church the Templars would spend the next two years erecting. By its very location on a mound atop the hill, the rotunda would be the first element of the surrounding terrain to be bathed by the light of the rising sun. The timing of the ceremony embodied the ancient Egyptian practice of performing the rite of resurrection at dawn.

The event also marked, to the day, the fortieth anniversary of the founding of the first Cistercian monastery in Portugale, at Tarouca, after the Templar knight Brother Roland and a group of monks from Clairvaux met with a young Afonso Henriques.

The rotunda's octagonal geometry would be an homage to both the Church of the Holy Sepulcher and Arabic sacred architecture; its interior was devoid of all ornament, precisely as Bernard de Clairvaux prescribed: "There must be no decoration, only proportion."[1]

During this period the Templars undertook no other project. It was a singular focus, a great work, a total and synergistic enterprise as though integral to their purpose. Only after the rotunda was complete did they turn to defensive and civic matters, first enclosing the rotunda within an extensive citadel, then focusing on Thamar and the attention the town obviously needed.

The town was practically rebuilt from scratch, requiring the import of vast quantities of artists and stonemasons, and in the decade that followed, the Templars devoted their entire efforts to its resurrection.[2] It was to become their headquarters in Portugal, the portal of the Order, containing perhaps the most significant Templar monuments in Europe.

Whatever the Templars brought here must have been noteworthy because on a sultry July morning twenty years later, they'd wake up to find the castle besieged by a Muslim army of four hundred thousand horsemen and five hundred thousand infantrymen.[*3] Even dropping a couple of zeros from such preposterous figures still leaves a disproportionate army of men eager to dispossess the Templars from a castle, an orchard, and a chapel! Certainly, the Arabs had not marched all the way from southern Spain just for the view. In any event, despite a six-day attack the Arabs were repelled, and the invading army retreated empty-handed.

POR TU, O GRAL. "Through you, the Grail." The same phrase inscribed beside the image of the Ark of the Covenant on the Door of Initiates at Chartres cathedral. Could the castle on the hill above Thamar be the same "castle of the wild mount" described in the Graal legend? Whether by coincidence or design, just as Gualdino's ceremony is taking place in Thamar, Chrétien de Troyes is settling down to write his Graal story in Champagne.

The origin behind the naming of Thamar is as intriguing as the reason why the Templars should have chosen a spot so far removed from their original homeland to give birth to their golden age. Thamara or Ta'amarah was the name given by its Arab habitants around the ninth century,[4] and its choice shines some light on why the location was important beyond the site of a former Benedictine monastery where a divine virgin was martyred.

---

*Verbatim from the lapidary on the wall of the rotunda.

Tamar or Tamara was the name of King David's daughter,*[5] just as it was the daughter of the union between Jesus and Mary Magdalene.[6] The name means "palm tree," and to anyone acquainted with esoteric symbolism this has a profound connection with the cult of raising the dead.

It has already been noted just how many of the Templar's pursuits have decidedly esoteric or ancient Egyptian overtones. One of the central pillars of the Egyptian Mysteries schools is the resurrection myth featuring Osiris and his consort, Isis. Osiris ruled the kingdom until his jealous brother, Set, and seventy-two co-conspirators cut him into little pieces and unceremoniously dispersed them into the Nile. Because Osiris produced no heir, Isis was left with no son to dispose of the evil Set. In effect, she was the divine virgin presiding over a kingdom gone to ruin. Resourceful to the end, Isis sets off to gather up her husband's body parts, magically reassembles them, and after fashioning him a new phallus made of solid gold she uses the sound of her voice, whereupon Osiris is resurrected and Isis impregnated.

After his ordeal, Osiris returns to restore life to a barren land and shines forever as a bright star. The myth essentially outlines the ritual of living resurrection, and the symbol of Osiris's experience is the palm tree. Osiris himself is depicted with green skin, making him the oldest expression of the cult of the Green Man, the tutelary deity of fertility who revitalizes the land and raises it from the dead.

One of the many visualizations of the Green Man. Roslin Chapel.

---

*It was also the name of a town built by King Solomon.

The god Amun. Note the two tablets of wisdom on his head.

It seems Osiris was adept at magic, perhaps because the priest-god who assists him in the ritual is the ibis-headed Djehuti (the Greek Thoth-Hermes), who is credited "as the author of every branch of knowledge, both human and divine . . . the inventor of astronomy and astrology, the science of numbers and mathematics, geometry and land surveying, medicine and botany."[7] Djehuti is nothing less than the personification of the mind of God. He is a half-human/half-divine encyclopedia, a skin-and-bones representation of the stone tablets written by God. As it happens, Djehuti's knowledge descended from heaven from the god Amun, whose image is depicted on temple walls wearing a crown of two tablets, suspiciously identical in shape to those handed to Moses.

After the Templars recovered the knowledge secreted beneath Temple Mount, they swore to "rebuild the temple," physically and symbolically. This they did by specifically selecting Thamar, in the land of

Ceras, a lifeless piece of land they held out for after a lengthy controversy with the Bishop of Lisbon. And now we know why.

The crowning of the hill with a round church gave it the appearance of Mount Sion and its curved basilica, the location where the Essenes once performed their secret ministries. If the Templars aimed to re-create the essence of Mount Sion, did they also re-create the rites of resurrection? For one thing, the unusual structure above Thamar was never a church to begin with; it never contained an altar inside or adjacent to it.[8] And why should the Templars require a second place of worship when they already had the nearby church of Santa Maria do Olival, where their prayers and sacred offices were conducted on a daily basis?

Even more curious, during sieges, the people of Thamar were never permitted inside the rotunda, arguably the safest, most secure building inside the citadel. And had they been allowed, getting inside would have proved awkward, for this rotunda had no door.[9]

40

**PRESENT ERA. APRIL.
INSIDE THE ROTUNDA
OF TOMAR . . .**

The plain Cistercian interior of the rotunda lasted four centuries until it became unfashionable for a house of God to resemble the domicile of a hermit.[1] What once was a soaring arc of eight plain columns within a circular ambulatory eventually became a decadence of decor and polychrome statues, proving the Baroque maxim that what is worth doing is worth overdoing. Bernard de Clairvaux would be venting liquid magma were he standing beside me right now. I could almost hear his famous admonition of the Benedictines bouncing off the rotunda's lofty walls: "I say naught of . . . the costly polishings, the curious carvings and paintings which attract the worshipper's gaze and hinder his attention of God."[2]

It had been fifteen years since I asked myself, "Why did the Templars come to my country of origin?" The silent reply was a slow and soaring hill of research. Looking under one stone led to a maze of roots, each connected to an ever-expanding and boundless body of a benevolent monster whose intricacies became as multifaceted as the three faces of Hermes. I had asked an honest question. I had not anticipated the loudness of the reply or the controversial nature of the material I unearthed. Now I had to complete the journey by returning to the

Interior of the rotunda. The decor was added four centuries later.

rotunda of Tomar (as it is spelled today) and the labyrinthine convent that sprouted around its core.

It is a maiden I adore. Only now did I become profoundly aware I had been inadvertently following a Graal quest.

One aspect of the Graal is a search for secret knowledge capable of raising an individual from the spiritual death that is life on the material plane. This knowledge derives from an ancient system of teachings spanning incalculable ages, brotherhoods, and continents, and its source material is often linked to the Ark of the Covenant. Perhaps elements of the Graal or the Ark were deposited right here. Perhaps inside the rotunda was the same marble keystone with an iron ring leading to a chamber of Mysteries, as it once did on Temple Mount. Certainly the founding of the rotunda became such a potent symbol that it remains the civic day for the town of Tomar, and until the change of calendars from Julian to Gregorian it even marked the first day of Portugal's official civil calendar.

The rotunda, Tomar.

To reach the rotunda it is necessary to walk up the hill along a meandering old cobblestone track that leads to the Gate of the Sun. Once inside the castle walls and its well-manicured courtyard, the aroma of lavender, lemon, and orange is as intoxicating to the senses as the sight of the round temple the knights erected. Indeed, it does bear a passing resemblance to the church of the Holy Sepulcher, even the old basilica of Mount Sion—the sacred places whose allure captivated the imagination of Godefroi de Bouillon, Hugues de Payns, Count Dom Henrique, and so many other protagonists in this Templar-Cistercian drama.

The building is not so much attractive as it is bewitching and entrancing.

Its exterior circular look is in fact an optical illusion; it is a sixteen-sided polygonal structure held by reassuring buttresses. Inside, the ceiling rests on a central arcade of eight slender columns, gathered like quatrefoils and arranged in accordance to the eight-sided octagon. The space between the columns and the gallery wall is defined by the invisible geometry of a hexagram: two intertwined triangles each representing nature's complementary opposites in perfect equilibrium, much like the symbolism behind the Templar emblem of two knights riding a horse.

The octagonal motif of the churches the Templars erected is heavily indebted to Arabic sacred architecture, which uses this geometry because it represents the fully illuminated human. It is a square unfolded twice, and just as the circle represents spirit and all that exists, so the square represents its physical counterpart, matter, and the four elements that make it so: earth, air, fire, water. The four remaining faces are representative of the invisible realm. Thus, by working with this talisman one strives to achieve utmost harmony between the material and spiritual. This was, and continues to be, the aim of all esoteric and gnostic sects.

The octagon's derivatives are the infinity symbol and the number 8. Notable avatars associated with these talismans are Jesus, Mohammed, the archangel Michael, the Arthurian wizard Merlin, and last but certainly not least, Djehuti, patron of scribes and god of magic, healing, and wisdom. His temple is situated in Khmun (eight-town), after the group of eight Egyptian deities or natural forces who represent the world before creation.*

The Templar inner brotherhood followed a secret doctrine,[3] and so their ceremonies appropriately took place in small, secret chapels inside their temples, such as the one below their preceptory in Paris.[4] What rituals were performed required total devotion to the craft, and the contents were revealed strictly to this inner brotherhood, and then only after a period of observation, typically one year. This law was broken on pain of death, as graphically described in Article 29 of the Rule of the Elected Brothers:

> If a Brother forgets, either by carelessness or by gossip, and makes known the smallest part of the secret rules or what happens in Chapters at night, let him be punished according to the greatness of his fault, with detention time in chains and exclusion from the chapters. If treason is proven and he has spoken with malicious intent, he is condemned to life imprisonment or even secretly put to death if it serves the best interests of all.[5]

The Templars were utterly devoted to Tomar, and given what we know so far about their tendencies to follow an ancient system of knowledge, it would have been uncharacteristic if they had not adopted these practices in, around, or under the rotunda itself.

In the Copper Scroll, one of the most important buildings described in the Inner Temple court is the House of Tribute. The entrance was still known in the first century BC as the Gate of Offering, and it stood on a stone platform, each of its four corners bearing a small chamber, one of which was the Chamber of the Hearth.[6] Inset into the floor was a marble slab that could be raised by a fixed metal ring to reveal an opening into a deep cavern below.[7] In an adjacent chamber, the Staircase of Refuge led to an underground passageway and into the Chamber of

---

*The Greeks renamed it Hermopolis, after the god Hermes, whom they identified with Djehuti.

Immersion, where, presumably, rituals such as the "raising of the dead" were performed. This may be the same chamber that stood out from the others and merited Captain Warren, the British excavator, to be lowered by rope into its rectangular form; it is the same chamber once described in the Talmud as a secret room kept for special ceremonies.

The Book of Ezekiel similarly describes how the elders of Jerusalem "engaged in secret mysteries . . . of Egyptian provenance" in darkness under the Temple of Solomon.[8] Such chambers still exist beneath the altars of early churches and cathedrals throughout Europe, particularly those erected above preexisting ancient temples where identical rituals were performed. Some are well known: Chartres cathedral, Mont Saint Michel, Roslin Chapel, and so forth. In Egypt, there exists a narrow, claustrophobic chamber beneath the temple of Dendera decorated with one-of-a-kind reliefs depicting a kind of rebirthing process. Just to the west, the chapel of Osiris in Abydos contains a mural depicting the

Resurrection ritual. Abydos.

same ceremony in graphic terms, while in the adjacent Osirion—an underground temple made from cyclopean blocks of red granite—the Mysteries of birth and rebirth were also taught and conducted, and although the whole site lies five hundred miles southwest of Jerusalem, the Osirion and the Templars are linked.

The prime Templar locations in Jerusalem are marked by the Church of the Holy Sepulcher and Solomon's stables, where the knights resided; the third is the Abbey de Notre Dame du Mont de Sion. The

Church of the Holy Sepulcher.

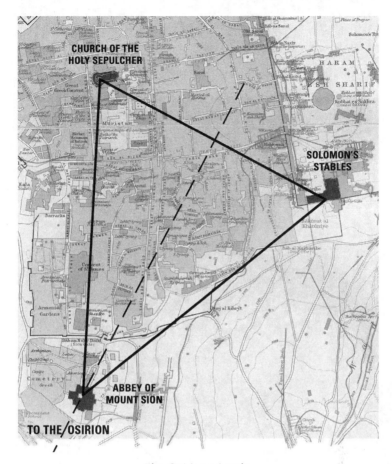

The Osirion triangle.

three sites form a perfect isosceles triangle, a symbolic holy trinity. When this triangle is bisected, an imaginary line extends all the way into the Osirion.

Geodesy on a continental scale.

Likewise, the Essenes conducted their Mysteries teachings in underground chambers on Mount Sion, and after their church fell into a state of disrepair Godefroi de Bouillon made additions to the original floor plan in the form of the Chamber of Mysteries, which was supported on a foundation of eight pillars, a room where the initiate ate a meal prior to the living resurrection ritual, also known as the Last Supper.[9]

Interior of the rotunda.

Godefroi therefore may have been maintaining a tradition upon which Sion is based, because the word *sion* is related to the Arabic *sahi* (ascend to the top), suggesting the location is interconnected with the process of "raising."[10] This Arabic interpretation is echoed in Jewish Kaballah, where the reference to Sion assumes an esoteric mantle as Tzion (a spiritual point from which all reality emerges).

By far the most direct reference to Templar secret chambers lies in Gisors, France, whose own rotunda is indistinguishable from the one in Tomar. The Gisors structure sits atop a Neolithic mound on which the Romans built a temple. Beneath its floor, an extensive tunnel system links two nearby churches, one possessing an underground initiation chamber.[11] Because such rooms are fundamental to the structural integrity of the building, they cannot be removed without making the structure above unsafe. It follows that if the Templars practiced the Mysteries in Portugal they must have built a similar chamber under the rotunda, and that chamber must still exist.

Alas, poverty and ignorance, the twin devils of conservation, have not been kind to the rotunda of Tomar. Details that would help the quest for a hidden chamber have been covered or replaced by well-intended attempts at preservation and, worse, by a lack of documentation. When its flagstone floor was refurbished in the mid-twentieth century no notes were made (at least none are known to have survived), nor were photographs taken of details that might appear out of the ordinary. If I had hoped to find a replica of the rectangular keystone with an iron ring and a staircase leading to an underground chamber, my quest was temporarily thwarted.

I retired to the adjacent courtyard and comforted myself with an orange freshly plucked from one of the four trees. Hope was in need of resuscitation. This was provided later that afternoon during a visit to the town archives, where a brief, yet tantalizing newspaper account from the 1940s describes how the exterior of the rotunda had been coated with reinforced concrete that hid or destroyed the entrance to what was then described as a kind of crypt.

ope Pius IX quickly made his point as he launched *Multiplices inter*, a fulmination against the Order of the Freemasons, in which its predecessors, the Knights Templar, were said to have followed a Johannite heresy from the very beginning: "The Templars, like all other Secret Orders and Associations, had two doctrines, one concealed and reserved for the Masters, which was Johannism; the other public, which was the Roman Catholic. Thus they deceived the adversaries whom they sought to supplant."[1]

One of the ringleaders of this heresy—the original meaning of *heretic* being "someone in possession of facts who is able to choose"— was Hugues de Payns, which the pope soon confirmed:

The Johannites ascribed to Saint John [the Baptist] the foundation of their Secret Church, and the Grand Pontiffs of their Sect assumed the title of Christos, Anointed, or Consecrated, and claimed to have succeeded one another from Saint John by an uninterrupted succession of pontifical powers. He, who, at the period of the foundation of the Order of the Temple, claimed these imaginary prerogatives, was named Theoclet; he knew Hugues de Payns, he installed him into the Mysteries . . . and finally designated him as his successor.[2]

It was also alleged that the Grand Masters of the Ordre de Sion were secret Johannites.[3]

That this should have raised the ire of the Catholic Church is explained by the fact the Knights Templar, as well as any number of gnostic sects around the time of John the Baptist, were following the gnostic Gospel of John rather than the church's canon, which confers power unto Jesus as a messiah and a god. It seems everyone except the Catholics were following a truer version of Christianity. This would explain why initiates into the Templar Order were requested to stomp and spit on the cross.* "Set not much faith in this," they were told, "for it is too young."[4] For them, the cross was a symbol of torture, an emblem of a fake religious institution that promulgated one of the greatest lies ever told. Even the debauched Pope Leo X admitted as much in what must rank as one of the biggest gaffes in history: "All ages can testifie enough how profitable that fable of Christ hath ben to us and our companie."[5]

The authority of the Catholic Church was further undermined by the gnostic Apocalypse of Peter, another of a set of hidden scrolls discovered in a cave, this time by the Nile: "Those who name themselves bishop and deacon and act as if they had received their authority from God are in reality waterless canals. Although they do not understand the mystery they boast that the mystery of truth belongs to them alone. They have misinterpreted the apostle's teaching and have set up an imitation church in place of the true Christian brotherhood."[6] Even the notorious Catholic theologian Iraneus was well aware of the power of the gnostic sects: "No one can be compared with them in the greatness of their gnosis, not even if you mention Peter or Paul or any of the disciples."[7]

The Templars' allegiance to John the Baptist rather than the

---

*Article 13, Rule of the Elected Brothers: The neophyte will tread on the cross and spit upon it; he will receive the white tunic with belt.

ministry of Jesus needs little convincing. One of the rare pieces of information extracted from the knights under torture was their alleged worship of a devil called Baphomet. They also were charged with practicing
the cult of the head, and indeed a bearded, silver-plated head was one of
the items confiscated by the Holy Inquisition from the Templar preceptory in Paris.[8] As sinister as this might seem, *baphomet* is merely a corruption of the Arabic *abufihamet,** meaning "father of wisdom," which
in its native Arabic tongue is also taken to mean "source." And when
decoded using the cipher discovered in the Essene scrolls, the word simply transliterates as *sophis* (wisdom).

This relic, the only one of special significance to the Templars, was
purported to have been the mummified head of John the Baptist, the
priest-messiah who baptized initiates into the Mysteries and the living
resurrection that followed.

The cult of the head is an ancient practice predating Druidism. It
is nothing more baleful than the veneration of the fertility principle in
nature once identified with the god Pan—whom the church overturned
into Satan—and the Green Man, whose image as a carved head
sprouting a healthy bout of vegetation from its mouth can be found in
churches in England more often than statues of Jesus.[9]

Since the skull was believed to contain the seat of the soul, it was
common practice for a deceased leader to have his head preserved or
buried in a place of spiritual significance. Because all sacred sites are
founded at locations where the Earth's telluric pathways converge, the
power in the severed head permeated the sacred site and flowed along
the invisible conduits throughout the land, protecting people and life.
The cult of the head is a staple of Celtic mythology, as it is in the
Arthurian legend of Sir Gawain and the Green Knight, even the life of
Saint Denis, who is said to have carried his own decapitated noggin two
miles to the location in Paris where the Templars built one of the first
Gothic cathedrals.

---

*Pronounced in Moorish Spanish as *bufihimat.*

One of the earliest and most notable legends involving this ritual occurred in London—a city founded by the Trojans[10]—where the head of King Bran the Blessed was interred in the sacred mound that later became the seat of the White Tower. As long as the head remained interred the kingdom was protected, but when successive leaders finally removed it, England's fortunes began to wane.

There are a number of similarities between Bran the Blessed and the Graal legend. The keeper of the Graal is mortally wounded in the leg (Bran's wound was in the foot); both are associated with a mystical castle; Bran possessed a magic cauldron that restored the dead back to life; and just like the Templars on Temple Mount, the small band of warriors protecting Bran's head stayed together for seven years before departing to a far-off place where they live for a further eighty, impervious to the passing of time as though by magic.

Perhaps the most iconic of decapitated people is John the Baptist, regarded by the Essenes and similar gnostic sects as a priest-messiah. John was one of two expected messiahs, the other being the king messiah, Jesus, yet all authority was deferred to John.[11] He was said to have lived simply on a diet of locusts and wild honey, a characteristic no doubt applauded by the Cistercians. He lived in the settlement of Bethany; the place where he performed baptisms was marked by a sacred mound where four springs intersected, thereby reflecting Bethany's other name, Bethabara (house of the crossing).

Bethany, of course, was also the domicile of Mary Magdalene, and the epithets by which the gnostics describe her—"the woman who knew the All" and "the one who is the inheritor of the Light"—clearly identify her as having been indoctrinated into the Mysteries too.[12] So when Bernard de Clairvaux wrote that the Templars should vow allegiance to "Bethany, the castle of Mary and Martha," it was an allegiance to both Mary Magdalene and her sister Martha, and the priestly line of their mentor, John the Baptist. This is what the cryptologist Lambert de Saint-Omer was conveying in his illustration of *The Heavenly Jerusalem,* which credits the founder of this kingdom of conscience to be John the Baptist, and not, as the world has been led to believe, Jesus.[13]

All this is very familiar to one particular group of John the Baptist's followers called the Mughtasilah (Those Who Wash Themselves), or as the sect is known today, the Mandeans. The name originates from the root word *manda* (secret knowledge). Often called the Christians of Saint John, the Mandaeans trace their origins to Palestine, but within forty years of the decapitation of John they were persecuted, so they moved north to Harran, a center of gnosticism usually associated with another sect called the Sabeans, who emerged from southern Arabia and Ethiopia.

Mandean gnosis is characterized by nine features, all of which echo Templar-Cistercian beliefs. For example:

> The soul is in exile while inhabiting the physical body.
>
> Savior spirits assist the soul's journey through life and afterward return it to the Light.
>
> The use of a language of symbol and metaphor.
>
> The practice of Mysteries to assist and purify the soul, ensuring its rebirth into a spiritual body.
>
> The maintaining of a culture of absolute secrecy with regard to disclosure of the Mysteries so that only those able to understand the truths, and ethical enough to promulgate them, are allowed admission into an inner brotherhood.[14]

According to the Mandean's credo, God is a formless entity known as the King of Light or the Great Mana (magic).[15] To this day, they maintain that John was the true prophet[16] and new Christianity, even rabbinical Judaism are false religions that impede the soul's release from bondage. And no wonder they believe this: they claim to have been in possession of a collection of original sacred books called the Ginza (Treasure), written in Aramaic, the language used at the time of John the Baptist. Among these was the Book of John (also known as the Book of Kings), which contains a legendary account of the Baptist's original message, the one censored by the church.[17]

In the course of their activities in the Near East the Templars undoubtedly established contact with such Johannite sects because the brotherhood's beliefs so mirror those of the Mandeans and the Essenes. It is feasible that the Templar's mandate consisted of nothing more than revitalizing the ministry of John the Baptist and the ancient system of philosophy he so clearly personified. This would explain why Templars who fell under the hammer of the Inquisition admitted that their Order was protecting a great secret, and if this secret included evidence of a surviving holy bloodline, not to mention a tradition of gospels preceding and contradicting the official canon (which they do), the Catholic Church would be outed as an impostor. Such a secret would indeed precipitate a profound change in society.

This alone does not explain a doctrine that allowed initiates "to come in to the joys of Paradise" nor why people so readily made huge donations to the Order. The wording by candidates joining the Templar fraternity implies an experience that was both liberating and self-empowering, so the emerging conclusion is that the secret ultimately revolves around a *revealed* knowledge through the ritual of physical initiation—the raising of the dead—the experience of which leads to personal revelation. According to insinuations throughout esoteric books, scrolls, and sacred buildings, this was achievable through selective knowledge and the practical application of natural laws.[18]

When the Templars found the Essene scrolls they tapped into this tradition, the fruits of thousands of years of knowledge.[19] Their work suggests it was applied in the particular design of buildings and their deliberate choice of location, as well as the strategic application of geometry, which, as science has discovered, is capable of influencing the human body to a significant degree.[20]

Bernard de Clairvaux was considerably partial to John the Baptist, as were the Portuguese Templars, who, under Afonso Henriques, sealed Portugal's day of independence on his feast day, June 24. They erected a disproportionate number of churches dedicated to him, and within earshot they placed an equal amount—at least fourteen in Portugal—dedicated to Notre Dame, the Divine Virgin, who is as synonymous with Isis as she is with Mary Magdalene.

In Tomar, the Templars built three places of veneration: the church dedicated to Notre Dame at Olival, the rotunda, and a third, in the central plaza of the town, the church of John the Baptist. Inside this church, several columns are marked by the figures of the Green Man and the dragon, two potent talismans of the life force. And between them aligns an invisible arrow pointing directly to Jerusalem.

42

PRESENT ERA. APRIL.
BY THE ROTUNDA,
AMID THE SECRETS OF
THE BEEHIVE . . .

There was something distinctly narcotic about sitting in the stillness of the cloister, and it had little to do with the whiff of lavender drifting from the octagonal flowerbed. Whoever created this courtyard certainly intended its geometry to induce a soporific assault on the senses. I soon found out the responsible party was Henry the Navigator, Templar Master during the fifteenth century. Across the square courtyard, the rotunda (or as the Portuguese refer to it, *charola*) stared back beyond the canopy of red roof tiles.

Access to the rotunda used to be restricted solely for initiates within the Templar Order. Even during times of siege, not even the townspeople were allowed refuge inside the safety of its six-foot-thick walls, despite it being arguably the most secure building in the citadel.[1]

If it never contained an altar, clearly the building was designed for a purpose other than worship. If it had no door, how did anyone get in?

Questions. Puzzles. Enigmas.

The first alterations to the rotunda were made after the dissolution of the Order of the Temple in the early fourteenth century by Pope Clement V, after which the site was temporarily abandoned. The first doorway was added perhaps a century later by Henry the Navigator when he incorporated a sacristy, or more likely by Manuel the Fortunate, who annexed an actual church as well as a chapter house, essentially mating the rotunda to a body.[2] Prior to that point, access was via secret underground passageways designed as part of the initiatory practices of the Order.[3]

Local traditions insist that the Templars built tunnels below the rotunda leading to their mother church of Santa Maria do Olival and elsewhere throughout Tomar. Older residents I spoke with not only swear to this, they recall how their grandparents saw the tunnels when some collapsed under the town's pavements. Some accounts were recorded. A guard who lived during the time of the last monks at the convent, in the mid-nineteenth century, claimed he himself descended a stairwell with several of the monks to a point below the town, but their progress was impeded by the fragile state of construction and the decay of the subterranean passageways, not to mention the poor quality of air, whereupon it became necessary to extinguish the torches. Later that century, the ground gave way beside the Church of the Misericords in central Tomar to reveal a tunnel leading up to the castle, and the opposite way, under the river.[4]

In the 1940s restorations were made to the mother church at Olival. A partly roofed tunnel was discovered, marked by a procession of air shafts aboveground.[5] The passage branched off in two directions, one toward the old convent of Saint Erea, the other beneath the riverbed and toward the main plaza of Tomar, where stands the unusual church dedicated to John the Baptist. Just as the tunnel veered toward the rotunda, progress was again impeded by decay. Consequently, the entrances and exits were sealed with stone as a safety precaution.[6]

As recently as the 1970s a local journalist and his cameraman reportedly entered an underground chamber near a well at the entrance to the seminary adjacent to the rotunda, only to be confronted by a ghostly presence like a vapor (which was filmed), after which the journalist became very ill. Another investigative researcher was permitted by a guard to enter a subterranean chapel via a doorway inside one of the castle's towers.[7]

*The rotunda, and the bell tower and convent
that grew around it after the fourteenth century.*

It seemed as though a number of people over the centuries had come in contact with the periphery of the rotunda's chamber of Mysteries, the only missing piece being definitive proof of the chamber itself. But at least I was not alone in my frustration. In 1988 an international group of experts wanted to know what lay in the basement of the Convent of Tomar, knowing there are entries, now sealed, and that elsewhere the Templars built a tunnel ninety feet below the ground. They liaised with the Institute of Geophysics, whose ground-penetrating radar was capable of detecting cavities up to 120 feet deep without leaving as much as a pinprick on the floor, yet despite this obviously unobtrusive and non-destructive scientific technique, the Portuguese Ministry of Culture inexplicably prohibited all investigations.[8]

Having made an appointment to see the director of the Convent of Christ (as the entire site is known today), I brought up the question of a secret underground chamber below the rotunda, but she could not help any further; in fact, what I had managed to dig up so far in archives seemed to put my own research ahead of the curve. She also had no knowledge of the proposed ground-penetrating radar experiments, but informed me of a second experiment in 2011, the results of which were somewhat inconclusive. I pressed for details of the institute pursuing this work, but the replies ceased, as though my nose had reached deep enough into the honeypot. After that, all follow-up communications were ignored by the director, as were those to the convent's architect and technical advisor.

It is easy to claim a conspiracy of silence is at play in Tomar even centuries after the Knights Templar and the Ordre de Sion colluded to establish a piece of the Graal in Portugal, as insinuated by the cryptic seal of Afonso Henriques on the charter that gave the knights this very parcel of land. Given how so many knights paid with their lives to maintain its secrecy, this is not surprising. What is both surprising and reassuring is that the secret may be alive and well.

The problem with conspiracies is they tend to dilate relative to the lack of solid facts. What I needed was more information.

Ancient places—such as Jerusalem—are riddled with secret underground passages, complicated vaults, cisterns, and aqueducts, and thanks to the efforts of Captains Warren and Wilson and their surveyors in 1867, their existence was brought to light.[9] However, just because something hides in the dark does not imply a great mystery or secret is at work. Relative to the times in which they were built, such subterranean passages were essential to the survival of local people; some were used for mundane affairs such as the collection of water and food, the provision of shelter, or as a means of escape. It's those that fall outside such categories that are of interest, and both physical and scriptural evidence does show how specific chambers in sacred places were reserved for special ritual purposes.

Signs that an esoteric tradition was once practiced lie scattered all around the periphery of the rotunda in Tomar. Adjacent to the building's foundation stands the Cloister of Cleansing, the term implying ablution, whiteness, and spiritual purification. Sects who honored the ritual of baptism (such as the Essenes, Nasoreans, Mandeans, Sabeans, Cathars, and so on) maintained a morning ritual of daily bathing before entering their sanctuaries. Being situated on the basement level, the

Templar gravestones, the convenient official explanation.

Cloister of Cleansing sits two floors below the level of the floor of the rotunda, and it does not require a leap of imagination to visualize initiates ritually washing themselves of impure thoughts prior to immersing themselves in the Mysteries.* Dispersed throughout this cloister is a collection of unusual circular limestone blocks, each carved with the figures of sacred geometry—pentagrams, hexagrams, heptagrams. Archaeologists are hard-pressed to explain them, so officially they have been given the designation of gravestones, even though they resemble teaching aids; after all, understanding sacred geometry was fundamental to esoteric schools.

The cloister's relative position on the eastern quadrant of the rotunda may provide an answer, for in the tradition of temple design this compass position corresponds with rebirth, when the clean light of

---

*It was in the later centuries that the cloister was literally used for the monks' washing.

the sun reappears at dawn following its immersion in the underworld, hence, why it was the direction associated with resurrection rituals performed in ancient Mysteries schools and temples.[10]

But as for a smoking gun proving that elusive chamber of Mysteries, well, there's nothing quite like an itch you can't scratch.

By the time I'd spent several days wandering the convent, the staff and I had gotten to know each other well. In the morning they would waive the normal entrance formalities and beckon me to resume my musings. One day was devoted entirely to looking at the ceiling of every chamber, and notes were made on the hundreds of bosses and capitals holding up every vault and pillar. Never did I realize how staring at ceilings could be so educational. There were laurels and quatrefoils, Templar crosses and armillary spheres, cherubs and oak leaves, all repeated aplenty throughout. But three carvings appeared only once above ground, and purposefully so. They sit in a small rectangular antechamber adjacent to the monks' refectory to the west of the rotunda. Except for a locked, dark-green door added in recent times there is nothing of interest to warrant passing tourists to pause; only by looking up at the ceiling does the chamber stop you dead in your tracks: two arches, each held up by effigies of a dismembered head spouting vegetation—the Green Man himself, tutelary god of regeneration. Between them, and the only time it appears throughout the entire property, a boss depicting the three faces of Hermes Trismegistus, the thrice-great god of wisdom, Djehuti. If I were to build a chamber dedicated to the Mysteries, it would be right beneath this vault.

Whatever lay there was blocked by that dark-green door. After gaining permission to unlock it, behold, a narrow limestone staircase spiraled downward. Walking into the darkness my footsteps echoed with a kind of timbre only heard in perfectly toned acoustic environments. A small passageway led to an empty stone balcony, beyond which lay a

The three faces of Hermes Trismegistus. Rotunda of Tomar.

plain stone staircase of eight steps leading down to a large hall shrouded in the half-light from a doorway 112-feet away.

The hall was allegedly used as a wine cellar. However, the storage of wine requires a cool, dry environment, and yet this is easily one of the dampest parts of the convent. While it is not unusual for buildings of this age to be reused according to the evolving needs of the times, I was skeptical that the builders should have identified its access point (which I was not even aware of) with the only image of the god of wisdom, then coincidentally placed a clockwise spiral staircase underneath (symbolic of inward journeying), leading to a hall whose mathematical footprint transposes to the musical equivalent of a double octave—all for the purpose of storing fermented grapes. It does not add up.

Sacred places the world over were built with the application of natural laws relative to the environment the architect wished to generate. Each measurement, color, and motif, the building's apparent and concealed geometry, even its alignment to reflect certain stars were all carefully considered to reinforce the purpose for which the temple was created.[11] No detail was superfluous.[12] It is a science called

Logo of the Ordre de Sion. Rotunda of Tomar.

the Law of Correspondence, one of the many forms of the knowledge contained in the curriculum of the Mysteries schools.[13]

This alleged wine cellar sits three to four levels below the floor of the rotunda. The more I walked around, the more the clues pointed to an altogether different and original function. There are nine bosses cemented to the spine of the ceiling, the esoteric number equated with perfection. Of these, two differ in design. The fourth boss bears a Templar cross with a rose in the center—the rose cross, emblem of the Abbey of Notre Dame du Mont de Sion at the time of its inception.[14]

I could hardly believe I was staring at the logo of a brotherhood with roots dating back to the Egyptian Mysteries school of Tuthmosis III,[15] whose teachings were promulgated by Plato, the Samaritan magi (founded by the grandfather of Mary Magdalene), and a gnostic brotherhood in old Alexandria called the Brothers of the Red Cross,* established by a mystic named Ormus.[16]

---

*Also called the Sages of Light.

Ormus* is an adopted name, a word synonymous with the principle of Light, and its earliest reference appears in Zoroastrian teachings. It is highly likely Godefroi de Bouillon was familiar with *ormus* as a concept of enlightenment because it later became the nickname adopted by the Ordre de Sion.[†17] A curious anagram was designed to express this word: an *M* with an added appendage, where two of its "legs" are crossed to form the astrological sign of Virgo, and the symbol of Notre Dame and Mary Magdalene.[‡] In-between this curious *M* sit the letters *OURS,* the French word for "bear," or in Latin, Ursus,[18] the name of the leader of the monks residing at Orval with whom Godefroi de Bouillon was associated.

The technique used for this anagram is identical in method to the seal designed by Afonso Henriques to encode the word *Graal* in PORTUGRAL.

Staring at the ceiling was getting me somewhere, so I continued. On either side of the rose cross, and the only time they appear in this hall, are two bosses depicting the Green Man.

As I approached the ninth and final boss, it too differed significantly from the others: a circular sunburst of seventeen rays, not unlike the Buddhist symbol of the total unfolding of the crown, with a small rose at the center.

Dividing a circle into seventeen makes for awkward mathematics and deviates from a standard stonemason's practice. However, to a Scottish Rite Freemason (whose foundation dates to 1314 with the arrival in Scotland of Templar knight, Robert of Heredom),[19] seventeen represents one of the Order's most profound degrees, the Knight of the East and West, dealing as it does with the raw spiritual power of the initiate, a kind of personal resurrection.

There exists another structure where this number is highly significant: the Osirion, the underground chamber at Abydos whose

---

Or is French for "gold."

†In 1188, when it changed its name to Priuré de Sion, or in English, the Priory of Sion.

‡Many Templar tombs depict knights with their feet similarly crossed below the calf.

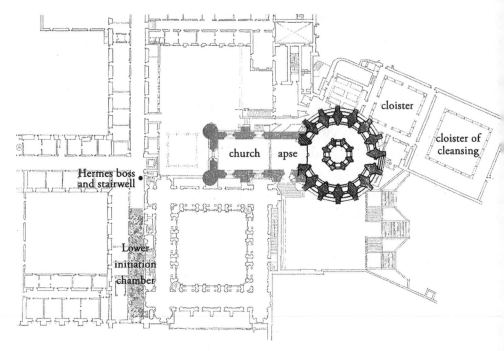

Plan of the rotunda and the later additions that became the convent.

side chambers number seventeen and where the Mysteries teachings of Osiris were once practiced.

Beneath the boss of the "wine cellar" lies an exposed shaft that sits inconveniently, and dangerously, in front of a doorway leading out to the orchard. It is not known where the shaft leads to, but given what we do know so far, if this unusual room really was originally designed to function as a wine cellar then I am the barber of Seville!

Encouraged by these discoveries, I ventured out into the orchard to absorb their implications. The Templars and the Ordre de Sion had obviously been collaborating here in Tomar, and since both the "wine cellar" and the room above it (the one with the boss of Hermes) are of later construction, obviously the Orders' rituals were continued by subsequent members.

Strolling beneath the canopy of lemon and orange trees I made my way to what used to be the principal entrance into the castle, the

Lower level hall, originally used for the Mysteries.

Almedina Gate. This south gate is today hardly visited, its staircase lies in a state of disrepair, and beyond it, vines and undergrowth have conquered the citadel's wall. However, one detail is visible above the gate, a stone carved with a large Templar rose cross. The surrounding inscription reveals its date, 1160, the year of the founding of the rotunda.[20] The presence in Tomar of the Knights Templar and the Ordre de Sion is once again reinforced. But it is the symbol to the top left of the rose cross that is of greater interest: a master mason's mark depicting, in stylized form, the three arrows "shot" by Gualdino Paes that established the location for the rotunda.

I returned to the rotunda to conclude what was turning out to be a long yet productive day. The overcast sky finally dissolved to allow a few rays of sunlight to penetrate the windows high along the rotunda's curving walls. It was at that moment I gazed up and noticed something found nowhere else throughout the convent or the Templar

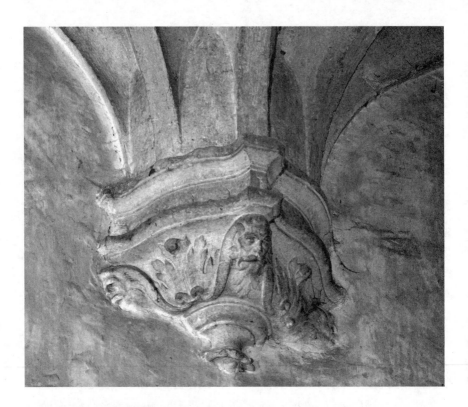

Images of the Green Man flank the boss of the Rose Cross.

Mason's mark to the top left of the rose cross and,
below, variations of the same mark.

monuments of Tomar: the opaque white-and-gold glass was made entirely of honeycombs.

All this time I had been standing inside the beehive.

I walked under the central octagonal canopy. So many clues leading to the chamber of Mysteries I was certain lay right beneath my feet. If only I could lift the flagstone floor, even for just one second.

The window of the beehive.

Perhaps I didn't have to. There exists an oral account by an elderly resident of Valado dos Frades who recalled an incident sometime around the end of the nineteenth century:

> It was said in old times that master masons and carpenters were hired from the town to work on the maintenance of the castle of Thomar. This was many generations ago. It was the habit of one of these masters to return home and register the alterations made inside the castle, because these would continue until much of what was old would be made unrecognizable or made to disappear. One of the things that riled him the most was the disfiguration of the beautiful and intriguing Arab pathway that the old monks of the Temple used in their ceremonies and led directly to the basement of the Temple church [the rotunda].
>
> Even in those days the brothers living in the convent used to share, from memory, stories with the masons of how Gualdino Paes brought back from the Holy Land the plans of the Holy Sepulcher which were to be used for the construction of the rotunda. Master Gualdino also ordered a pathway leading to it to be constructed in the Arabic style, and that both were used not just for religious ceremonies but also for the investiture of new knights.[21]

The monks also spoke of the Templar Master returning from the Holy Land with many scrolls. He kept them safely in a room excavated out of the rock, which was to the right of its main entrance and had a doorway the monks referred to as the "gate to the underworld." This doorway rested on very old stonework upon whose uprights the Templars carved dragons, and on the supported lintel, a kind of winged serpent.[22]

Tradition states that an old Jew was the only person permitted to enter the cave to work on the translation of the scrolls. Later, this man spoke of the results of his labor and how several volumes of manuscripts had been translated into Latin: "Much later, the stonework was dismantled and everything was patched, including much of the Arab pathway, which was never seen again."[23]

The master mason left a descriptive record of the construction work performed at the rotunda and the castle of Tomar, but the whereabouts of the book were forgotten. "Then in 1936 the parish priest of Valado found an old book behind the altar of the chapel of S. Sebastian that may have belonged to the master mason, but the priest threw it into a fire. Nevertheless, the stories have long since spread through oral tradition."[24]

During recent attempts to beautify the perimeter of the castle of Tomar, an area was cleared around the original Almedina Gate. A chunk of the pathway that once accessed the gate from the outside has been eroded or destroyed, revealing a twenty-foot drop in the terrain around the base of the wall. Right under where the pathway used to be lies a doorway into a cave. The official position is that this cave is a mine, yet who in their right mind would open a mine in a location that undermines the foundations of a castle wall?

The lintel stone is still in place, and indeed a kind of winged serpent is carved upon it, flanked by the heads of two dragons from whose mouths emanate a series of circles, now badly eroded, and two crescent moons.

The two uprights that would have constituted the body of each dragon are missing. However, a drawing made in 1918 shows the engravings still in their entirety, accompanied by a description of which parts of the Arab pathway were visible inside the subterranean passages and led to the chamber beneath the rotunda.*[25]

---

*Curiously, during the restorations that took place later, in the 1940s, many of the stonemasons working on the project were threatened and harassed by the people in charge of the restoration.

Entrance below the Almedina Gate, whose tunnels lead to a chamber under the rotunda; the lintel with carved dragons remains in situ.

PRESENT ERA. APRIL.
MUSING OUTSIDE
THE BEEHIVE . . .

hat could possibly have happened to the scrolls Master Gualdino secreted in that underground chamber? Not to mention their decoded text, from which one lone, old Jewish scholar extracted copious manuscripts?

On occasion, knowledge and drinking go together rather well. To understand the Mysteries, and specifically the ritual of resurrection, it is first necessary to "drink" of the knowledge, to imbibe from the "cup of everlasting life." The Chinese referred to the process as Dao, the Essenes as the Way, the Greeks called it *sophis,* and the Templars, *baphomet.*

One emblem representing this tradition is the three faces of Hermes, the Greek personification of Djehuti, thrice great scribe of the gods.[1] Luminaries such as Copernicus and Kepler claimed their achievements were a result of studying the concealed sacred arts of Djehuti,[2] Kepler himself admitting he was merely "stealing the golden vessels of the Egyptians."[3] Even the seventeenth-century scientist Isaac Newton stated that his law of gravity was not new, that it had been decoded in antiquity, and his knowledge of universal processes as well as his own conclusions in physics stemmed from esoteric wisdom, specifically from the decrypting of hermetic and alchemical treatises, not to mention the cryptic language of prophetic biblical scriptures.[4] Newton went so far as to unravel codes hidden within the books of Ezekiel and Revelations, even learning Hebrew so he could get it right. He reconstructed the floor plan of the Temple of Solomon, convinced that the edifice deliberately built to house the Ark of the Covenant was a cryptogram of the universe and by understanding it one would know the mind of God—precisely as it was claimed of the teachings of Djehuti.[5] As Newton said himself, "The

Djehuti. And later, Thoth-Hermes.

Egyptians concealed mysteries that were above the capacity of the common herd, under the veil of religious rites and hieroglyphic symbols."[6]

Newton was a prolific writer, a member of a Masonic-style institution, and alleged Grand Master of the Priuré de Sion, the name by which the Ordre de Sion became known after 1188 following a historically documented ceremony.[7] Given the associations between these fraternities and the Knights Templar, it is revealing that when Newton's hitherto unknown private manuscripts came to light, the economist John Maynard Keynes commented on the significance of Newton's sources and in so doing may have revealed the kind of knowledge the Templars and Bernard de Clairvaux had been privy to: "[He saw] the whole universe and all that is in it as a riddle, as a secret which could be read by applying pure thought to certain evidence, certain mystic clues which God had hid about the world to allow a sort of philosopher's treasure hunt to the esoteric brotherhood. He believed that these clues were to be found . . . in certain papers and traditions handed down by the brethren in an unbroken chain back to the original cryptic revelation."[8]

During their formative years in Jerusalem, the Templars would have had time to absorb local esoteric influences, particularly those from the descendents of a group of gnostics called the Sabeans who compiled a great hermetic book on magic called *Ghayat al hakim* (The Goal of the Wise). This valuable work was translated into Latin in Moorish Spain during the same period the Templars were settling down in Portugal. It was renamed *Picatrix*.[9] Much like the Templar scroll decrypted by Lambert de Saint-Omer, it too contained a blueprint for the utopian hermetic city,[10] along with 224 manuscripts on hermeticism, Kaballah, astrology, magic, and alchemy—the kind of tome one would dedicate seven quiet years in Jerusalem to read, absorb, and understand. Not surprisingly, it is considered one of the most exhaustive works on talismanic magic in existence.

The Sabeans were an Arabic sect living in Harran, a province in modern-day southeastern Turkey and not far from some of the world's oldest sacred sites. Sabean comes from *saba'ia,* (star people). They venerated the moon—symbol of Djehuti—and were known to have undertaken yearly pilgrimages to the Giza Plateau to conduct astronomical observations, recognizing the pyramids as monuments mirroring the stars, which ultimately proved to be a correct deduction.[11]

Derived from the word *saba'ia* is the Portuguese word *sabia* (scholar); its extensions are *saber* (knowledge) and *sabedoria* (wisdom).

Where did the Sabeans acquire their knowledge?

After the library and light of Alexandria were extinguished at the end of the fourth century AD by a rampaging mob of Christian fundamentalists (who were not much fun but certainly very mental), the knowledge moved north to Edessa and then to Harran, where an academy was established to enable the hermetic teachings of alchemy and symbolism to permeate the Islamic world and, by extension, the area in and around Jerusalem.

Alchemy comes from the Arabic *al-khem,* ironically the old name for Egypt. So to practice alchemy is to know "matter that comes from Egypt." The Greeks acknowledged their gratitude to the Egyptian Mysteries by calling that land Khemet, and *khemia,* the art of transmuting an ordinary metal into gold. Except that in the esoteric world such alchemy has little to do with transforming minerals and all to do with altering the individual through knowledge, and when such a person is "transformed into gold," so it is said he or she is "risen from the dead."

Old Thamara would have been an ideal place to drink or imbibe such knowledge. The town's oldest known iteration is *atamarmah,* an Arabic word meaning "sweet waters," a description of the river flowing through it. The Templars' adapted the name to Thomar, and it too is a play on words in Portuguese, for it literally means "to drink, to imbibe, to ingest." For the Templars, then, Tomar was *sabedoria,* the location where wisdom is to be imbibed.

Although I had not found the central item on my agenda—namely the Chamber of Mysteries under the rotunda—I was satisfied with the amount of surviving evidence in support of its existence, and that all around the rotunda's periphery remain enough signs pointing to something of great import having been taught here, generation after generation, enough to warrant the Arab caliph Yaqub al-Mansur and his million-man army to come looking for it. Perhaps he too was searching for this Graal; after all, the rambunctious young Arab leader came from the same time and place where *Picatrix* was translated.

All these possibilities rumbled through my mind as I passed the time beneath a group of mature trees on the hill overlooking Tomar, waiting for an early evening rainstorm to conclude its business. Below, the octagonal gothic tower of the church of John the Baptist, built on the site of a former temple of forgotten provenance,* rose above the rooftops like a needle emerging from its square stone box. The castle gates closed for the day, and behind them, the enchantment of the rotunda, whose invisible arms refused to soften their clasp as though another element of this Templar mystery was hiding in plain sight.[12]

Like the sphinx on the Giza Plateau, the rotunda and its adjacent chapel expectantly point to an object of distant significance besides the rising sun. The axis through these two buildings is offset by a few imperceptible degrees from true east. If this invisible line is extended, it descends into the plaza of Tomar, to the bell tower of the church of John the Baptist, and specifically to a small pyramidal bas relief along its foundation. People walk by this strange carving every day, they snap pictures, but no one has the slightest idea why it is there or what it means. The well-worn relief depicts a sapling out of which sprouts a fleur-de-lys; a dog and a lion stand on either side. If I were an ancient Egyptian, the dog would represent Sirius, the dog star, the embodiment of knowledge; the lion would be Regulus, the brightest star in the constellation of Leo, referred to as the royal star, which has long been described as a gateway to the records of all knowledge, the key to the Mysteries. Vedic astronomy identifies Regulus with the summer solstice, thus associating it with John the Baptist. In Sanskrit they call the

---

*The spire appears to have been built by King Manuel I, a later Templar Master.

Church of John the Baptist. And the unusual stone relief below the spire.

*The dragon and Green Man pillars inside the church of John the Baptist.
The gap through the two aligns to the rotunda and, 2,886 miles away,
the Abbey de Notre Dame du Mont Sion.*

star Magha (the Mighty One), from which are derived the word *magi* and the title Magda, as in Magdal-eder—as in Mary Magdalene.

Like threading a needle, the line bisects two columns inside the church, each bearing effigies, of a dragon and a Green Man, respectively; then it extends straight as an arrow for 2,886 miles until it strikes a hill bearing a remarkable similarity to Tomar and its rotunda—the Abbey de Notre Dame du Mont Sion.

44

1165.
MONSANTO. PECULIAR BEHAVIOR
ON AN UNUSUAL HILL . . .

ith Gualdino Paes and the Templars busying themselves with the rebuilding of Thomar, Afonso Henriques occupied himself in eastern Portugal with the reconquering of a vertiginous outcrop of granite from the Moors.

Mons Sanctus, or Monsanto, rises abruptly out of its surrounding plain, and the conglomeration of boulders continues climbing until it reaches 2,500 feet. Below its summit a tiny settlement of great antiquity has nestled among the stones since at least Paleolithic times, its stone houses having developed organically around the gargantuan and miraculously balanced granite boulders. For the Lusitanians it was probably their most prized place of veneration. As with all true pagans, the villagers conducted a festival every May, on the Celtic fertility feast of Beltane, when the women carried clay jars full of flowers to the top of the hill and threw them from the walls of the ruined fort.

Successive Portuguese kings and Templar Masters also conducted a strange ritual of their own here: they granted Monsanto no less than four charters, which is oddly disproportionate to the size of the settlement.

Once the Templars concluded their work in Thomar their focus

Templar castle. Monsanto.

shifted to the construction of a citadel on top of this enigmatic hill. Any warrior certifiable enough to climb Monsanto would likely drop dead from exhaustion by the time he reached the summit, and so the walls of the fortress are understandably low.

Erecting a fortification on top of a mountain requires considerable effort. What is worrisome is that Gualdino Paes and the Templars should have placed it below the level of the outcrops of rock immediately adjacent to the walls, making the entire site vulnerable to both enemy spying and arrows. The Templars were expert castle builders par excellence; such an oversight would be unthinkable.

Aside from the obvious strategic location of the site—from which the Templars kept an eye on the continuously troublesome king of Castilla e Léon—they once again devoted a disproportionate amount of effort attending to spiritual matters, and this on a summit where, for a good part of the year, the prevailing features are mist, bitterly cold winds, and snow. Inside the citadel they erected a church dedicated to Mary Magdalene and aligned it to reference the summer solstice sunrise; a few yards *outside* the protective wall they erected another, a chapel dedicated to

John the Baptist, while a farther dozen yards away they rebuilt a third church, possibly of Visigothic origin but in ruins at the time.

Ever since their inception, whatever locations the Templars chose, each came with a long history of veneration. Monsanto was no different, but there are three clues that the knights also conducted secret rituals here.

The first is a series of anthropomorphic graves cut out of the granite bedrock. Although at first glance they suggest a funerary function, most are too shallow to house a body and thus of little practical use as graves. If they were used for cremation, the rock shows no effects from the application of heat. The "graves" are impossible to date, but the various styles suggest the idea was continued across many cultures.

These oddities rest on the eastern side of the summit, the traditional cardinal direction associated with the rite of spiritual resurrection. Could these granite sarcophagi, then, have been used for something other than burial?

One of the many anthropomorphic shallow sarcophagi carved out of living rock.

The answer lies at the base of the mountain, on the west side, the direction followed by initiates preparing for a ritual entrance into the Otherworld. Here, adjacent to another Templar church, lie two massive sarcophagi hewn out of the granite, each surrounded by a protruding uneven lip that must have required a time-consuming removal of bedrock. If a lid were placed on top, the resulting gap would not prevent rodents from entering and feasting on the body, essentially nullifying the purpose for which the graves were intended. The feature would be useful, however, for someone requiring little light but enough air to breathe. What is more, the interior measurements of these granite enclosures are identical to those of a famous red granite box in Egypt: the one inside the King's Chamber of the Great Pyramid.

Not a shred of evidence exits to support the fact that the Great Pyramid's "sarcophagus" was ever designed for funerary purposes. There is, however, substantial evidence pointing to the chamber having been a fundamental component of resurrection rituals.[1] The interior harmonic of the box is shown to resonate at a frequency of 117 Hz,[2]

Additional carved sarcophagi on the west side of the mountain.

a characteristic shared with megalithic stone chambers from Malta to Ireland, many of which are known to be acoustically tuned to resonate at a common frequency of 110 Hz.[3] These frequencies fall within a range that triggers a shift of activity in the prefrontal cortex of the brain and induces trance and altered states of awareness.[4]

The second clue is that the citadel of Monsanto neatly encloses a monolith the size of a small chapel, on whose surface is carved what appears to be the symbol of a womb. Beneath the monolith lies a hollow chamber dug out of the bedrock and soil. The deep hole is dysfunctional as a cistern, nor is it a well, but above it spread two stone arches for no obvious structural purpose except that they visibly mark the path of two intersecting telluric currents. That the site is ritually significant—besides the obvious symbolism that a person is lowered into an underground room or womb—is the way in which the fortification wall behind this "cosmic egg" has been deliberately lowered by three feet, contradicting its defensive purpose. Yet the attentive visitor will note how, as the sun rises on the equinox, the day associated with

Boulder above the arched underground chamber. Note the womb carving on its face. The church dedicated to Mary Magdalene looks on.

ancient resurrection rituals, it is the lower height of this wall that allows the first rays of sunlight to hit the flattened top of the boulder.

As to the third clue, it lies in the words of Bernard de Clairvaux.

Looking down into the interior of the chamber.

Strategic referencing between the "egg" stone, the lowered wall, the distant mountain, and the equinox sunrise.

PRESENT ERA.
MONSANTO. AND OTHER PLACES
FOR MUSING . . .

ernard de Clairvaux was adamant that attention be paid first and foremost to a spiritual life and the mystical contemplation of the soul. It was this grace that led to enlightenment. One of the many positive virtues of the Cistercians was their focus on the common good, with the emphasis on fraternal charity and unity in the spirit of divine love. Much of this was achieved by adopting a submissive and charitable will.

The other was by frequenting sacred places, and Bernard's exhortation to the Templars—to every knight, even—focuses on the importance of visiting and protecting the holy places, that they should not waste the opportunity to meditate on the deeper mysteries of life that unfold at these special locations.

It was with this advice in mind that he wrote a series of excellent meditations on positive experiences associated with personal transformation in ancient temples, particularly where avatars such as John the Baptist had demonstrated the virtue of love; in the Near East, emphasis was placed on the Holy Sepulcher as the symbol of resurrection that reveals the physical world to be a temporary stage for the transition of matter. In describing the spiritual significance of these sites, Bernard hoped the Templars would see their lives as a pilgrimage and that upon their visits they would look at sacred places with spiritual rather than material eyes.[1]

The overarching principle in the Cistercian ethos was the achievement of the sacred marriage between the soul and its source, a bond that launches a journey of self-discovery as a route to self-empowerment. By extension, this Cistercian ideal was also the driving force behind the Knights Templar. In this respect Bernard de Clairvaux was following a recipe that once kept ancient cultures in equilibrium for thousands of years, be they Tibetan, Zoroastrian, Egyptian, Sabean, Lusitanian, Bogomil, Cathar, or Celt. As Bernard wrote in *De Laude Novae Militae*, his letter in praise of the Knights Templar:

> A new knighthood has appeared in the land of the Incarnation, a knighthood which fights a double battle, against adversaries of flesh and blood and against the spirit of evil. I do not think it a marvellous thing that these knights resist physical enemies with physical force, because that, I know, is not rare. But they take up arms with forces of the spirit against vices and demons and that I call not only marvellous but worthy of all the praise given to men of God . . . the knight who protects his soul with the armour of faith, as he covers his body with a coat of mail, is truly above fear and reproach. Doubly armed, he fears neither men nor demons.[2]

If Bernard de Clairvaux recognized immersion into sacred places as integral to personal transformation, he must have been equally aware of the mechanism at work in such locations.

A crucial component in the enactment of the Mysteries, particularly the component dealing with the "raising of the dead," was the strategic placement of the temple. Like the Cistercians, who regularly chose areas that veered from architectural norm, the Templars also took great care in deciding the locations of their chapter houses and preceptories, as though they were sourcing a subtle element in the land.[3] Without doubt they chose locations, especially in Portugal, that were richly associated with ancient traditions, particularly pre-Christian cults who honored the Earth mother Ceres, the Divine Virgin, Inanna, and Isis. The province covering most of Portugal in their time—and coincidentally the *exact* area donated to the Templars—was named after the goddess of Celtic creation myths, Beira. She appears in Scotland (another major Templar stronghold) as Cailleach Bheur, goddess of winter and the mother of the gods, the name nowadays simplified as Beira.[4]

The same applies to the Templar's final home, Tomar, the old Nabancia. The name derives from Nabia, Lusitanian goddess of water and rivers. The body of water most associated with her cult was the one river (Neiva) honored by the people of Braga and Fonte Arcada, coincidentally the first two Templar homes in Portugale, and obviously, the river Nabão in Tomar itself. This specific attraction by the Templars to the sanctity and purity of water harmonizes with John the Baptist's teachings on the importance of ritual bathing and baptism.

The second attention the Templars paid to location was the siting beside or on top of ancient places of veneration. The preceptories at Paris, Gisors, and London, for example, were built on Roman chapels above earlier Druid temples, even Neolithic stone circles. They followed the same practice in Portugal, as their chosen sites show:

- Loures. Church dedicated to Notre Dame built on the ruins of an early Celtic temple.
- Ceras. Named after the goddess of fertility, site of an ancient temple honored by the Lusitanians.[5]
- Castelo de Bode. The "castle of the goat," associated with the pagan cult of Proserpina, daughter of Ceres, whose ritual is associated with springtime, hence the root of the word *proserpere,* "to emerge," with respect to the ripening of the seed.
- Souré. Site of former monastery built with reused stones from a former Visigothic temple.[6]
- Faria and Idanha-a-Nova. Both on Neolithic sacred sites.

- Idanha-a-Velha, Braga, and Almourol. On temples dedicated to Venus and Isis.[7]
- Pombal. On a pre–AD 200 chapel dedicated to the archangel Michael.[8]
- Monsaraz. Hub of a metropolis of megalithic monuments.
- Santa Maria de Feira. On the Lusitanian temple of Tueraeus-Lugo, and one of the earliest places taken by Afonso Henriques in 1128.
- Castelo Branco. Already venerated in Neolithic times; the Templars built a church dedicated to Notre Dame above an underground chamber.

The list is extensive.

Such locations have a second major theme in common: they are known to coincide with the crossing points of the Earth's natural streams of electromagnetic energy, what the ancients referred to as spirit roads. Many of these places even mark gravitational anomalies,[9] and all ancient sacred sites, without exception, are founded on such hotspots.[10]

Simply put, the Earth's telluric current is a kind of life force, a blending of the intertwined forces of electricity and magnetism. As the anthropologist William Howells attempted to classify it, "It was the basic force of nature through which everything was done . . . [its] comparison with electricity, or physical energy, is here inescapable. [It] was believed to be indestructible, although it might be dissipated by improper practices. . . . It flowed continuously from one thing to another and, since the cosmos was built on a dualistic idea, it flowed through heavenly things to earthbound things, just as though from a positive to negative pole."[11]

When NASA scientists discovered magnetic energy spiraling like tubes linking the Earth to the sun—even employing the metaphysical term *portals*[12]—they essentially validated the ancient master geomancers and temple builders who sourced these very same flux events on the land because they were all too aware of their connection to territories far and beyond the confines of this physical sphere. The image the ancients chose to represent this elusive telluric force was the serpent or dragon, and it became a culturally shared archetype describing the energy's winding behavior along its earthly course.

The Egyptian Building Texts provide actual instructions for establishing a sacred space, the principal component being the "piercing of the snake," which serves to root these currents to a desired spot.[13] Typically, when a serpent motif is displayed in a temple it is an instruction that the telluric current passes through the site, it is the X that marks the spot.[14] Neolithic temple builders did the same by placing standing stones wherever telluric currents flow. These monoliths sometimes depict a serpent wound around them; the standing stones of Portugal, the *betilos* (literally "house of God"), often have carved snakes rising from the bottom of these stone sentinels.

This serpent energy is a natural force that can be harnessed for all manner of beneficial purposes; in Chinese geomancy such dragons were never slain, rather their electrical energy was kept in the realm and utilized for all manner of shamanic purposes.[15]

In 1983 a comprehensive study was undertaken to validate the existence of this energy in sacred sites. Using a magnetometer, the Rollright stone circle in England became the test subject. It was discovered that telluric currents are drawn into the stone circle in a spiral pattern. The leading project scientist also noted how "the average intensity of the [geomagnetic] field within the circle was significantly lower than that measured outside, as if the stones acted as a shield."[16] Identical readings have been found at temples throughout Europe, Egypt, and India, where the Earth's energy field appears to stretch around the sites like a protective membrane.[17] Celebrated primordial mounds such as Saqqara, Karnak, Luxor, and the pyramids control the energy into an interior neutral zone in a manner that is beneficial to people. Identical energy hotspots exist in Gothic cathedrals such as Chartres.[18]

The idea that sacred places are encircled by a force field has been widely explored. Measurements reveal how the current running through

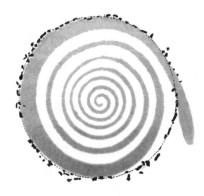

Magnetomer image shows how telluric forces behave at the Rollright stone circle.

the entrance of the sites is double the rate of the surrounding countryside, making them not just doorways but also entrances. The magnetic readings at temples die away at night to a far greater level than can be accounted for under natural circumstances, only to charge back at sunrise, with the ground current from the surrounding land attracted to the temple just as magnetic fluctuations within reach their maximum.[19] The voltage and magnetic variations are related and follow the phenomenon known in physics as electric induction,[20] leading to the realization that sacred places behave like concentrators of electromagnetic energy.[21]

There is one more thing. Temples, including the more recent Gothic cathedrals, are typically sited at locations that have been in continuous use for millennia, and they are unique in the sense that a second anomaly occurs at these hotspots. Every dawn the Earth is subjected to a rise in the solar wind, which intensifies the planet's geomagnetic field; at night this field weakens, then picks up at dawn, and the cycle repeats ad infinitum. But there are places on the ground where the geomagnetic field interacts with the telluric currents.[22] This action generates a hotspot known to science as a *conductivity discontinuity,* and even though ancient people did not own magnetometers they were able to source this energy long before scientists built machines that proved them right. Hence the name given to such sensitives: *sourcerers.*

The Sioux call this energy *skan,* and when concentrated at sacred sites it is claimed to influence the mind and creativity, as well as elevate personal power in the form of spiritual attuning. In essence, the energy raises the body's resonance. Constant contact with multiple power places builds up a kind of numinous state of mind, what Chinese Daoists describe as "awakening the Great Man within."

This has a profound effect on the human body, which is now widely accepted as composed of particles of energy, a walking electromagnetic edifice sensitive to minute fluctuations in the local geomagnetic field. With electromagnetism playing such a pivotal role in temples, its influence on the body is immediate. And since blood flowing through the veins and arteries carries a fair amount of iron, magnetism will work on it like a magnet reorganizes iron filings sprinkled on a sheet on paper. The same is true of the brain. Substantial amounts of magnetite are found in brain tissue and the cerebral cortex, and under the right conditions, magnetic stimulation of the brain induces dreamlike states, even in waking consciousness.[23]

Lastly, and possibly most importantly, is the effect that telluric energies in temples may have on the pineal gland, a pine cone–shaped protuberance located near the center of the brain. Fluctuations in the geomagnetic field affect the production of chemicals made by the pineal, such as pinoline, which interacts with another neurochemical, seratonin, the end result being the creation of DMT, a hallucinogen. It is believed that this is the neurochemical trigger for the dream state—the hallucinogenic state of consciousness that allows information to be received. In an environment where geomagnetic field intensity is decreased, people are known to experience psychic and shamanic states.[24]

This blending of modern science with ancient esoteric practices and beliefs helps explain why temples are built where they are and why the Templars and Cistercians followed the same formula by regularly erecting their sites in places that were either architecturally unsuitable or atop preexisting places of veneration.

It is perfectly feasible that such information was part of the knowledge decoded by the Kabalists working in Troyes. This spiritual technology was a component of the Mysteries teachings, whose central pillar concerned shamanic and ecstatic practices that led to a personal experience of God, in a nonreligious sense, and the strategic placement of the temple plus its geometry facilitated the process.

One of these hotspots is Jerusalem, one of the many so-called primordial mounds throughout the ancient world. In the time of the pharaoh Akhenaten it was known as Garesalem, which breaks down as *gar* (stone), *esa* (Isis), and *salem* or *shalem* (perfect). Thus, Jerusalem is "the stone that embodies the perfection of Isis"; it is a place of reconnection with the essence of the Divine Virgin.

Interestingly, telluric currents tend to be attracted to water, and water is a prerequisite in establishing a sacred site, quite beyond the obvious need for human sustenance. The place where John the Baptist performed baptisms, Bethany, was marked by a sacred mound where four springs intersect, thereby reflecting Bethany's other name, Bethabara (House of the Crossing).

The same crossing is evidenced at Monsanto, where the two enigmatic arches inside its shaft mark the exact crossing point of two telluric currents.

An identical situation exists under the rotunda of Tomar. The site marks the crossing of four underground water courses, while the diameter of the building itself defines the precise width of two crossing telluric currents. Several indicators marking the path of this earth energy still exist in adjacent cloisters and chambers. One is an effigy carved on a low wall that is used as a seat for meditating monks, resembling a hand pointing downward or, seen another way, an energy descending from the sky; two capitals depicting the Green Man in the underground hall of Mysteries (the alleged wine cellar) mark another edge of the current, as does its underground shaft and the seventeen-rayed boss strategically placed above it.

And yet Tomar is not alone when it comes to the Templars sourcing this exotic energy. Geomagnetic anomalies around sacred places in Portugal have been observed since the seventeenth century, and in recent times Portugal's National Geological Survey found three major

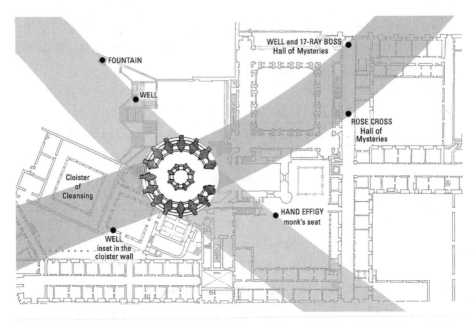

Relationship between telluric currents and the position of the rotunda of Tomar. Several surviving features mark the edges of these pathways, including the monk's seat with its carved effigy.

concentrations of magnetism in the Iberian Peninsula: the area of megaliths around the city of Évora, the promontory of Sagres, and the mountain of Sintra.[25] Coincidentally, all three were prime Templar locations.

Évora, a center of the cult of Isis-Diana, became the home of the affiliated Templar Order of the Knights of São Bento de Avis, created in 1162 at the Council of Coimbra, when the Cistercian Rule came into effect in Portugal.[26] Its first Grand Master was Pedro, brother of King Afonso Henriques.

Sagres, already described in the time of the scholar Strabo as the Sacred Promontory and home to a group of dolmens,[27] later become the focal point of the Templars' maritime exploits under Henry the Navigator. What no one can explain to this day is what the Templars were doing with a curious three-hundred-foot-wide wheel made of radial lines of stones, the purpose of which is a complete mystery; beside it they erected a chapel dedicated to Notre Dame, designed with an octagonal roof and perfectly located at the intersection of two telluric currents.

As for Sintra, this was the village donated by Afonso Henriques to Gualdino Paes in absentia. It was the only such donation of its kind, which makes this unique offering all the more intriguing.

Sagres. The asymmetric radial structure left behind by the Templars.

Castle of Sintra.

46

**1147.
SINTRA. A FUNNY THING
HAPPENS ON THE WAY TO THE
CASTLE . . .**

While the Crusaders were preparing to ransack the city of Lisbon, Afonso Henriques quietly marched his knights into the village of Sintra, fourteen miles to the west, taking back what had once marked the southernmost limit of his late father's land until the Moors captured it once more.

Afonso and his knights took the meandering path up the vertiginous hill toward the castle where the Moors were camped. Using the gigantic boulders and lush vegetation as cover, they overran the fortification with absolutely no resistance; in fact, its inhabitants were nowhere to be seen. Even the mosque was stripped of relics.

Sintra was of immense strategic importance, and yet the Arabs left without a fight. How could an entire garrison just vaporize?

Stories say they escaped via underground tunnels and galleries leading from the watchtower, some emerging by the sea to the west, others three miles east, where Moorish men were witnessed emerging from within the mountain: "Heading to the first tower was a granary that was five feet in diameter, through which it is said there was a hidden road that went to Rio Mouro [River of the Moors], and it is called that for on the right side was seen a doorway through which they say was the actual entry."[1]

Even Moorish chroniclers stated categorically that Xentra (as the Arabs called it) is a hollow mountain, with one of its hilltops connected by a honeycomb of underground galleries to another hill thirty-five miles away, so much so that even the sea is able to penetrate these inland caverns.[2] Although a good number of cavities are of natural volcanic origin, the rest were purposefully carved out with both defensive and ceremonial purposes in mind. According to a caretaker of the Moorish castle, the hill is one big subterranean city with miles of underground tunnels, one linking the castle with a Capuchin monastery three miles away.[3] When the Templars arrived—or returned—they made good use of such features and added a few of their own. At Penha Verde, on the northern slope of Sintra, they built a round church upon a dilapidated lunar temple from circa 5000 BC and dedicated it to Mary of Sion. Beneath the foundations were discovered various underground galleries once used for the practice of chthonic mysteries. These galleries connected to other passageways extending for two miles before emerging by a river.[4] Similar chambers exist nearby at the monastery of Penha Longa, "a cave that was once closed by crystallization, which was discovered by a monk in the Convent. . . . Descent into this cave is by a door (which once served to protect it) which is seven or eight feet high . . . there is a gap through which the sun, its rays penetrating with a wonderful effect, makes this a house of shining crystal."[5]

This bewitching sacredness of Sintra had a particular effect on one of the king of Portugal's knights, Pêro Pais, who upon arrival was so overwhelmed that he retired from secular soldiery and moved to one of its peaks to continue life as a penitent. There he founded a chapel dedicated to Saturn (the god representing the rational evaluation of life, particularly negative forces) to better gain mastery of himself.*[6]

Coincidentally, Saturn's mythological father, Jupiter, built a Golden Age, not unlike what the Templars and the Cistercians were attempting to fashion in Portugal.

---

*It became the chapel of Saint Saturnino.

Inside one of Sintra's narrow passageways carved out of solid granite bedrock.

Five years later (in 1152) Afonso issued a charter in which the village of Sintra and thirteen of its properties are donated,[7] with exceptional privileges, "to Gualdino Paes, Templar Master General of Portugal, we give you the aforesaid houses, with their estates cultivated and uncultivated, so that you may have and possess all the days of your life."[8] A later document is more explicit about the details of the property.[9] It identifies the houses as those defining the village square and its public right of way, and states that in addition to "a few good houses in the village" the Templars were awarded "two vineyards, a water mill, several homesteads on the coast . . . and an orchard in *almosquer*," that is to say, in Arabic, a suburb, which was then a mere ten minutes walk from the center of the village.[10]

The charter also provides for the town's residents, putting everyone on equal footing, "both the highest class as the inferior," be they Christian, Jew, or Moor, and the responsibility for upholding this equitable justice was entrusted to the Templars alone.

At face value such a donation from the king to the Templars seems typical enough, and yet unconventional insofar as it is awarded to Gualdino while he is away in the Holy Land experiencing the sacred places, and the manner in which he is addressed as "Templar Master," a full five years before he is officially awarded the title, appears as though the knight's promotion upon his expected return was a foregone conclusion.

Meanwhile, the "orchard in *almosquer*" provides a big clue in understanding the nature of this donation. A surviving document states that more than two hundred years later, in 1371, the Templars still owned rights to this "forest of Almosquer,"[11] which by then comprised a wood called the Forest of Angels, and below it, a truly bewitching place called the Estate of the Tower. It is this piece of property that reveals much about the spiritual/esoteric motives the core brotherhood was pursuing in Portugal.

PRESENT ERA.
SINTRA. IN THE FOREST
OF ANGELS . . .

rticle 7. "Build in your houses meeting places that are large and hidden that can be accessed by underground tunnels so that the brothers can go to meetings without the risk of getting into trouble. . . . In the houses of unelected Brothers, it is prohibited to conduct certain materials pertaining to the philosophical sciences, or the transmutation of base metals into gold and silver. This shall only be undertaken in secret and hidden places.[1]

Talk about a smoking gun! This instruction to the Brothers of the Temple comes from a document listing the two secret Rules of the Knights Templar—the Rule of the Elected Brothers and the Rule of the Brothers Consulate. It was originally found in the possession of Templar Master Roncelin de Fos[2] and rediscovered by accident in the Vatican archives by a Danish bishop. It unequivocally proves that the Templars followed a tradition of using crypts for the strict use of initiation into the Mysteries, intensifying the words of the Templar Preceptor Gervais de Beauvais to the Inquisition of how "there exists in the Order a law so extraordinary on which such a secret should be kept, that any knight would prefer his head cut off rather than reveal it to anyone."[3]

A copy of these Rules was preserved by Brother Mathieu de Tramlay until 1205, then passed to Robert de Samfort, proxy of the Temple in England, in 1240, and finally to Master Roncelin de Fos. They were kept only by the inner brotherhood, forbidden "to be kept by the brothers, because the squires found them once and read them, and disclosed them to secular men, which could have been harmful to our Order."[4] The document describes how only true initiates of the Order knew of a secret that "remains hidden from the children of the New Babylon," even the king of France, and that no prince or high priest of the time knew the truth: "If they had known it, they would not have worshiped the wooden cross and burned those who possessed the true spirit of the true Christ." This truth alludes to a transformation of the soul and the establishment of a kingdom united and presided over only by God.[5]

Article 18, in particular, reveals much about the content of the Mysteries the Templars found and how, like the Essenes, this knowledge was revealed only to a select few: "The neophyte will be taken to the archives where he will be taught the mysteries of the divine science, of God, of infant Jesus, of the true Bafomet, of the New Babylon, of the nature of things, of eternal life as well as the secret science, the Great Philosophy, Abraxas [the Source of everything] and the talismans—all things that must be carefully hidden from ecclesiastics admitted to the Order."[6]

One of the extensive articles illustrates the universal appeal of the brotherhood to ordinary people: "Know that God sees no differences between people, Christians, Saracens, Jews, Greeks, Romans, French, Bulgarians [referring to the Bogomils] because every man who prays to God is saved."[7] This utopian vision clearly undermined the religious authority of the Catholic Church and its stated doctrine that "outside the church there can be no salvation." But to a medieval populace whose daily diet consisted of perpetual war, an economy based on plunder, and religious intolerance and corruption, the ethos expounded by the Templars must have seemed like honey cascading from heaven.

Such utopian thinking would have been perfectly at home in Sintra.

Throughout this bucolic hill there is no shortage of immersions and disappearances into empyrean worlds. Two local legends speak of Templar knights falling in love with enchanted Moorish princesses shortly before vanishing through secret doors into the bowels of the mountain; another describes the Cave of the Fairy,* "formed by a large granite rock balanced on two rocks. Legend has it that every night a fairy will mourn her fate there."[8] This Neolithic passage chamber stands near another place of immersion called Anta do Monge (Dolmen of the Monk); *anta*† means "to mark," it describes how such man-made monolithic structures deliberately reference hot spots whose energy differs from the surrounding land.[9] Its association with a monk comes from a local legend of a Capuchin brother who became lost in one of Sintra's famous mists and took refuge inside the stone chamber only to suddenly find himself "in another world."

One reason why the memory of magic persists in Sintra is due to its consecration to lunar and chthonic cults since at least the Mesolithic era. Throughout this verdant mountain lie steps carved out of cyclopean granite boulders as though made for giants. There are Neolithic dolmens, caves for initiates and reclusive monks, and serene old hermitages draped in fern and moss. Sintra is, to quote Byron, a "glorious Eden," and he ought to know; the poet overstayed his vacation there by three years precisely because Sintra is as close to paradise as one will get while alive.

In remote times the region was known as Promontorio Ofiússa (Promontory of the Serpent), its residents being the Ofiússa (People of the Serpent).[10] The name has nothing to do with the physical worship of snakes and all to do with the honoring of the profusion of earth energies that were later proven to congregate in this area.[11] The local Celts associated the mountain with Chyntia, the lunar goddess, from whom Sintra derives its name.[12] Since the prefix *sin* is Babylonian for moon, it links Sintra with Sinai (Mountain of the Moon), where Moses once

---

*The Cave of the Fairy is situated near the main gate of the Parque da Pena.
†From the Latin *anotare*.

Steps leading to the Cave of the Monk. Such places of veneration and introspection have attracted chthonic cults to Sintra since at least 5000 BC.

watched a pillar of light descend from heaven and offer a treasure of words carved on stone tablets. Hence, to be "a sinner" is to worship the moon along with its feminine connotations.

One of Sintra's oldest known prehistoric temples dedicated to the moon dates to at least 4000 BC. It is located on one of its many peaks, and various megaliths still lie scattered there. Beside it stands a temple* of unknown origin whose columns survived into the nineteenth century; a few yards away, Santa Eufemia church marks the spot where a sacred spring was virtuous even in the twelfth century,[13] its water considered miraculous for curing "scabies of the liver and of other deformations of the body," and was still thus in 1787.[14]

When the Greeks ventured here they regarded Sintra as Mons Sacer (Sacred Mount),[15] and they amplified the tradition by building at least one temple dedicated to Militha, goddess of the moon.† The hermitage of Melides was subsequently erected on its ruins.

Thus, Sintra has been a veritable refuge for seekers of a terrestrial paradise, a sacred mount for reflecting on the bigger mysteries of life. Seekers such as the inner brotherhood of the Knights Templar.

Centuries of well-intended restorations in Tomar may have left few, yet undeniable signs of the knowledge the Templars brought back from the Holy Land, but Sintra is an entirely different matter. Secret societies understandably do not openly advertise their wares, yet vestiges of the Templar's craft remain scattered all around this area, and in one property in particular. And since this property lies precisely

---

*One lunar temple stood by the beach at the very western tip of the mountain where it meets the Atlantic. By the time of André de Resende, the sixteenth-century father of Portuguese archaeology, all that remained were romantic ruins covered in vines. The Roman historian Pliny the Elder stated that the mountain used to extend a further sixty miles into the sea, corroborating esoteric traditions that a citadel existed on its promontory but was destroyed around 9700 BC during a violent upheaval of the ocean. Certainly, Ptolemy states there having been an island there to which the Lusitanians moved when fleeing from the Roman occupation. While the island no longer exists, underwater maps show a large seamount in the area.

†The nickname of Athena.

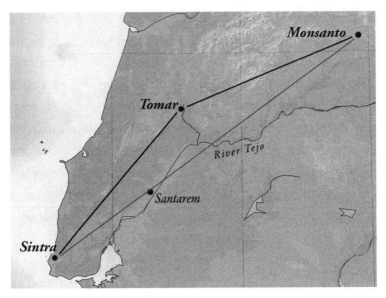

*Equidistant geodetic placement of Templar sites on
Sintra, Tomar, and Monsanto.*

the same distance from the rotunda of Tomar as does the ritual center on the summit of that other sacred mount, Monsanto, such deliberate triangular referencing was all too tempting to ignore.

The Templar homes around the main square in Sintra were adjacent to the former Arabic palace, whose entire ground floor the knights rebuilt.[16] Hundreds of years of earthquakes, neglect, and time made their mark on the properties, but their original foundations remain and now serve modern-day businesses, such as the Hotel Central and Café Paris.* In 1970, a hypogeum, or ritual chamber, with access tunnels was discovered beneath said café, with a connecting passageway leading one way to the nearby palace and the other uphill toward the castle; another

---

*Many of these properties survived the catastrophic earthquake of 1755 and were still standing in 1850 before gentrification removed them.

was found behind the Café da Avozinha.[17] It seems espresso and secret Templar places are magnetically drawn to each other.

In 1904 Sintra attracted one notable figure to its womb as though by magical impulse, a rich merchant named Carvalho Monteiro, who bought a large sylvan estate named Regaleira. Barely ten minutes' walk from the village's central square, the property's extensive reputation must have sparked his interest, for its status as a sacred place was known as far back as 1717, when reference is made to a *via sacra* running through the estate, which back then was known as Quinta da Torre (Estate of the Tower).*[18] Even when Afonso Henriques and the Templars rode in, a sacred spring was known to exist there, its waters so efficacious they caused one eyewitness to write, "The use of which is said to stop coughs and ally consumption. Hence, if the inhabitants should hear anyone coughing, they might discern that he was not a native."[19] The resident Arabs discovered these healing properties for themselves, even noting how many of the local rocks possessed medicinal benefits, especially for curing kidney ailments.

The estate produced an abundance of fruit and other staples, but by 1904 the owners had fallen on hard times, and so Quinta da Regaleira, as it became known, was auctioned and Carvalho Monteiro was the winning bidder. He was a man of prodigious culture, with a degree in law from the University of Coimbra. He was also a Freemason, and as coincidence would have it, he followed a long tradition of Freemasons who had previously owned the property: the brother of the former owner in 1840 was a Freemason, while the owner before her, Manuel Bernardo, was both a Freemason and a member of the Royal Academy of Sciences.

An absence of paperwork then bridges the history of the estate between the fourteenth and eighteenth centuries, but given how Freemasonry is the progeny of the Knights Templar,[20] habits would indicate the property most likely remained "in the family" throughout

---

*There were three towers running through the property.

those centuries. And once one realizes what exists on the property it is not hard to see why.

Monteiro made sizeable improvements to the estate, and judging by the symbolism employed throughout the villa he built, the chapel he erected, and the gardens he refurbished, every inch was designed to be an open invitation for immersion into the Mysteries. Masquerading as a scene from a divine opera, each corner and alcove of Regaleira is filled with alchemical and sacred symbolism. It is a complex environment of sacred spaces and mythical and magical talismans, with grottoes, towers, and temples set in a scenographic landscape that leads a pilgrim deep into contemplation of hermetic knowledge.

Carvalho Monteiro was a stout man, a doyen of perfect health, so clearly he did not move here to imbibe the miraculous waters. The images, themes, and emblems in Regaleira follow the themes throughout Tomar's Convent of Christ, their placement throughout the estate reflecting a profound philosophical and esoteric wisdom. Upon his death, his prodigious collection of books was bought by America's Library of Congress.

Near his villa stands a compact, rectangular chapel resembling a white castle in miniature, brimming with Templar, Hospitaller, and Masonic symbolism, including a haloed triangle with a central eye above the entrance—the all-seeing eye of God. An imposing Templar cross made from tiny colored tiles commands the floor of the chapel; in the gallery above, several more Templar crosses are interspersed with the cross of the Monteiro family. A narrow and intricately carved limestone spiral staircase descends into a basement whose marble floor is covered from wall to wall in a checkerboard pattern, the eternal play between light and dark, good and evil, emblem of the Knights Templar and, later, the Freemasons. A second staircase leads farther down into a deeper subterranean recess connecting a labyrinth of tunnels that burrow deep into the side of the mountain.

After eventually reemerging into the light of day behind a statue of the Divine Virgin, a cursory look at the rear of the chapel reveals a

The white chapel.

Chapel interior. Mosaic floor featuring the later Portuguese Templar cross over the armillary sphere, symbol of the Templar's maritime exploration.

The castle of Mary and Martha, symbol of the Magdalene, to whom the Knights Templar pledged allegiance; it stands over a Green Man, tutelary spirit of nature.

subtle sculpture depicting a castle with two towers—the castle of Mary and Martha, to whom the Templars pledged allegiance, resting on an effigy of the Green Man.

Being a mere seven miles from my place of birth, I have visited this property numerous times, sometimes on consecutive days, and each time a new wonder presents itself. Since one of the focal points of my investigation centers on the reason behind the Templar's presence in Portugal, my attention was drawn to a dolmen-like structure farther up the hill, which is reached after ascending the meandering garden paths filled with statues of solar and lunar deities, a reflecting pool for stargazing, and a grotto protected by two enormous dragons. Finally, the monoliths appear, heavily encrusted with soft, damp moss.

At first, there appears to be no door, but closer inspection reveals

Entrance to the initiatory well disguised as a Neolithic stone chamber.

*The concealed
entrance into
the top of an
initiation well.*

a seven-foot-tall stone slab, and with a little effort, the slab pivots to allow passage through the upright stones. Inside, one is confronted with the remarkable sight of an eighty-foot well circumscribed by an arched spiral staircase.

The bottom of the shaft sits in the half-light reflected from the diffused sunlight drifting through the trees above, but the symbol on the marble floor is unmistakable, a combination of the heraldic emblem of the Monteiro family and the cross of the Knights Templar.

After a reality check, I took a compass reading of the doorway through the megalith. It faces west, in esoteric tradition the direction the initiate follows during the final ritual of living resurrection. Ritual descent is traditionally made clockwise, and indeed the paved staircase descends just so. The builder knew what he was doing. One-third of the way down, a tunnel carved out of the limestone burrows through the hill, at the end of which appear two dragons guarding the entrance into daylight. I retraced my steps and continued my descent; the Templar cross below was by now glistening from the beads of falling drizzle. At the bottom, another carved doorway marked a further passage into the unknown, and a journey into a labyrinth of tunnels ensued. Cut into the limestone and granite, several passageways of indeterminable age branch in several directions; in some places it is clear the passages have been blocked, and beyond lies a network of tunnels still unexplored.

Some niches and chambers are large enough to accommodate someone wishing to spend time in a hermitlike solitary environment, contemplating the Mysteries in total sensory deprivation, meditating in the peace and quiet and darkness of the womb to the point where the ego is dissolved and only the soul remains. It is a favored alchemical method by which incalculable numbers of adepts through the ages have experienced personal revelation.

Immersion complete, one continues wandering the maze of tunnels, each decorated with chunks of coralline limestone imported from the coast and glued by hand to the walls, eventually to emerge under

The first well.

*Part of the endless subterranean passageways at Regaleira
that burrow deep inside the mountain of Sintra.*

a waterfall as though engaging in a kind of baptism, and finally, out into the light. To make the point that the experience was designed to be both initiatory as well as symbolic, a pond stands between you and solid ground, and only after carefully negotiating a set of stones barely concealed below the level of the water does one reach the other side.

Walking on water. Point taken.

Clearly, the well was never designed to hold water. It is a ritual well, a component of a deliberately designed ritual landscape. But a ritual landscape created by an early-twentieth-century merchant is no proof the Templars were here or that they engaged in similar practices. Or were they?

A stupendous feat of construction it may be, but the architecture of the well of Regaleira is incongruous with the rest of the estate. While the structures throughout were built in the romantic revivalist Manueline style common to Carvalho Monteiro's time, the well is Romanesque, the general style in the era of the Templars. However, the condition of the structure does not suggest it is eight hundred years of age either. There is no doubt restorations have taken place. The Romanesque arches are not dissimilar in style to early-twentieth-century reproductions, and the level, unworn steps and mosaic well floor also appear to be recent. But once again, something just did not add up.

While I wondered and wandered the maze of tunnels, I took a right turn into one unlit section and, confined within its obsidian darkness, finally discovered a practical use for my iPhone—a flashlight. After bumping my head and shoulders here and there, a faint glow of gray light penetrated the black beyond. I emerged at the bottom of a second shaft and inside another mystery.

Unlike the previous "well," this second shaft was primitive of construction. Five levels of unevenly stacked and undressed limestone blocks, here and there patched and repaired. Behind the blocks hid five low and narrow circular galleries, each accessed through claustrophobic spiral stairs set into the rough wall and in a measured style that suggests a later refurbishment. The top of the shaft is literally an eighteen-foot-diameter hole, level with the ground and surrounded by a rough, drystone wall in the shape of a horseshoe.

The architectural style of this shaft could not be more removed from the first; in fact, its style of construction has more in common with habitations found nearby at Castro de Ovil dating to circa 100 BC.

Despite an abundance of architect's drawings for the entire estate, including the features found throughout the gardens, not a single blueprint exists for either of the "wells."

The following day was spent in Sintra's archival offices, which for a small town are surprisingly well maintained; some of its original records date back to the time Afonso Henriques rode through town with his Templars. The sheer scale of manual labor performed at Regaleira would have left a paper trail; it was impossible for it not to. It was this researcher's dream and the town archivist's nightmare when I placed a request for every available scrap of paper and bill of sale between the arrival of writing and Monteiro's time, and the folders just kept coming. Somewhere: an impressive newspaper report, a bill of sale for large quantities of building material, dynamite, horses, hired labor—anything that would link the wells to the early-twentieth-century merchant.

Nothing. No evidence exists that Carvalho Monteiro built either one. More architect's drawings materialized; not one showed a well or a shaft. Two possibilities now presented themselves. First, if the wells were indeed part of secret initiations into the Mysteries, then obviously their existence would have been a matter of discretion. And yet once Monteiro's work at Regaleira was complete the property was opened to the public, rendering all secrecy redundant. A second possibility is that the shafts, or at the very least the more primitive of the two, were already on the property before Monteiro's time. Monteiro bought Regaleira in a state of disrepair; unquestionably, he made immense contributions and improvements to the site, and yet by the same token he may also have restored a portion of whatever was already on the property.

The available evidence and the circumstances surrounding the provenance of the property favor the latter argument, and local

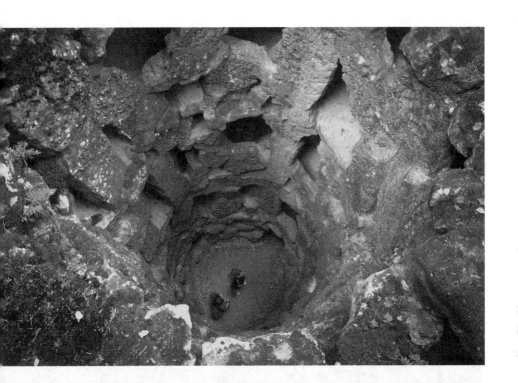

The second well.

One of two megalithic passage chambers at either end of Sintra. They are aligned to the equinox sunrise and sunset, respectively, the ritual directions used in resurrection rituals across the world. Both structures essentially form portals on the east and west sides of the mountain.

researchers have independently reached the same conclusion: "It is not known for certain, but it is probable that both the large and small wells already existed before the acquisition of the property by Carvalho Monteiro."[21] Regaleira's previous owners were also Freemasons, and by 1830 the estate was already well developed. Freemasons and their Templar precursors share a history of close bonds and family ties, it would be inconceivable for the property to have been sold to "outsiders" between the last recorded Templar owners in 1371[22] and its documented use as a sacred ceremonial route three centuries later. And there's the rub: the property was spiritually significant even before the day Afonso Henriques rediscovered it. After all, there must have been a very good reason why it once was named the Forest of Angels.

Evidence that the Templars realized its spiritual significance lies in the anomalous donation of Sintra by the king to Master Gualdino Paes in absentia. No one could have guaranteed Paes's safe return from Jerusalem; for all he knew, Afonso Henriques could have been awarding the property to a dead man, and yet he followed through on the certainty of his conviction. Could it be that Afonso—an initiate of the inner brotherhood himself—awarded Regaleira to the person most likely to appreciate its sanctity, a man who went to the Holy Land, was initiated into the Mysteries, and shone "as a star"?

Two things are certain about the second, primitive "well." One, the horseshoe entrance faces northeast, the summer solstice sunrise, the highest position of the light, the esoteric reference to ancient wisdom, and coincidentally, the feast day of John the Baptist. And two, the entire structure is so plain, so devoid of any decoration it is as though built by people for whom ornamentation was superfluous, a distraction from the total experience of God—as though the architect had not been a twentieth-century Manueline revivalist but a Cistercian monk.

PRESENT ERA. APRIL.
IN THE SHADOW OF A
STATUE IN TOMAR . . .

y now, I was confident that the Knights Templar, in cooperation with the Cistercians and the Ordre de Sion, had pursued two primary objectives in Portugal. The first was the creation of an
independent nation-state, which, once achieved, allowed for the development of a kingdom within a kingdom, a temporal New Jerusalem;
the second was the practice of the Mysteries, particularly the ritual of
"raising the dead," promulgated by an inner brotherhood from knowledge obtained under Temple Mount, thanks in part to the decoding of
texts by learned individuals in Flanders and Champagne.

There are, in addition, insinuations of the preservation of a holy
bloodline, the most blatant evidence being the oath sworn by every new
Templar Master and Procurator in Portugal, who each vowed "to protect the bloodline of David."[1]

Right from the very beginning the quest undertaken by Godefroi
de Bouillon, Hugues de Payns, Count Dom Henrique, Bernard de
Clairvaux, and their supporting cast inevitably leads to the same
conclusion: the improvement of the human condition. Their guide was
knowledge of a revelatory nature that fashions the individual into a
metaphorical vessel of gold. As the ancient Egyptians describe it, once

the individual becomes a suitable receptacle for this knowledge, he or she imbibes the knowledge and becomes the knowledge. Many cultures throughout the world speak of this process of self-empowerment, how such information is timeless, transmitted long ago by a god or an individual of godly stature, the words inscribed on special icons or sacred stones and housed in suitable vessels or temples.

Ages may change, but basic human traits do not. No person involved with such a quest could possibly have resisted the temptation to seek out its source material, especially since wondrous things came to those who interact with it. To quote a Templar initiate, it led them "to experience the joys of Paradise."

Admittedly, I had by now become equally as curious, and although my original purpose never intended to raise controversial subjects such as the Graal or the Ark, by merely stroking the Templar urn one resuscitates them by default. In any event, I came to understand that in 1210 the Graal legends were compiled into one work titled *The Vulgate Cycle,* most likely by Cistercian monks.[2] In one of its five sections—the Queste del Saint Graal—an intriguing dimension is added to the legend when the quest is completed by Galahad, a virgin knight destined from birth to achieve it.

The parallel to the gilded path of Gualdino Paes is here inescapable. While one chronicler claims this knight was a Templar Master right from the beginning—although unlikely—if the claim is taken figuratively the implication is that Paes was destined, like Galahad, to undertake the quest from a very young age, which in Gualdino's case might have begun as an infant, for when he returned from Jerusalem with Arnaldo da Rocha and three other Templar Procurators in the winter of 1125, he was barely eight years old.

In light of the donation of Sintra to Gualdino, and the esoteric discoveries made there, I could not help but wonder to what degree the aspects of both the Graal and the Ark of the Covenant were played out in Portugal, especially given Afonso Henriques's cryptic seal on the charter of Ceras, the property that Master Gualdino and the Templars put to good use by creating an Elysian oasis in Tomar, the focal point being its enigmatic rotunda.

The Ark and the Graal share similar characteristics, especially in Wolfram von Eschenbach's later and more complete story. They are both receptacles, they serve as oracles, they offer information, to the pure of heart they are light in weight but to others become unbearably heavy, they are stones that fell from heaven, they emit a dazzling radiance, they produce fertility or a cornucopia of abundance, they are associated with a salver or tray, they are made of gold, and they are symbolized by the emblem of the dove. It can be argued, then, that to search for the Ark—or what was deposited inside it—is to pursue the Graal.

Tradition describes how the Ark was secreted away from the Temple of Solomon by Menelik, son of the Ethiopian queen of Sheba and King Solomon,* shortly before a Babylonian army razed the building to the ground.[3] Menelik is said to have transported it to Ethiopia by way of the river Nile, and he afterward became that kingdom's first Jewish emperor. Research into the physical whereabouts of the Ark was carried out in the 1990s, leading to a thoroughly convincing argument for its present resting place to be the unassuming church of Our Lady Mary of Sion in the town of Aksum.[†4] Simple logic dictates, therefore, that if the precious object is in Ethiopia, then it cannot be in Portugal as well.

Nor had I expected it to be. But an *aspect* of the Ark, now that is another story. If, like the Graal, the concept of the Ark depends very much on how it is interpreted, there is no reason why information once deposited in this container—scrolls, sacred geometry, rituals, and so forth—should not have been applied in Tomar by Gualdino Paes, especially if a million man Arab army came all the way from southern Spain to remove it from him.

This much was running through my mind as I found shade beneath the focal point in Tomar's central plaza, a bronze statue of Gualdino

---

*The genomes of Ethiopian people hold echoes of the meeting between a legendary king and queen.

†The original church having been destroyed by a Muslim army.

Paes, his right hand firmly clutching a scroll as though its sculptor wished to convey a message.

Every four years, the plaza itself becomes the focus of an old tradition, the Feast of Tabuleiros. In a long procession, men and women parade side by side through the town, each woman balancing on her head a decorated *tabuleiro* to which is attached an unfeasibly tall vertical shaft bearing thirty loaves of bread. The structures are crowned either with a dove or an armillary sphere. The feast is unique to Tomar and has been enacted since at least the reign of Dom Dinis, a thirteenth-century Portuguese king and Templar protector,[5] and up until 1895, it was celebrated on or close to the feast day of John the Baptist.

Such folk festivals reveal a lot about the history of a place, for they often commemorate a truth or an event of sufficient importance as to be maintained in the local consciousness long after the event itself. What struck me about this one was its blatant Templar roots and symbolism: thirty loaves of bread, synonymous with the thirty pieces of silver for which Jesus's—and by implication John the Baptist's—lineage was betrayed, later to become the symbolic entry fee into the Templar Order itself; the armillary sphere, an emblem unique to the maritime discoveries of the Order of the Temple in Portugal; and the dove, representing the holy spirit, an important symbol in the Graal story of Parzival, in which a secretive and spiritual group within the Templars, symbolized by this bird, protect the Graal and a castle on a hill, much like the one on top of the hill behind me protects the rotunda.

Incidentally, the seal of the Ordre de Sion also depicts a dove.

Perhaps I was starting to read too much into what may be nothing more than an innocent feast honoring the summer solstice, but then why perform it every fourth year when the solstice is a yearly event? I also could not help but take note of the disproportionately tall *tabuleiros* balanced precariously on the women's heads and how the combination bears an uncanny resemblance to the unusually extended crown of twin tablets worn by Amun, the Egyptian god who once handed the knowledge of heaven to the god of wisdom, Djehuti.

The seal of the Ordre de Sion.

The Portuguese word *tabuleiro* means "tray," and the feast shares many similarities with the Ethiopian feast of Timbuk, a celebration practiced since the time when Menelik placed the Ark in the church of Our Lady Mary of Sion. During Timbuk the priests balance on their heads a tray called a *tabotat,* and that word shares the same etymological root as *tabuleiro.*

How did Ethiopia come to be in Portugal?

tories of the existence of an Ethiopian ruler named Presbyter John had been circulating around the city for eight years now. Gualdino Paes, recently arrived from Portugal to join the newly appointed Templar Grand Master, André de Montbard, would have been privy to these rumors, even though he would return to his native land by the time envoys representing this king finally arrived to request an altar in the Church of the Holy Sepulcher from the patriarch of Jerusalem.

Seeing as the Ethiopian king was "a direct descendant of the Magi, who are mentioned in the Gospel,"[1] and one of the leaders of that sect had been grandfather to Mary Magdalene, the request was granted in 1177.[2] Pilgrims describe the monks and priests in the Church of the Holy Sepulcher at the time as Copts, Egyptian Christians from the city of Alexandria.

A century passes and the story picks up in Bavaria when a writer by the name of Albrech von Scharfenberg adds the final component to the Graal legend originally begun by Chrétien de Troyes. In it, he mentions the final resting place of the Ark as the land of a priest-king nicknamed Prester John. Although that kingdom is eventually identi-fied as Ethiopia, never did the Ethiopians refer to their king by that name. "Prester John" was an unfortunate artifact of translation, Prester being a contraction of the Latin *pretiosus* (exalted), while John was in actual fact pronounced *gyam,* which in Ethiopian means "powerful."[3]

Ethiopia had a long tradition of black female monarchs who were often referred to as Virgin Queens. They ruled a vast empire stretching along the Nile, through Egypt and all the way to the Mediterranean, covering parts of Eritrea, Nubia, Yemen, and southern Arabia. It was a province considered as large as India, so much so that cartographers often confused the two.[4] The focal center of the kingdom was Meroe, an ancient city on the eastern bank of the Nile centered on an area presided by no less than two hundred pyramids.

Meroe inevitably brings up connotations with Merovingian, the holy bloodline of Trojan kings and the line of Kings David and Solomon, which reemerged in central Europe around the fifth century AD with Merovech, king of the Franks, whose territory included the duchy of Burgundy. The focal point of these connections is Solomon and his lover, the queen of Sheba.

The queen of Sheba bore the title Maqueda, or as it appears in the Middle East, Magda, as in Magdalene. The attribute translates as "magnificent one." In Arabian, Sheba is Saba, and may be linguistically linked to the Sabeans, the gnostic sect who once migrated from Ethiopia around 690 BC.[5] In Ethiopian history, this consort of King Solomon was addressed as Negesta Sabia, with the word *sabia* surviving intact in the Portuguese language and meaning "a wise woman."

The curiosity of the Knights Templar led them to trace the resting place of the Ark of the Covenant to the queen of Sheba's former kingdom,[6] because around 1181 Emperor Lalibela of Ethiopia is said to have given them permission to build round churches in his land. This they did, and they progressed to create eleven others carved entirely out of the volcanic bedrock, one of them in the shape of a Templar cross. An eyewitness account describes how some of the churches "hide in the open mouths of huge quarried caves. Connecting them all is a complex and bewildering labyrinth of tunnels and narrow passageways with offset crypts, grottoes and galleries . . . a subterranean world, shaded and damp, silent but for the faint echoes of distant footfalls as priests and deacons go about their timeless business."[7]

That Emperor Lalibela was somehow involved with a holy bloodline lies in the nature of his name, which literally translates as "the bees recognize his sovereignty," the bee being the adopted symbol of Merovingians through the centuries.[8] Like other Ethiopian monarchs, Lalibela also held the title Neguse Tsion (King of Sion); thus, he may have been involved with the Ordre of Sion in Jerusalem, given its original relationship with the Church of the Holy Sepulcher.

Three and one-half centuries passes, and the story picks up again in the sixteenth century, when unusual processional staffs are witnessed in Ethiopia's Coptic Christian community. One comprises a large central cross identical in design to the first dynasty Portuguese Templar cross, while the other bears the unmistakable emblem of the Templar cross surmounted with the fleur-de-lys, emblem of the Portuguese Order of

Left, first dynasty Portuguese Templar cross,
and right, cross of the Order of Avis, atop Ethiopian processional staffs.

Avis, the splinter Templar group created by Afonso Henriques, whose leader was the king's brother, Dom Pedro.[9]

All this is most odd. How did the Portuguese Templars become involved in remote Ethiopia, especially since the entire Order had supposedly been extinguished two centuries earlier throughout Europe by order of the pope?

50

ith the Inquisition taking root in Spain, Pope Clement V issued the bull *Regnas in coelis,* ordering the Portuguese monarch to investigate the Knights Templar in neighboring Portugal. It had been five years since orders were issued on the night of October 13 to arrest all Templars and confiscate their property. The pope's actions sought to extinguish the Templars' power along with their secret teachings, for the obvious reason that both were undermining the authority of the church.

The second party to the issuing of arrests was the French king, Phillippe le Bel, who was merely keen to get his hands on their vast wealth, seeing as he had amassed a colossal debt in unpaid loans from the Templars. There was also that small grievance he harbored after requesting admittance into their inner brotherhood, but being as honest as a three-libre note, the Templars flatly refused him.

King Dinis of Portugal did not accept the pope's accusations, in fact, his reaction to the pontiff's letter requesting the Templar's imprisonment was derisory. Nevertheless, Dinis paid lip service and requested the archbishop of Lisbon look into the charges by way of procedure. Predictably, the archbishop found no wrongdoing, and the king exonerated the Templars.

Four quiet years passed, and the Portuguese Templars remained unmolested, so an understandably fuming Pope Clement pushed the issue with a follow-up bull, *Vox in excelso,* this time suppressing the Templar Order and ordering all Templar assets be handed over to the Hospitallers, who had since been reorganized into a military arm of the Catholic Church, with notable exceptions in Portugal and Scotland, where they still cooperated with the Templars and generally pursued their original charitable aim.[*1]

Dinis the Farmer King, and his queen, Isabel, were stout proponents of the Cistercian model and encouraged its ideals and practices throughout their reign. Under pressure, Dinis reasoned with Rome that the Templars had simply been granted perpetual use of lands that actually belonged to the Portuguese crown.[2] When the ruse failed to convince, the king summoned the Templars to his court to explain another cunning plan.

What happened next ranks as one of history's biggest practical jokes. Dinis proposed the Templars transfer their entire assets to the Portuguese crown, then take a sabbatical in the Algarve. In the meantime, a letter would be issued to the pope indicating the Order of the Temple in Portugal had ceased to exist.[3]

The Templars packed their belongings, left Tomar for Castro Marim, and laid low for a while, but to prove old habits die hard, they established the town's municipal day on June 24, the feast day of John the Baptist.

Six years later, on the Feast of the Assumption (the same day Godefroi de Bouillon marched to Jerusalem), the ex-Templars returned from their extended vacation and met with the king, to discover he had rebranded the Knights Templar as the Order of Christ, all former

---

[*]The Hospitallers and the Templars were still cooperating in 1156, proved by a donation by Maria Paes (apparently the widow of Archbishop Payo Mendes) that states that upon her death her properties should be split, two-thirds to be given to her sons and the rest to be divided equally between the Knights of the Temple of Solomon and the Order of the Hospital; another donation that year by Soeyro Ordeniz agreed to the exact same terms.

Templars were now members of this Order, and all their former holdings and funds were transferred intact.[4]

In a manner of speaking, the Knights Templar died and were raised from the dead.

All knights remained unscathed in Portugal. And in Scotland, too, where many persecuted French Templars were given safe harbor by King Robert the Bruce, rebranding themselves as Scottish Rite Freemasons.

Back in Tomar, the "new" Order of Christ returned to its objectives and developed a strange alliance bordering on obsession with Ethiopia.

Ethiopia was a kingdom on the other side of the world and required a considerable effort to reach. It offered no obvious financial incentive to anyone willing to make the perilous journey; it was a land to which, up to that period, no known maritime route was known. But the Portuguese persevered, and with two exceptions, all known early visitors to Ethiopia were Portuguese.[5] Why should the Templars/Order of Christ develop this irrational obsession?

A century later, in 1452, a group of Coptic emissaries arrived in Lisbon to meet with the new king, Afonso V. Shortly after, the king published an unusual book called *Arte Magna,* an alchemical treatise in which he mentions having been initiated into the magical arts by a man of knowledge who came from the lands of Egypt and taught him the secrets of what by then had become known as the Stone of Philosophy—formerly known as the Stones of Testimony, the very same ones associated with the Ark of the Covenant. Whether the two events are related or not, the truth is that two years after the meeting, the enlightened Afonso V granted spiritual jurisdiction over Ethiopia to the Order of Christ![6]

These same emissaries then spent a considerable time in the company of the king's uncle, Infante Dom Henrique (or Henry the Navigator, as he is most famously known), Grand Master of the rebranded Order of Christ and the mind behind Portugal's unprecedented maritime achievements, which he oversaw from his office adjacent to the rotunda of Tomar.

Tomar became especially important in the fifteenth century as the nucleus of Portuguese overseas expansion, and Henry applied the knowledge and resources of the Templar Order with great success in his enterprises throughout Africa and the Atlantic. The distinctive red cross of the Order of Christ was painted on the sails of Portuguese *caravelas,* and missions in the new lands came under the authority of Tomar.

Enriched by his overseas endeavors, Henry became the first person since Gualdino Paes to ameliorate the original buildings of the Convent of Christ—as the area surrounding the rotunda had been rebranded—and he subsequently moved into the new quarters. Henry's nickname, "the Navigator," stemmed in part from his maritime exploits, although he himself spent little time aboard a ship. The term *navigator* or *helmsman* in French is *nautonnier,* a term familiar to the Ordre of Sion, which in 1188 changed its name to Priuré de Sion, and ever since then its Grand Masters have carried the official title Nautonnier.[7] The Priuré also adopted the emblem of the rose cross, just like the ones engraved around the periphery of the rotunda of Tomar.[8]

Could Henry the Navigator have served two brotherhoods,* just as Hugues de Payns and Prior Arnaldo da Rocha had done before him?[9]

The language in the correspondence maintained throughout this period expresses a brotherly love and appreciation by the Ethiopians for the Portuguese.[10] For his part, Henry admitted to dedicating a disproportionate part of his career to finding a maritime route around Africa so as to reach the kingdom of Presbyter John, with every effort conducted under absolute secrecy.[11] Facts, maps, even instructions to the ships' captains and their reports were suppressed, and any man disobeying this commitment to secrecy was to be punished by death.[12]

---

*Charters show that King Louis VII (of the House of Capet, from which Afonso Henriques was descended) installed the Ordre de Sion in the priory of Saint-Samson at Orléans, which he donated to the Ordre in 1152. Ninety-five members of the Ordre sailed with him back from Jerusalem, sixty-two of whom were installed at Saint-Samson; seven joined the Knights Templar, and the remainder entered the small priory du Mont de Sion one mile away in Saint Jean le Blanc.

Perhaps Henry's privileged position as Grand Master of the Temple opened his eyes to the inner knowledge secreted by the brotherhood in Tomar, or maybe the rotunda was exercising its own magical effect. The learned man surrounded himself with the best savants of the period—astronomers, mathematicians, cosmologists—all of whom assumed the secretive behavior of a similar group of seekers in the Graal legends.[13] It is possible that his meeting with the Copts from "the Egyptian lands" may have reawakened a dormant Templar plan. Maybe the Copts came with hope that whatever the Templars had once pursued in that remote corner of the world, but was rendered inert from three centuries of hostilities with the Muslims, was now worth pursuing once more.

Certainly, the opportunity was denied Henry, for he passed away in 1460, shortly after making his will on October 13.[14]

It would be two decades before the new king, João II of the Order of Avis, sent an envoy to Ethiopia by the name of Afonso de Paiva. A few years passed until Afonso was found to have died from a fever along the way in Cairo. A second envoy, Pero de Covilhã, followed in his footsteps, not knowing if his predecessor had succeeded in making contact with the court of Presbyter John.

Covilhã took a circuitous route, visiting the Ka'Ba in Mecca and Saint Catherine's Chapel in Sinai. Three years later, the Portuguese man finally arrived at the king of Ethiopia's court, where he was greeted most warmly. When a traveling Portuguese priest later met Covilhã, he wrote, "He is liked by the Presbyter and all his court."[15] This Presbyter John would have by now been more than three hundred years old, so clearly the name identified was not that of an individual but a shared title; indeed, Ethiopian monarchs did carry both a birth name as well as a throne name, in addition to the epithet Abd es Salib (Servant of the Cross).[16]

Meanwhile in Portugal, time passed, and the next Templar Master also ascended the throne, as King Manuel I. One of his first instructions was to commission a fellow knight of the Order of Christ, the explorer Vasco da Gama, to sail his four ships eastward. After disembarking in

Mozambique, a member of da Gama's crew wrote the following entry in his journal: "We were told that Presbyter John resided not far from this place . . . far in the interior, and could only be reached on the backs of camels." News that the Portuguese finally and safely reached their goal came in the form of a letter from Queen Eleni of Ethiopia to King Manuel I in 1509. She followed up with an ambassador from her court, who conveyed a second letter suggesting, among other items, marriages between princes and princesses of the Ethiopian court with members of the Order of Avis, the offshoot Templar Order.

King Manuel encouragingly replied by sending the Ethiopians the most unusual of items: an extensive library of one thousand books, and a printing press—significant in that it would be the first one outside of Europe to be free of the Vatican's censorship. The Portuguese king also sent a token army of 450 men under the command of Dom Cristovão (another knight of the Order of Christ and the son of Vasco da Gama) to assist the court of the Ethiopian king. At one point this small contingent faced ten thousand spearmen and, against all odds, won. The Portuguese stayed long enough to build a stone bridge, the first of its kind, across the Nile, as well as several stone churches and castles.[17]

It was tradition for the king of Ethiopia never to show himself to his people except veiled behind silk muslins, yet eventually the Portuguese priest Francisco Alvarez of Coimbra did get to see Presbyter John: "We dressed ourselves and arranged ourselves very well . . . and many people came to accompany us on foot and on horseback, so we went in order from the place we started from as far as a great portal, where we saw innumerable pavilions and tents pitched like a city in a great plain."[18] Alvarez described him as "a young man, not very black. His complexion might be chestnut and bay, not very dark in color."[19]

Presbyter John wrote several letters to the Portuguese king in which he addressed himself as "son of Solomon, son of the Pillar of Sion . . . son of the Hand of Mary."[20] The bundle was tied up, placed in a small brocaded bag, and packed in a leather-lined basket ready for Alvarez to bring back to Portugal, along with the presbyter's gift of his own crown made of gold and silver. Alvarez himself was awarded thirty ounces of gold for his efforts, and on February 12, 1521, together with fellow Portuguese travelers, he began to make his way back home.

The Portuguese were forced to wait a whole year before favorable winds in the Red Sea allowed their ship to leave, so Alvarez took the opportunity to attend the sacred places. He noted many hermitages

Beta Ghiorghis.

where holy men passed their lives in a state of privation. He also visited the extraordinary rock-carved churches at Lalibela, eleven of them. The most striking, Beta Giorghis, was carved into the bedrock itself. "I weary of writing more about those buildings, because it seems to me that I shall not be believed if I write more, and because regarding what I have already written they may blame me for untruth. Therefore I swear by God, in whose power I am, that all I have written is the truth . . . and there is more than what I have written, and I have left it that they may not tax me with it being falsehood, so great was my desire to make known this splendour to the world."[21]

Alvarez's astonishment was understandable. The structure descended forty feet below ground, and the remaining freestanding cube of volcanic tuff was then hollowed externally and internally in the shape of a cross. "A double cross," Alvarez noted, "that is, one within the other, like the crosses of the Order of Christ."[22]

The priest asked his sources who had been responsible for this outstanding masonic craft, to which they replied, "They were made by white men."[23]

The Knights Templar had carved them in the twelfth century.

51

The church of Our Lady Mary of Sion in Aksum claims to house the Tabota Zion, the Ethiopian name for the Ark of the Covenant.[1] Copies of the Ark, or *tabot,* reside throughout other Coptic churches, particularly in the Lake Tana region, where the churches were built in circular fashion. The *tabot* spend much of the year resting behind a curtain of veils inside their inner sanctum. But for one special day their contents are brought out of the churches during Timkat, a feast celebrating the rite of baptism.

The feast of Timkat is referenced in the Bible and is still practiced throughout Ethiopia by black Jews who honor the Old Testament traditions, independent of later Judaism. During the celebrations the priests balance on their heads a stone tablet called a *tabotat,* a copy of the tablets contained within the Ark.[2] These tabotat resemble trays, about fifteen inches square, each draped with a cloth embroidered with the emblem of a dove.

The ritual bears an uncanny similarity to an old Egyptian ceremony, the Festival of Apep, that took place in ancient times in a township by the Nile called Thebes, which back then was formerly called Tapet,[3] a word sharing linguistic similarities with *tabot.* In this ceremony a miniature boat was carried on staves between the temples of Luxor and Karnak. The boat was curved much like the crescent moon, symbol of the god of wisdom, Djehuti; at its center rested a box-like repository inside of which was placed a sacred stone or veiled statues of gods made of stone.[4] One scholar says of the connection between the ceremonial stone objects and the Ark, "The tradition of two sacred stone tablets within the Ark would point strongly to the conclusion that the original contents of the Ark must have been sacred stone . . . [which] was either conceived of as the deity himself, or as the object in which the deity was thought to reside permanently."[5]

The original Ark would have passed through Thebes on its exodus from Jerusalem to Ethiopia, because its custodians built a temple to protect it on the island of Elephantine, to the south of Thebes.[6]

It would seem that Thebes is named for a celebration of the Ark, the memory of which was preserved in the form of a local folk tradition, while the event itself is depicted on the walls of the temple of Luxor.

Although no such mural exists in Tomar, its Feast of Tabuleiros records the memory of an event. Whether the Templars brought a copy of the Ark to Tomar is not possible to prove, but the remarkable thing is how an etymological trail connects these stories.

Linguistically, *tabot* descends from the Hebrew word *tebah* via the Aramaic *tebuta,* which refers to a container.[7] Portuguese is a language rich in characteristics that reflect the myriad of peoples who settled in Portugal, such as Arabs, Jews, Egyptians, and particularly Phoenicians, whose language shares many common traits with Aramaic and old Hebrew. The Phoenician word *thabilitho* (a wooden slab), is also the origin of the Portuguese word *tabuleiro;* its variant, *tablete,* literally means "a tablet."

Its first syllables, *tabu,* mean "something that is designated as sacred, set apart, or denoted as restricted." Thus, the Feast of Tabuleiros in Tomar can be accurately described as "the feast of a tray on which rests a restricted holy or sacred object."

The Feast of Tabuleiros in Tomar, during which women parade through town balancing a tabuleiro, a tall vertical shaft bearing thirty loaves of bread.

The visual symbolism of the Feast of the Tabuleiros bears an uncanny resemblance to the stella of Amun and the two oversized tablets of wisdom that make up his crown.

52

PRESENT ERA.
TOMAR. STARING AT
THE ROTUNDA . . .

The Templars may have once deposited something of great spiritual importance in Tomar after all, something associated with the Ark of the Covenant or its contents. And just like the cryptic phrase carved beside the image of the Ark on the Door of Initiates in Chartres cathedral, its exact location in Tomar, like its nature, remains elusive, while its inviolable halo has been kept alive by way of a folk tradition.

What struck me most about Francisco Alvarez's eyewitness account from Ethiopia is not so much the record of advanced construction techniques the Templars employed in their churches in Ethiopia—which no modern expert has solved, by the way—but the description of the labyrinth of tunnels, crypts, and galleries connected to the churches and used for religious purposes, all of which seamlessly resonates with the Regaleira estate in Sintra, already a sacred place by the time Master Gualdino Paes inherited it on behalf of the Templars.

Perhaps Sintra's maze of tunnels and the two mysterious shafts are an imprint of methods the Templars learned abroad, possibly implemented by the Templar Master based on knowledge and experiences acquired during his years of preparation in the Holy Land.

Like the secrets of the Mysteries, the absolute truth remains obscured by veils.

As for the actual secrets for "raising the dead," that "law so extraordinary on which such a secret should be kept," they too remain occulted (hidden from the eye), appearing here and there in ripples and echoes like a benevolent ghost. What is certain is that, in the end, the Templars were protecting the pilgrim trail after all. Not in its literal sense but in the manner in which they guarded the path for every inquiring journeyman wishing to come into contact with the Mysteries, the path to personal revelation that opens a metaphorical door to the kingdom of heaven.

To paradise.

53

PRESENT ERA.
A CIRCULAR HALL IN A SMALL
COUNTRY NAMED PORTUGAL . . .

Once upon a time, the kingdom known as Portugal was called Lusitania. The name is an amalgam of *lux* (light) and Tanit,[1] a Phoenician lunar goddess and divine virgin equated with Isis. Her emblem is a fusion of the Egyptian symbol of eternal life—the ankh—and an isosceles triangle beneath a crescent moon.[2]

In its Latin form, *lux tanit* means "a storehouse of light" or "a place of concealment."[3] Lusitania, then, is "a place where the knowledge (light) is stored or concealed."

In the medieval legend, the Graal is described as a gold object carried on a salver, a silver tray used in a formal ceremony. It is similar to the Portuguese root word *salvar* (to save) from which arises the term *salvation*. And salvation by imbibing the knowledge contained in the Graal—the Sophia, that beautiful woman of knowledge—adequately describes the Templar quest.

In Tomar, the Templars could have named their circular "church" the rotunda. The same word exists in Portuguese, even carries the same meaning. But they did not. Instead, they named it something else—*charola,* an unusual choice of word to ascribe a building, for it literally translates as "a salver."

Who would have thought it, the rotunda is the resting place for the Graal?

And by creating a kingdom within a kingdom and erecting this salver in the town whose name means "to drink," the Templars provided a safe haven where one could imbibe the Graal, through a secret ritual, to experience that ultimate of journeys: the discovery of the nature of reality and the self, a timeless experience once given its own unique symbol, the cup of everlasting life.

END

EPILOGUE

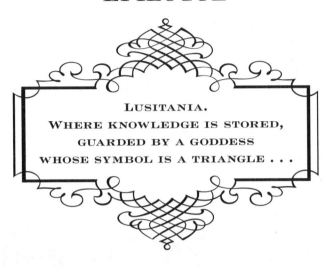

LUSITANIA.
WHERE KNOWLEDGE IS STORED,
GUARDED BY A GODDESS
WHOSE SYMBOL IS A TRIANGLE . . .

ust how wide did the Templar plan in Portugal extend? Consider the following connections . . .

In her grant of 1139, Eleanor of Aquitaine gave the Knights Templar a building and a mill in the western French port town of La Rochelle, "entirely free and quit of all custom, infraction, and tolte and taille [levies] and the violence of all officials, except for our toll." She suggested her vassals make similar donations. More importantly, she granted the Templars freedom to transport anything through her lands "freely and securely without all customs and all exactions."[1]

Almost two hundred years later, this foresight would save the lives of countless knights and ensure the survival of the Order of the Temple beyond the borders of France and the grasp of Pope Clement V. That was the eve of Friday, October 13, 1307. A statement by a Templar named Jean de Chalon declares that three carts containing the Templar treasure (gold and documents) left the Paris temple that evening following a tip-off that the king's henchmen were out to arrest all members of the Order. The intent was to move the contents of their preceptory to La Rochelle, where the Templars owned a fleet of large ships for the ferrying of passengers and cargo between Europe and the Mediterranean.

However, by the time the carts reached the Templar castle at Gisors the roads were already under surveillance, so the contents were hidden in subterranean passages under the castle's keep.

The statement was obtained under torture and may have been a red herring. Nevertheless, a document associating Gisors with the Templar treasure was found in the Vatican library and obtained at the request of the French ambassador to Rome.[2]

Eighteen ships filled up with fleeing Templars at La Rochelle while other knights made their way down the Seine (a river from which they were exempt from tolls and thus not subject to search) to the port of Le Havre. Once loaded, the ships sailed into the Bay of Biscay and disappeared from all documented history. It is a notable omission given how such a considerable fleet would have been of significant value.

In truth the fleet split into two. One arm sailed west to Portugal,[3] making good use of the water routes made available since the days of 1125 when the Templars used the estuary of the Mondego to reach the castle of Souré.[4] Upon reaching Portugal, to ensure anonymity, they disembarked at a small fishing village on a peninsula near Serra d'El Rei. Some of the ships' names were Temple Rose, Great Adventure, and Falcon of the Temple (a salute to the god Horus, son of the resurrected Osiris).[5] It is rumored that part of a treasure was offloaded here and transported to nearby Obidos, a town patronized by the queens of Portugal.[6] The remaining ships and their cargo continued down the coast to Lisbon. The river Tejo was navigable in those days all the way to Spain, as were many of its tributaries, one being the Nabão, which leads right onto the quay opposite the Arab waterwheel in Tomar.

Meanwhile, the second fleet sailed north to Scottish Templar strongholds in Kilmartin, Kilmory, and Castle Sweet. Essentially, the Templars took up positions on the extreme points of Europe, from which the only rational place to expand was across the Atlantic.

Framing the sunrise side of the town square of Tomar, the church of John the Baptist looks out over a pavement of large black-and-white checkerboard mosaics made of small cobblestones, as though the entire plaza is the center of a Masonic stage. And yet the play is real enough, for it was from here that the Knights Templar—as the rebranded Order of Christ—set out on bold maritime explorations that changed the world as we know it. This great work was conducted patiently and over the course of centuries, initially with the building of Europe's first independent nation-state, then a kingdom within the kingdom of Portugal, and following the disbandment of the Order throughout Europe, a cooperation with brothers taking refuge in Scotland to resume an ongoing mission.

Like all esoteric sects, the Templars were master geometers. If we recall, an axis runs through the rotunda, through two marked pillars in the church of John the Baptist, continuing as the crow flies to the abbey on Mount Sion. Could the Templars have applied the talisman of triangular geometry to a third notable landmark to form a geometric trinity?

A number of shared similarities exist between events in Portugal and Scotland: the protection offered the Templars by King Dinis was similarly offered by his counterpart, King Robert the Bruce, who never legally ratified the dissolution of the Scottish temple;[7] both countries' move toward independence occurred in battles on the feast day of John the Baptist;[8] the Templars in Portugal were renamed Order of Christ, and in Scotland, Scottish Rite Freemasonry. On the infamous night of October 13, Templar ships slipped out of French ports, split up, and sailed to these two respective safe havens.

Following the Council of Troyes in 1128, the Templars under Prince Afonso Henriques set in motion a chain of events that led to Portuguese independence. As this was unfolding, Hugues de Payns was in Scotland meeting with King David I, who granted the Grand Master the chapelry and manor of Balantrodach, a small hamlet whose name means "stead of the warrior." The land around Balantrodach had earlier been awarded as a gift of gratitude to William the Seemly, of the Sainte Clair family, for bravery and loyalty to the Scottish crown;[9] his son Henri de Sainte Clair played an active role in the first Crusade and the conquest of Jerusalem by King Malcolm.[10]

The Sainte Clair family originated from Normandie, a county adjoining Flanders, the place of origin of a number of original Knights Templar; the Sainte Clairs were themselves linked by blood and marriage to the family of the Counts of Champagne and the Duke of Burgundy.[11]

Hugues de Payns set up a preceptory at Balantrodach in 1129, to which was added a church and a Cistercian cloister and mill.* In essence, it became a focal center of operations for the Templars in Scotland. Contact between Scotland and Flanders became very active thanks to the partnership between King David and the Flemish comte Philippe d'Alsace, cousin of the Templar knight Payen de Mont-Didier;[12] the king also surrounded himself with Templars and appointed them as "Guardians of his morals by day and night."

After the night of October 13, the Templars escaped to enclaves throughout Scotland, and in time amassed no less than 519 properties.[13] They would have been fascinated to discover the Graal legends had become popular there too, not least because Celtic mythology is rife with quests by a group of chivalric warriors seeking a mysterious sacred object of mystifying power, along with a remote castle and a crippled king ruling over a land similarly fallen on hard times. In one of the original Graal stories—specifically the one written by Chrétien de Troyes—the Graal knights defend a castle guarding the gates "de Galvoie," which is a specific reference to a real Scottish castle in Galloway, where the Bruce clan was seated after being made lords by King David I.[14] Chrétien also makes a reference to a religious site at Mons Dolorosus, which at the time was the actual name of the Cistercian abbey of Melrose in Northumberland, where Robert the Bruce's heart was buried.[15]

One hundred and fifty years go by, when in 1446, Earl William St. Clair[†] founds an unusual chapel just three miles from Balantrodach, at Roslin, and it shares a number of similarities with the rotunda of Tomar:

Both never originally housed an altar.[‡]
Both were built adjacent to castles.

---

*The village is today called Temple. Only the walls of the church remain. Excavations in 1989 revealed additional foundations surrounded by graves, many bearing the Templars' maritime battle insignia, the skull and bones.
†Also spelled Sinclair and Sainteclaire.
‡Roslin's was added later, in the sixteenth century, then destroyed, and only added again in the Victorian era.

Both sit on promentories above fabled rivers.

Both sit over a warren of tunnels, those at Roslin accessed only by the lowering of a person down a well, much like the one inside Tomar's Chamber of Mysteries.

Both are rumored to be the final repositories of the Templar treasure. (Roslin's ships having sailed up the Esk,[16] while Tomar's used the Nabão.)

The obvious similarities end there, for while the original interior of the rotunda was as plain as a Cistercian, the same cannot be said of Roslin chapel, which can only be described as a coded esoteric library of stone housing the beliefs and traditions of the Knights Templar and just about every faith in the world.[17] However, Roslin was founded at the same time Henry the Navigator was adding an apse to the rotunda of Tomar, a project later completed by King Manuel I, who also added a nave. From this point the similarities continue:

Both buildings make prominent features of the Widowed Mother and the Green Man.

Both feature a similar style of architecture, which in itself is not unusual given they share the same period, except that Roslin's outstanding feature is a curved column called the Apprentice Pillar, the "model of this beautiful pillar having been sent from Rome, or some foreign place."[18]

It is possible this "foreign place" may have been Tomar, because the anomalous pillar so closely matches the unique Manueline style in which its nave is built.

And here is where the geometrical connection with Tomar and Mount Sion comes in. One of the details that struck me from Warren's excavations beneath Temple Mount is an anomaly he found on the northeast point of the sanctuary: ". . . a perforated stone. The uprights of the wall are formed by megaliths up to 14 ft tall and of extreme age."

More recent marks on the stone show a cross of the type used by early Christians. The stone that closes the end of the passage has "a recess cut into it four inches deep. Within this recess are three cylindrical holes arranged in the form of a triangle."[19]

No explanation exists for this unusual feature. So let us assume for a moment the anomalous triangle suggests a triangulation of points or places, because if we link Mount Sion, Roslin, and Tomar, interesting commonalities emerge: all three places are associated with ancient wisdom: Jerusalem speaks for itself; Roslin, or *ros linn* (a name chosen by Henry St. Clair), translates from Gaelic as "ancient knowledge passed down the generations";[20] and Tomar means "a place of imbibing," in the land of Lusitania, "the place where the knowledge is stored."

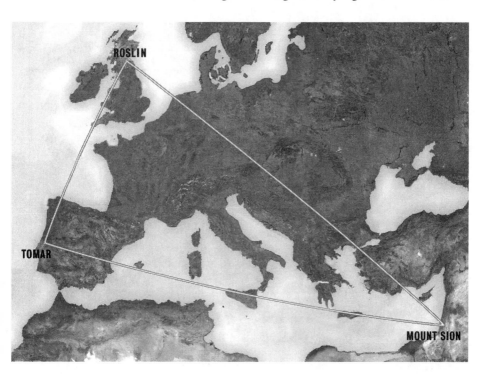

It was ancient practice to locate temples sharing similar purposes according to perfect triangles,[21] the triangle being a two-dimensional representation of the tetrahedron, the fundamental geometry of matter. Thus, by linking sacred places across sometimes-vast distances in perfect triangular relationships, it was believed the sites were imbued with the power of nature's most elemental geometric form.[22]

The link between the rotunda of Tomar and the basilica of Notre Dame du Mont de Sion can now be extended to Roslin Chapel, and as such, the three temples form a perfect isosceles triangle, with a margin of error of just 0.1 percent.*

Suddenly the triangular symbol of Tanit, a presiding goddess of Lusitania and Palestine, takes on a whole new perspective.

---

*Tomar to Sion is 2,488 miles, and Sion to Roslin is 2,485 miles, an error of just 0.12 percent.

Sion, Switzerland.

When a mound was excavated in Suffolk, England, it was found to contain the sixth-century ritual burial of a ship along with a trove of gold coins belonging to the Merovingian family dynasty, one coin in particular linking the items to Theodebert II, a Merovingian king. The coins were minted in Sion, Switzerland.[23]

The diocese of Sion is the oldest in Switzerland, when in 999 the last king of Burgundy, Rudolph III, granted the county of Valais to its bishop, and Sion became the capital. At that time, a Carolingian church stood on a prominent mount above the village. After its destruction by fire it was rebuilt as a fortified church in the twelfth century and became the basilica of Notre Dame de Valere; as for the hill, it was dedicated to Saint Catherine, patron saint of the Knights Templar.

If a bearing is taken from the basilica of Mount Sion in Jerusalem to its counterpart in Sion, Switzerland, the line bisects the Tomar-Roslin-Sion triangle and extends across the Atlantic, making its first landfall

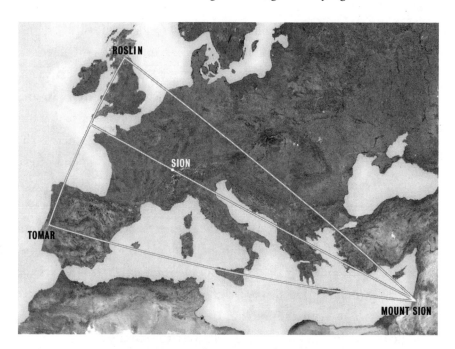

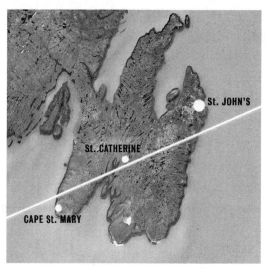

in Newfoundland, by the city St. John's, named after, you guessed it, John the Baptist. It then continues past the towns of St. Catherine's, and St. Mary's.

Henry St. Clair was the grandfather of the founder of Roslin Chapel. Inside this curious building there are stone carvings of North American plants supposedly not seen by Europeans until Columbus's arrival in that part of the world. Since the chapel was completed in 1486 and Columbus made his first voyage six years later, common sense dictates that Henry St. Clair or members of his court made a voyage across the Atlantic first. Although stories and letters circulated at the end of the fourteenth century outlining such an expedition, the evidence has been hard to substantiate.[24] However, there exists an anomalous round tower in what is today Newport, Rhode Island, in a style of architecture common to medieval Europe. Further inland, in Westford, Massachusetts, someone carved an effigy on a large boulder of a knight. He wears the habit of a military order, a sword with a pommeled hilt commensurate with the style used in the fourteenth century, and a shield depicting a single-masted medieval vessel sailing west toward a star. The style is virtually identical to carvings on grave-posts in the Templar cemetery in Kilmartin, Scotland, which date to the same period. Lending weight to the argument that Templar knights may have crossed the Atlantic are testimonies from the only two Templars arrested in Scotland, who stated how their brothers at Balantrodoch "threw off their habits" and fled "across the sea."[25] If so, they would have lived and died there, and a number of old gravestones in Nova Scotia (Latin for New Scotland) do incorporate Templar devices such as the skull and crossbones, the symbol of the Templar's maritime fleet, just as they do on Scottish graves.[26]

It is speculated that the Scottish Templars shared information of this voyage with their Portuguese brethren and that the knowledge found its way to Columbus via Portuguese navigators in Lisbon. Certainly, Columbus solicited the sponsorship of the Portuguese court for an expedition to the Indies—even his father-in-law was a knight of the Order of Christ—but still the Portuguese king acquiesced to his request, possibly because the Portuguese, particularly Henry the Navigator, kept their maritime ventures close to their chests.

There is good support for this. There exists a long seafaring tradition between Genoa and the Portuguese monarchy, dating to as early as 1099 when Dom Henrique twice sailed to Palestine with the Genoese.[27] The relationship was still strong two centuries later when shipbuilders and thirty sea captains were recruited from Genoa to rebuild the Portuguese fleet. Then in the early fifteenth century, the Portuguese ambassador Damião de Goes sailed to Italy to study in Padua, where he befriended the Italian cartographer Giovanni Ramusio; Goes was also the Commander of the Order of Christ, and he shared with Ramusio various Templar maritime discoveries, which the Italian illustrated in *Raccolta di Navigationi et Viaggi*. One of the maps in this opus shows the coast of Labrador dotted with Portuguese fishing boats and what appears to be the drying of salt cod, while the Portuguese shield and coat of arms feature prominently on this North American territory, suggesting these lands were already—and unofficially—known to the Portuguese crown.[28]

Which brings us to the carving of that knight, the ship, and the star. In his *History of the Jews,* Josephus points out how the Essenes placed the origin of good souls in an idyllic land in the West. They mention this again in the Copper Scrolls and associate this land with a star of the Orient; the same concept is found in the esoteric traditions of the Celts, Jews, and Greeks. West is the place of the setting sun, so to figuratively follow the path of the setting sun is to enter into the Otherworld, the place of spirit. The Mandeans—successors to the Essenes and Nasoreans—added that this land is identified by a star called Merika.

Since the Templars found the scrolls written by their forebears, it stands to reason they would set sail for this land of paradise after a mass arrest essentially undermined their power as a group. Ensconced in their safe harbors in Scotland and Portugal, the members of the Order of the Temple made future plans to go west.

In Templar symbology, Merika is the western star toward which mounted knights ride and ships sail. This star, often depicted in the form of the five-pointed pentagram synonymous with Isis, is also the bright morning star Sirius, otherwise known as Sophis, the star of wisdom. The same symbol appears above the altar of the Templar's mother church in Tomar, the first structure obsessively built by Gualdino Paes, in a town created by the Templars that became the focal point of their overseas explorations.

The attribution of the name America to the newfound land in the West has long been wrongly attributed to the Italian explorer Amerigo Vespucci by a highly imaginative priest named Waldseemuller, who simply pieced together several unconnected facts and created an accidental myth.[29] So by the time Columbus reached the "New World," it was hardly so; Merika was already old news to the Templars.

Whether by design or coincidence, the imaginary line from Mount Sion, through Sion, Switzerland, and St. John's, Newfoundland, continues into Chesapeake Bay, near the birthplace of a Freemason by the name of George Washington, who laid the foundation stone for the White House on October 13, essentially commemorating the anniversary of the death of Portuguese Templar Master Gualdino Paes and, 112 years later, the day the Order of Temple was almost extinguished, along with its purpose.

It seems that, even at the very end, another chapter begins in the eternal quest to build that heavenly Jerusalem.

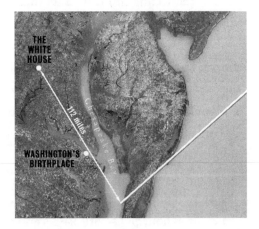

"Then he saw the rich Graal enter
through a door to serve the food;
it promptly put the bread down
in front of the knights."

—Chrétien de Troyes,
Perceval, the Story of the Grail

Notes

CHAPTER 1. 1125.
AN OAK TABLE IN A LARGE HALL IN
A SMALL COUNTY NAMED PORTUGALE . . .

1. Viterbo, *Elucidario das palavras,* 232.
2. Secco, *Escrituras de Thomar;* and Viterbo, *Elucidario das palavras,* 232.
3. *Livro dos mestrados,* 38, gaveta 7, maço 9.
4. da Costa, Bernardo, *Historia da Militar Ordem de Nosso Senhor Jesus Christo,* 1; and Viterbo, *Elucidario das palavras,* 233.

CHAPTER 2. 1095. NOVEMBER.
IN THE AUVERGNE, A MOUNTAINOUS
REGION IN CENTRAL FRANCE . . .

1. Urban II's speech at the Council of Claremont, in Fulcher de Chartres, *Fulcheri carnotensis historia hierosolymitana.* There are five versions of the speech.
2. In Robert the Monk, *Historia hierosolymitana.*
3. Ibid.
4. Ibid.
5. Fulcher de Chartres, *Fulcheri carnotensis historia hierosolymitana.*
6. Ibid.
7. Addison, *Knights Templars,* 6–8.
8. Hagenmeyer, *Le vrais et le faux,* 518.
9. Guizot, *France,* 304.

10. Ibid.

11. Ibid., 306.

CHAPTER 3. 1096. AUGUST.
CONSTANTINOPLE, CAPITAL OF
THE HOLY ROMAN EMPIRE . . .

1. In William of Tyre, *History of Deeds.*

2. Guibert de Nogent, *Deeds of God,* 43–45.

CHAPTER 4. 1096. AUGUST.
WITH THE NORTHERN ARMY,
PREPARING TO DEPART . . .

1. Baigent, Leigh, and Lincoln, *Holy Blood, Holy Grail,* 107.

CHAPTER 5. 1098.
ON THE DESERT ROAD NEAR ANTIOCH . . .

1. William of Tyre, *History of Deeds.*

2. Tyerman, *God's War,* 122.

CHAPTER 6. 140 BC.
IN A LAND IN WESTERN IBERIA
CALLED LUSITANIA . . .

1. Caesar, *Incerti avctoris de bello Hispaniensi liber.*

2. Diodorus the Sicilian, *Historical Library of Diodorus.*

3. Gordon, *Prehistoric London.*

4. Davies, *Celtic Linguistics.*

5. Igrejas, "Sobre a origem e significado"; and Markale, *Templar Treasure at Gisors.*

6. Marques, *Historia de Portugal,* 28.

7. Sousa, Manuel de Faria e, *Europa Portugueza.*

8. Brito, *Primeira parte,* and 1720 version by Pascoal da Sylva, vol. II, bk. VII, 387–89; and Sousa, Manuel de Faria e, *Europa Portugueza,* book 2, pt. 1, chap. 2, no. 10. p. 19; also cited Ferreira, *Memorias e noticias historicas,* 820.

9. Sousa, Manuel de Faria e, *Europa Portugueza,* book 3; and cited Ferreira, *Memorias e noticias historicas,* 798–99 (although his date is off by two years).

10. Also cited Ferreira, *Memorias e noticias historicas,* 820.

11. Brito, *Primeira parte;* and 1720 version by Pascoal da Sylva, pt. 1, book 5, chap. 3.

12. Zapater y Lopez, *Cister militante en la campana,* vol. 1, chaps. 1, 2, and 3.

13. Sousa, Manuel de Faria e, *Europa Portugueza,* book 3; and cited Ferreira, *Memorias e noticias historicas,* 820.

14. Herculano, *Historia de Portugal,* book 1, 201; and Ferreira, *Memorias e noticias historicas,* 800–12, 824–28.

15. Sousa, Manuel de Faria e, *Europa Portugueza,* book 3, pt. 1, cap. 2, no. 10, chap. 19; and cited Ferreira, *Memorias e noticias historicas,* 727–28.

16. Ferreira, *Memorias e noticias historicas,* 829; and document in the archives of the Monastery of Lorvão.

17. Sousa, Manuel de Faria e, *Europa Portugueza,* book 3; and cited Ferreira, *Memorias e noticias historicas,* 727–28.

CHAPTER 7. 1099. JUNE.
OUTSIDE THE GATES OF JERUSALEM . . .

1. Konstam, *Historical Atlas of the Crusades,* 133.

2. Tyerman, *God's War,* 153–57.

3. Ibid., 159.

4. Albert of Aachen, *Historia hierosolymitana.*

5. William of Tyre, *History of Deeds,* book 9, chap. 9.

6. Vogüé, *Les eglises de la Terre Sainte,* 326, citing Jacob Vitriac.

7. Paraschi, *Historia dos Templarios em Portugal,* 14.

8. Albert of Aachen, *Historia hierosolymitana.*

9. William of Tyre, *History of Deeds.*

10. Vogüé, *Les eglises de la Terre Sainte,* 326.

CHAPTER 8. THIRTY YEARS EARLIER.
ORVAL. A TOWN DOWNRIVER
FROM BOUILLON . . .

1. Tillière, *Histoire de l'Abbaye d'Orval,* 3 ff.

2. Baigent, Leigh, and Lincoln, *Holy Blood, Holy Grail,* 473–75.

3. Tillière, *Histoire de l'Abbaye d'Orval,* 3 ff.

4. Baigent, Leigh, and Lincoln, *Holy Blood, Holy Grail,* 107.

5. Jeantin, *Les chroniques de l'Ardenne,* 398.

6. Hagenmeyer, *Le vrais et le faux,* 518.

7. Hamblett, in Olsen, *Templar Papers.*

8. Paraschi, *Historia dos Templarios em Portugal,* 14.

9. Vincent, *Histoire de l'anciene image miraculeuse,* 92.

10. Vogüé, *Les eglises de la Terre Sainte,* 326.

11. Hebrews 12:22, Oxford King James Bible, 1769.

12. Book of Isaiah 28:16.

13. Wheeler, *Moses in the Quran,* 89–92.

14. Freund, *Digging through the Bible,* 141.

15. Bromiley, *International Standard Bible Encyclopedia,* vol. 2.

16. Rabbi Heshy Grossman in the *Weekly Parsha.*

17. Vogüé, *Les eglises de la Terre Sainte,* 322; see also Pixner, "Jerusalem's Essene Gateway," 18–22.

18. Pinkerfield, *Bishvili Omanut Yehudit.*

19. Grousset, *Histoire des Croisades,* vol. III, xiv; and de Sede, cited in Baigent, Leigh, and Lincoln, *Holy Blood, Holy Grail,* 112.

20. William of Tyre, *History of Deeds.*

21. Gardner, *Bloodline of the Holy Grail,* chap. 18, note 1.

22. In Baigent, Leigh, and Lincoln, *Holy Blood, Holy Grail,* see notes on chap. 51.

23. Gardner, *Bloodline of the Holy Grail;* also discussed in Baigent, Leigh, and Lincoln, *Holy Blood, Holy Grail.*

24. See Fredegar's *Chronicle,* seventh century, cited in Gardner, *Bloodline of the Holy Grail,* 142.

25. Gardner, *Bloodline of the Holy Grail,* 146.

26. Pinkham, *Guardians of the Holy Grail,* 132–33.

27. Ibid.; Baigent, Leigh, and Lincoln, *Holy Blood, Holy Grail,* 245–49; and Gardner, *Bloodline of the Holy Grail,* 145–50.

28. William of Tyre, *History of Deeds,* 380.

29. Baigent, Leigh, and Lincoln, *Holy Blood, Holy Grail,* 107.

30. Matthew of Edessa, *Armenia and the Crusades.*

31. Grousset, *Histoire des Croisades,* xiv.

32. Ibid.; and Sede, cited in Baigent, Leigh, and Lincoln, *Holy Blood, Holy Grail,* 112.

33. Cited Vogüé, *Les eglises de la Terre Sainte,* 323. Dated July 19, 1116.
34. Röhricht, *Regesta regni hierosolymitani,* 19, no. 83.

CHAPTER 9. 1114.
BRAGA. A VERY OLD CITY
IN PORTUGALE . . .

1. Herculano, *Historia de Portugal,* book 1, 230.
2. Cunha, *Historia ecclisiastica de Braga,* pt. 1, chap. 1.
3. Cited in Freitas, *Memorias de Braga,* 88–89.
4. Gordon, *Prehistoric London,* 5.
5. Cited in Freitas, *Memorias de Braga,* 8.
6. i.e., Freitas, *Memorias de Braga,* 88.
7. This name comes from the Chaldean god Belinus and the Babylonian Oannes, later Janus of the Romans. See, for example, William Betham's discussion in Fraser, *Proceedings of the Numismatic Society.*
8. Sulpicius Severus, *Chronica II,* 46.
9. McKenna, *Paganism and Pagan Survivals.*
10. Cited in Freitas, *Memorias de Braga,* 21.
11. Freitas, *Memorias de Braga,* 31–34. This occurred in 1103.
12. Ibid., 32.
13. Secco, *Escrituras de Thomar,* book 1, 5; and cited in Viterbo, *Elucidario das palavras,* 232.
14. Schaeffer, *Histoire de Portugal,* 37.
15. Vincent, *Histoire de l'anciene image miraculeuse,* 92.
16. Hamblett, in Olsen, *Templar Papers,* 39.
17. Latrie, *Chronique d'Ernoul,* 7–9.
18. Johann Starck, cited in Haagensen and Lincoln, *Templars' Secret Island.*
19. Latrie, *Chronique d'Ernoul.*
20. Map, *De nugis curialium,* 1.18, 54–55; and cited Barber and Bate, *Templars: Selected Sources,* 29–30.
21. i.e., Viterbo, *Elucidario das palavras.*
22. See Figueiredo, *Historia da Militaria Ordem de Malta,* 15.
23. Ibid., 28.
24. Ibid., 61–62.
25. Ibid., 66. Made in October 1123, deed in Maço da Frequesia do Rio de Gallinhas, no. 7.

26. Ibid., 63. In 1144, the monastery of Freiras de Aguas Santas.
27. Viterbo, *Elucidario das palavras,* 234.
28. Figueiredo, *Historia da Militaria Ordem de Malta,* 107.
29. Herculano, *Historia de Portugal,* book 1, 230.
30. Cited Viterbo, *Elucidario das palavras,* 233. Quote by the fourth Templar Master in Portugal.

CHAPTER 10. 1100.
JERUSALEM. IN THE PALACE
OF THE NEW KING . . .

1. William of Tyre, *History of Deeds.*
2. Barber, *New Knighthood.*
3. Smail, *Crusading Warfare,* chap. 5.
4. Brownlow, *Account of the Pilgrimage,* 8–9; also cited Barber, *Origins of the Order,* 220.
5. Latrie, *Chronique d'Ernoul.*

CHAPTER 11. 1100.
BRAGA. HEARING FOREIGN VOICES . . .

1. i.e., Reis, "O foral de Guimarães," note 106.
2. A property deed by Dona Sancha Viegas, the buyer being "a Friar of the Temple" by the name of Petrus Arnaldo, dated 1185 era of Caesar, equivalent to AD 1147; also cited Paraschi, *Historia dos Templarios em Portugal,* 10.
3. Ferreira, *Memorias e noticias historicas,* 751–52, 840.
4. Viterbo, *Elucidario das palavras.*
5. Ferreira, *Memorias e noticias historicas,* 808.
6. See article on Geoffroy de la Roche by Didier, *History of La Roche Vanneau,* ref. 194.
7. Röhricht, *Regesta regni hierosolymitani,* 19, no. 83.
8. Ibid.
9. Ferreira, *Memorias e noticias historicas,* 720, 749.
10. Sousa, Manuel de Faria e, *Europa Portugueza,* book 3, pt. 4, chap. 8, no. 13.
11. Brito, *Monarchia Lusytana,* IX, 81.
12. The number of eleven original knights was also cited by Ward, *Freemasonry and the Ancient Gods,* 204.

CHAPTER 12. 1117.
BETHLEHEM. AT A CEREMONY . . .

1. Baigent, Leigh, and Lincoln, *Holy Blood, Holy Grail,* 116.
2. Fulcher de Chartres, *Fulcheri carnotensis historia hierosolymitana.*
3. Ibid.
4. Michael the Syrian, *Chronique de Michel le Syrien.*
5. Saint Bruno, *Lettres des premiers Chartreux,* 154–61.
6. *Encyclopedia Brittanica,* 591; also cited Hancock, *Sign and the Seal,* 93.
7. William of Tyre, *History of Deeds,* 12.7, 553–55.
8. Johann Starck, cited in Haagersen and Lincoln, *Templars' Secret Island*; and Hamblett, in Olsen, *Templar Papers,* 28–29.
9. Latrie, *Chronique d'Ernoul,* 7–9; and cited in Barber and Bate, *Templars: Selected Sources.*
10. Charpentier, *Secrets of Chartres Cathedral,* 59.
11. d'Albon, *Cartulaire général,* 99, no. 141.
12. Wilson, cited in Knight and Lomas, *Hiram Key,* 29.
13. Delaforge, *Templar Tradition.*
14. Cited in Barber and Bate, *Templars: Selected Sources,* 30; and Hamblett, in Olsen, *Templar Papers,* 26.
15. Santos, José António, *Monumentos das ordens militares,* 1, quest. 2, 5, 6; and cited in Ferreira, *Memorias e noticias historicas,* pt. 1, p. 10.
16. Petel, *La commanderie de Payns,* x.
17. Bouquet, *Recueil des historiens,* 162, no. 245; and Jubainville, *Histoire de Bar-sur-Aube,* 113–14, no. 1.
18. Hopkins, Simmans, and Wallace-Murphy, *Rex Deus,* 114.
19. Lalore, C., *Collection des principeaux cartularies,* no. 3; and *Capitulaire de l'Abbaye de Montiéramey,* Paris, no. 18 (1890): 11–14, 23–25. The transactions were each witnessed by a Hugo de Peanz and a Hugo de Paeniciis. It was common in those days for a name to differ in writing according to dialect and the type of language used. Payns was written Péanz, Paens, Paence, Paenz, Paains, Paiens, and Payens in French, and its variants in Latin were Pagani, Paganus, Peancium, Paencia, and Paentium. See Socard, and Boutiot, *Dictionnaire topographique de l'aube,* 118–19.
20. Father Tamburino, cited in Ferreira, *Memorias e noticias historicas,* pt. 1, p. 13.
21. Gérard de Sède, cited in Baigent, Leigh and Lincoln, *Holy Blood, Holy Grail,* 111.
22. Hamblett, cited in Olsen, *Templar Papers,* 27.

23. Röhricht, *Regesta regni hierosolymitani*, 19, no. 83.
24. Ibid., 25, no. 105.

CHAPTER 13. 1117.
GUIMARÃES. IN THE COURT OF
COUNTESS TAREJA . . .

1. Figueiredo, *Historia da Militaria Ordem de Malta,* 109. A bill of sale for a property in Pega by Mayor Judia is made to "Dom Paayo de Leça": two similar transactions state the same. His name appears again on a donation of Leça made "to the Hospital."
2. Ibid., 107.
3. Freitas, *Memorias de Braga,* 141.
4. Ibid., 31–34.
5. By 1122.
6. Biggs, *Diego Gelmirez,* 43, 121–22.
7. Freitas, *Memorias de Braga,* 36; and Viterbo, *Elucidario das palavras,* 234.
8. Mann and Hollnsteiner, *Lives of the Popes,* 294.
9. Brandão, *Monarchia Lusitana,* 373.
10. Reilly, *Kingdom of Leon-Castilla,* 245.
11. i.e., Brandão, *Monarchia Lusitana,* 375, 377.
12. Secco, *Escrituras de Thomar,* 5; and Viterbo, *Elucidario das palavras,* vol. II, 581–83.
13. Figueiredo, *Historia da Militaria Ordem de Malta,* 107. Document in the registry of the monastery of Paço de Sousa dated 1145, in which they are referred to as Order of the Hospital.
14. Ibid., 106.
15. Herculano, *Historia de Portugal,* 278.
16. Ibid.

CHAPTER 14. 1126.
CLAIRVAUX. A VERY, VERY, VERY
MODEST ABBEY IN CHAMPAGNE . . .

1. Sucena, *A epopeia Templaria e Portugal.*
2. d'Albon, *Cartulaire général,* 1–2, no. 2.
3. Ibid, 1, no. 1; cited in Howarth, *Knights Templar,* 50.

4. Leclercq, "Un document," 81–91. The letter is likely by Hugues de Payns circa 1128, while soliciting in Europe.

5. Ibid.

6. Roserot, *Dictionnaire historique,* 1096. Hugues's family had at least seven land holdings, including one in Troyes.

7. Ferreira, *Memorias e noticias historicas,* pt. 1, 3.

8. According to Lobineau, *Dossiers secrets,* planche no. 4; and cited in Baigent, Leigh, and Lincoln, *Holy Blood, Holy Grail,* 116.

9. Viterbo, *Elucidario das palavras,* 582–83; cited in Paraschi, *Historia dos Templarios em Portugal,* 20–22; and Lamy, *Les Templiers.*

10. Williams, *Saint Bernard of Clairvaux,* 3.

11. Leclercq, "Un document," 15.

12. Gardner, *Bloodline of the Holy Grail,* 212.

13. Jubainville, *Histoire de Bar-sur-Aube,* XXIII, and Jubainville, *Histoire de ducs et comtes,* 80–89.

14. Jubainville, *Histoire de Bar-sur-Aube,* 103.

15. Jubainville, *Histoire de ducs et comtes,* 87.

16. Hopkins, Simmans, and Wallace-Murphy, *Rex Deus,* 114.

17. Jubainville, *Histoire de ducs et comtes,* 110.

18. Auberger, *L'Unanimite cistercienne primitive,* 103–7.

19. Begg, *Cult of the Black Virgin,* 103.

20. Jolibois, *Haute-Marne;* also in Didier, *History of La Roche Vanneau.*

21. Guillerme de Saint-Thierry, Arnald de Bonneval, and Geoffrey de Auxerre, *Vita prima sancti Bernardi,* 185, 225–368; and cited in Bredero, *Bernard of Clairvaux,* 198.

22. Rudolph, *Things of Greater Importance,* 10.

23. Van Hecke, *Le desir dans l'experience religieuse,* 44–45.

24. Guillerme de Saint-Thierry, Arnald de Bonneval, and Geoffrey de Auxerre, *Vita prima sancti Bernardi,* book III, ch. iii, 6; Migne, *Patrologia Latina tomus,* 185, 306; and cited in Bredero, *Bernard of Clairvaux,* 14.

25. Webb and Walker, *Saint Bernard of Clairvaux,* 45–46.

26. Epistola 64, c. 2. from Bernard's sermon *In septuagesimo.*

27. Bredero, *Bernard of Clairvaux,* 263.

28. Röhricht, *Regesta regni hierosolymitani,* 25, no. 105. On this same document appears the name Raimund Bernard, who wears the title of Procurator for the Hospitallers.

29. Santa Catarina, *Catalogo dos mestres,* 21.

30. This is implied in the biography by Vallery-Radot, *Bernard des Fontaines;* also cited in Page, *First Global Village.*

CHAPTER 15. SEVEN YEARS EARLIER.
CLAIRVAUX. A SPECIAL MOMENT ON JUNE 24 . . .

1. Brito, *Monarchia Lusytana,* vol. III, book IX, 77–81.
2. Ibid., 109–11.
3. Ibid., 77–81.
4. Ibid., 213.
5. Ibid., 77–81, 109–111.
6. Brito, *Primeira parte,* 338–40.
7. Matos, *A Ordem de Cister.*
8. Brito, *Monarchia Lusytana,* 126. He lists the date as 1124; an augmented charter was made in 1142.

CHAPTER 16. 1125. LATE AUTUMN.
PORTO. DISEMBARKING AFTER
A LONG SEA VOYAGE . . .

1. The Chronicler Catarina.
2. Cited in Viterbo, *Elucidario das palavras,* 233.
3. Figueiredo, *Historia da Militaria Ordem de Malta,* 106–7.
4. Viterbo, *Elucidario das palavras,* vol. II, 231.
5. Schaeffer, *Histoire de Portugal,* 37.
6. Herculano, *Historia de Portugal,* 21–24.
7. i.e., Brandão, *Monarchia Lusitana,* 375–57.
8. Secco, *Escrituras de Thomar,* 5.
9. Ibid.; and Viterbo, *Elucidario das palavras,* vol. II, 231, 581–83.
10. Denis, *Histoire et description,* 27.
11. da Costa, Miguel Manescal, *Definições e estatuto,* 23–24, the document, which by this time had disappeared, was in Torre do Tombo; transcript in Brandão, *Monarchia Lusitana,* 356.
12. Viterbo, *Elucidario das palavras,* 583.
13. da Costa, Bernardo, *Historia da Militar Ordem de Nosso Senhor Jesus Christo,* 2–3.
14. Facta Carta II, Doc. de Tomar, cited in Viterbo, *Elucidario das palavras,* 233.

The original document is dated 1114. The date on the document is 1152, but in the Iberian Peninsula of the twelfth century, documents were dated "era of Caesar"; only on August 22, 1422, was "anno domini" fully adopted in Portugal. This makes most documents of the period off by thirty-eight years relative to our established calendar, thus the donation was made to the Knights of the Temple in 1114.

15. Hopkins, Simmans, and Wallace-Murphy, *Rex Deus,* 113.

16. Viterbo, *Elucidario das palavras,* vol. II, 582–3; and Lamy, cited in Paraschi, *Historia dos Templarios em Portugal,* 20–22.

17. According to Lobineau, *Dossiers secrets,* planche 4; and cited in Baigent, Leigh, and Lincoln, *Holy Blood, Holy Grail,* 116.

18. da Costa, Bernardo, *Historia da Militar Ordem de Nosso Senhor Jesus Christo,* 3.

19. Cited in Viterbo, *Elucidario das palavras,* 232.

20. Secco, *Escrituras de Thomar,* part II; and cited in Viterbo, *Elucidario das palavras.*

21. da Costa, Bernardo, *Historia da Militar Ordem de Nosso Senhor Jesus Christo,* 16.

22. Santa Catarina, *Catalogo dos mestres.*

23. da Costa, Bernardo, *Historia da Militar Ordem de Nosso Senhor Jesus Christo,* 1; and Viterbo, *Elucidario das palavras,* 233.

24. *Livro dos mestrados,* gaveta 7, maço 9, Torre do Tombo, copied in vol. 38.

25. Figueiredo, *Historia da Militaria Ordem de Malta.*

26. Brito, *Monarchia Lusytana,* vol. III, book IX, 81.

CHAPTER 17. 1127. AUTUMN.
ABOARD A GALLEY IN THE MEDITERRANEAN . . .

1. Esquieu, "Les Templiers de Cahors," 147.

2. Hopkins, Simmans, and Wallace-Murphy, *Rex Deus,* 114.

3. Leroy, *Hugues de Payns.*

4. Gardner, *Bloodline of the Holy Grail,* 242.

5. *Fontes rarum Austriacarum,* t. XIII, no. 41, 94, cited in Rey, *Les familles d'outre-mer,* 870.

6. Barber, *Trial of the Templars,* 8; and Barber, *New Knighthood,* 12.

7. Santa Catarina, *Catalogo dos mestres;* and Paraschi, *Historia dos Templarios em Portugal,* 29.

8. Carrière, *Les débuts de l'Ordre du Temple,* 311–12.

9. Sucena, *A epopeia Templaria e Portugal.*

CHAPTER 18. 1128. APRIL.
BRAGA. AN OFFICE WHERE LOTS
OF DOCUMENTS ARE SIGNED . . .

1. Barbosa, Ignacio, *Monumentos de Portugal,* 127–28.

2. Viterbo, *Elucidario das palavras,* 232.

3. Ibid., 585.

4. Herculano, *Historia de Portugal,* 470.

5. da Costa, Bernardo, *Historia da Militar Ordem de Nosso Senhor Jesus Christo,* 6.

6. Herculano, *Historia de Portugal,* 212–14; and Schaeffer, *Histoire de Portugal,* 37.

7. Viterbo, *Elucidario das palavras.*

8. Brito, *Monarchia Lusytana,* 128–130.

9. Secco, *Escrituras de Thomar,* 5.

10. Brito, *Monarchia Lusytana,* vol. III, book IX, 81; and Brandão, *Monarchia Lusitana,* 355.

CHAPTER 19. 1128. JANUARY.
A MAJOR GATHERING AT TROYES,
A TOWN IN CHAMPAGNE . . .

1. See controversial discussion in Barber, *New Knighthood,* 9.

2. Esquieu, "Les Templiers de Cahors," 147.

3. Phillips, *Defenders of the Holy Land,* 21–28.

4. Hefele and Leclercq, *Histoire des conciles,* pt. 1, 668.

5. James, *Letters of St. Bernard of Clairvaux.*

6. Bernard de Clairvaux, *Episcolae,* in Bernard de Clairvaux, Leclercq, Talbot, and Rochais, *Sancti Bernardi Opera,* vol. III, no. XXI, col. 123.

7. Bernard de Clairvaux, Leclercq, Talbot, and Rochais, *Sancti Bernardi Opera.*

8. Bernard de Clairvaux, *Textes politiques,* 202.

9. David, Charles Wendell, *De expugnatione Lyxbonensi,* 117.

10. Curzon, *La règle du temple.*

11. Cited in Barber, *Origins of the Order,* 231.

12. Curzon, *La règle du temple.*

CHAPTER 20. 1128.
BACK IN CLAIRVAUX UPON
THE CONCLUSION OF THE CONCLAVE . . .

1. Migne, *Patrologia Latina tomus,* 182, col. 921.

2. Barber, *Trial of the Templars,* 10.

3. Charpentier, *Secrets of Chartres Cathedral,* 74.

4. Gardner, *Bloodline of the Holy Grail,* 147.

5. Harrison, *Prolegomena to the Study of Greek Religion,* 91.

6. Anderssohn, *Ancestry and Life of Godfrey of Bouillon,* 9; and Baigent, Leigh, and Lincoln, *Holy Blood, Holy Grail,* 107.

7. Lobineau, *Dossiers secrets;* and cited in Baigent, Leigh, and Lincoln, *Holy Blood, Holy Grail,* 116.

8. Bernard, *Epistolae,* vol. III, ep. 359, 305. In 1126.

9. i.e., Valery-Radot, Merton et al.

10. Lay, *The Reconquest Kings of Portugal,* 63.

11. Brito, *Primeira parte,* pt. 1, book 5, chap. 3.

12. Brito, *Monarchia Lusytana,* 253–57; dated April 27, 1143, the document is in the monastery of Alcobaça.

13. Ibid., 214–16.

14. Ibid.

15. i.e,. Michelet, *Le proces des Templiers,* 124.

16. Cited in Charpentier, *Secrets of Chartres Cathedral,* 65–66.

17. Gardner, *Bloodline of the Holy Grail,* 232–36.

18. Figueiredo, *Historia da Militaria Ordem de Malta,* 44.

19. Ibid., 27–28.

20. Ibid.

21. Figueiredo, José Anastasio, *Historia da Militar Ordem de Malta,* 44. Donation made by Countess Tareja and probably Afonso Henriques himself, July 28, 1122; he cites Santa Catarina, *Malta Portuguesa,* book II, 31–32, 59, 371; Figueiredo, *Historia da Militar Ordem de Malta,* 118; Figueiredo points out that in the homestead of Gontemir there lived twelve men at the time Master Dom Raimundo was Templar Master in Portugal, and since one-third of the property was owned by the Knights Hospitaller, it was also defended

by them; one-third was owned by the Order of the Temple. In 1134, Afonso Henriques expanded the donation to include the hermitage of S. Pedro da Cova in Gondomare. Cited in Mattoso, *Lusitania Sacra,* 12.

22. Brito, *Monarchia Lusytana,* 27.

23. Viterbo, *Elucidario das palavras,* vol. II, 582–83; Lamy, cited in Paraschi, *Historia dos Templarios em Portugal,* 20; and Barber, *Origins of the Order,* 228, although he lists him as Spanish.

CHAPTER 21. 1128. APRIL.
A CHAMBER IN THE ROYAL RESIDENCE
OF GUIMARÃES . . .

1. Galvão, *Chronica do D. Affonso Henriques,* 51.

CHAPTER 22. 1128. MEANWHILE IN CHAMPAGNE . . .

1. d'Albon, *Cartulaire général,* no. XXII, 6.
2. Ibid., 1–2; cited Hamblett, in Olsen, *Templar Papers,* 144.
3. Barbosa, Ignacio, *Monumentos de Portugal,* 127–28.
4. Dias, *Os Templarios em terras de Portugal,* 69.
5. Whitelock, Douglas, and Tucker, *Anglo-Saxon Chronicle,* 146–47.
6. See Anderssohn, *Ancestry and Life of Godfrey.*
7. Abbot Aelred of Rievaulx, cited Bob Mander, in Olsen. *Templar Papers,* 181.
8. Barber, *New Knighthood,* 13.
9. i.e., Viterbo, *Elucidario das palavras.*

CHAPTER 23. 1128. JUNE 24.
A BATTLEFIELD OUTSIDE GUIMARÃES . . .

1. Galvão, *Chronica do D. Affonso Henriques,* 51–52.
2. Viterbo, *Elucidario das palavras,* 235.
3. d'Albon, *Cartulaire général,* 1–2.
4. Herculano, *Historia de Portugal,* 493–94, maço 3, no. 8; and Reis, *O foral de Guimarães,* 55–77.
5. Azevedo, *Documentos medievais Portugueses,* vol. 1, 121; and Lay, *Reconquest Kings of Portugal,* 72.
6. i.e., Viterbo, *Elucidario das palavras;* and Secco, *Escrituras de Thomar.*

CHAPTER 24. 1129. MARCH.
AFONSO REVEALS HIMSELF . . .

1. Viterbo, *Elucidario das palavras,* 232.
2. Herculano, *Historia de Portugal,* 470.
3. March 30, 1129. Herculano, *Historia de Portugal,* 470; gaveta 15, maço 8, no. 20; and d'Albon, *Cartulaire général,* no. 10, 7; no. 24, 17.
4. Curzon, *La règle du temple,* 14.

CHAPTER 25. 1139.
OURIQUE. PREPARING TO BATTLE THE MOORS . . .

1. Lay, *Reconquest Kings of Portugal,* 69; and DMP vol. 1, 112.
2. i.e., Mattoso, *Lusitania Sacra,* 75–79.
3. Galvão, *Chronica do D. Affonso Henriques,* 72–73.
4. Ibid.
5. Galvão, *Chronica do D. Affonso Henriques,* 76.
6. Ibid., 77.
7. Jenkins and Sofos, *Nation and Identity,* 155, "A nation-state is a political artifact called into being by nationalist ideology and movement based on common language, religion, history, culture and ethnicity"; 11–15, "Portugal is the oldest nation-state in Europe, dated from as early as 1139."

CHAPTER 26. 1139.
CLAIRVAUX. EARLY DAWN,
OUTSIDE THE CHAPEL . . .

1. Matos, *A Ordem de Cister,* 27.
2. Brito, *Primeira parte,* book III, cap. IV, 249; cited Matos, *A Ordem de Cister,* 28.
3. For example, Herculano, *Historia de Portugal,* book II, 326, note 2; National Archive document gaveta 6, maço 29, dated March 30, 1140; Henric., fasc. 1, xix, cited Williams, *Saint Bernard of Clairvaux,* 64; and Merton, *Bernard de Clairvaux,* 253.
4. Catarina, cited in Paraschi, *Historia dos Templarios em Portugal.*
5. May 24, 1136, according to Barthelemy, *Obituaire de la commanderie,* 321.

6. Cited in da Costa, Bernardo, *Historia da Militar Ordem de Nosso Senhor Jesus Christo,* 15.
7. Viterbo, *Elucidario das palavras,* 236.
8. Ibid.
9. Ibid., 232.

CHAPTER 27. 1867.
JAFFA. A MULE TRAIN HEADING
TOWARD JERUSALEM . . .

1. Wilson and Warren, *Recovery of Jerusalem,* 39.
2. Knight and Lomas, *Second Messiah,* 22–26.
3. Ben-Dov, *Shadow of the Temple.*

CHAPTER 28. 1146.
COIMBRA. AT HOME WITH
AFONSO AND HIS NEW BRIDE . . .

1. Brochado, *D. Afonso Henriques,* 176, citing *Livro dos mestrados,* 61, in Torre do Tombo.
2. i.e., Mattoso, *Ricos homens, infanções e cavaleiros.*
3. Charter listed in d'Albon, *Cartulaire général,* no. 439, 275, dated 1185 era of Caesar.
4. da Costa, Bernardo, *Historia da Militar Ordem de Nosso Senhor Jesus Christo,* 10, "Ugo Martiniensis P. Templi, in iflis partibus Kartulam recepi."
5. Church of Alporão. *Figueiredo,* 120.
6. Guimarães, *A Ordem de Christo,* 9–10.
7. da Costa, Bernardo, *Historia da Militar Ordem de Nosso Senhor Jesus Christo,* 15; and Viterbo, *Elucidario das palavras,* vol. II, 588.
8. Viterbo, *Elucidario das palavras,* vol. II, 236.
9. Ibid., 237.
10. Brito, *Primeira parte,* book III, cap. IV, 249; cited Matos, *A Ordem de Cister,* 27–28.
11. Brito, *Primeira parte,* pt. 1, book 5, chap. 3.
12. In 1138, Henric., fasc. 1, xix, cited Williams, *Saint Bernard of Clairvaux,* 64.
13. Merton, *Thomas Merton on Saint Bernard,* 253.
14. Guimarães, *A Ordem de Christo,* 7.

15. Brito, *Primeira parte,* book III, cap. XI, 325–26.

16. Ibid., pt. 1, book 5, chap. 3.

17. Brito, *Monarchia Lusytana,* 213.

18. In Bernard de Clairvaux, *Apologia.*

19. Brito, *Monarchia Lusytana,* vol. III, book VIII, 34.

20. Santos, Manuel dos, *Alcobaca Illustrada,* folio 3, 60.

21. Page, *First Global Village,* 69–71.

22. Cocheril, *Routier des abbayes Cisterciennes,* 2.

23. Schmolders, *Essai sur les écoles philosophiques,* 54.

CHAPTER 29. 1147. APRIL.
BRAGA. THE MYSTERIOUS PRIOR ARNALDO
IN HIS NEW ABODE . . .

1. cited Viterbo, *Elucidario das palavras,* vol. II, 237. Date is April 1, 1185, era of Caesar, equiv. 1147.

2. Figueiredo, *Historia da Militaria Ordem de Malta,* 114; and Viterbo, *Elucidario das palavras,* vol. II, 237.

3. William of Tyre, "Arnaud, prieur du Mont de Sion 1120," in *History of Deeds,* book I, XII, c. XIII.

4. Sousa, *Europa Portugueza,* pat. 4, chap. 8, no. 13.

5. i.e., Röhricht, *Regesta Regni Hierosolymitani,* 19, no. 83.

6. Viterbo, *Elucidario das palavras,* vol. II, 582–83.

7. Santa Catarina, *Catalogo dos mestres.*

8. Paraschi, *Historia dos Templarios em Portugal,* 30.

9. Ibid.

10. da Costa, *Historia da Militar Ordem de Nosso Senhor Jesus Christo,* 153.

11. Document gaveta VII, maço XI, in Torre do Tombo.

12. Figueiredo, *Historia da Militaria Ordem de Malta,* 113.

CHAPTER 30. 1119.
TEMPLE MOUNT. A TUNNEL,
EIGHTY FEET BENEATH . . .

1. Runciman, *History of the Crusades,* vol. II, 157

2. Addison, *Knights Templars,* 34.

3. Markale, *Templar Treasure at Gisors,* 110.

4. Addison, *Knights Templars*, 34; see Figueiredo, *Historia da Militaria Ordem de Malta*, 1–2.
5. Robinson, *Born in Blood*, 66.

CHAPTER 31. 1147.
BRAGA. GUALDINO PAES ALSO
MOVES INTO HIS NEW DOMICILE . . .

1. d'Albon, *Cartulaire général*, no. 381, 241. Dated 1146.
2. Ibid.
3. In Brito, *Monarchia Lusytana*, IX, 82, document in the Book of Charters in Torre do Tombo, Livro da Leitura Nova, 135; also Brandão, *Monarchia Lusitana*, 356.
4. i.e., Brandão, *Monarchia Lusitana*, 357.
5. Ibid.
6. Also Paraschi, *Historia dos Templarios em Portugal*, 37.
7. Guimarães, *A Ordem de Christo*, 9–10.
8. Ibid., 11; and Viterbo, *Elucidario das palavras*, 590.
9. Cocheril, "Essai sur l'origine des ordres militaires," t. XXI, 310; cited Oliveira, *Castelos Templarios em Portugal 1120-1314*, 82.
10. Ferros, cited in Viterbo, *Elucidario das palavras*, 237.
11. Ibid.
12. In Lizerand, *La dossier de l'affaire*.
13. David, Charles Wendell, *De expugnatione Lyxbonensi*, 69.
14. Ibid.
15. Ibid., 93.
16. James, *Letters of St. Bernard of Clairvaux*, 469.
17. Brito, *Monarchia Lusytana*, vol. III, book VIII, 34; see Murray, *Handbook for Travellers in Portugal*, xxxiiii.
18. Phillips, Jonathan, *Defenders of the Holy Land*, cited in Page, *First Global Village*, 75.
19. Paraschi, *Historia dos Templarios em Portugal*, 43.
20. Charter cited Viterbo, *Elucidario das palavras*, 590; and Almeida, Fernando, *Pedras Visigoticas em Souré*, vol. I, doc. 4.
21. i.e., Almeida, M. Lopes de, *Ferreira da Costa, and Dinis*, doc. 3.
22. Lobineau, cited in Baigent, Leigh, and Lincoln, *Holy Blood, Holy Grail*, 115–17.

CHAPTER 32. 1121.
SAINT-OMER. IN THE HOME OF
A CRYPTOGRAPHER NAMED LAMBERT . . .

1. Knight and Lomas, *Second Messiah*, 83.
2. d'Albon, *Cartulaire general,* no. 295, 193.
3. Plantard, cited in Baigent, Leigh, and Lincoln, *Holy Blood, Holy Grail,* 225. The Ordre de Sion oday operates as Priuré de Sion.

CHAPTER 33. 1947.
QUMRAN. TWO GOATHERDS,
IN A CAVE, BY THE DEAD SEA . . .

1. Knight and Lomas, *Hiram Key,* 260–63.
2. Ibid.
3. i.e., Freitas, *Memorias de Braga,* 40, 79.
4. Vilnay, *Legends of Jerusalem,* 11.
5. Exodus 24:12.
6. See also Gardner, *Bloodline of the Holy Grail.*
7. Acts 7:22.
8. See Zuckerman, *Jewish Princedom in Feudal France.*
9. Wigoder, *Encyclopedia of Judaism,* 583.
10. Gardner, *Bloodline of the Holy Grail,* 260.
11. See, for example, Kaplan, *Sefer Yetzirah;* 199; and Hall, *Secret Teachings of All Ages.*
12. Lamy, *Les Templiers,* 45.
13. Bernard de Clairvaux, *On Consideration,* 163.
14. i.e., Silva, *Common Wealth;* Lawlor, *Sacred Geometry*; and Chritchlow, *Islamic Patterns.*
15. i.e., Scarre and Lawson, *Archaeoacoustics.*
16. i.e., Eneix, "Ancient Architects of Sound"; Jahn, Devereux, and Ibison, "Acoustical Resonances of Assorted Ancient Structures"; Devereux, et al., "Acoustical Properties of Ancient Ceremonial Sites"; and Cook, Pajot, and Leuchter, "Ancient Architectural Acoustic Resonance Patterns and Regional Brain Activity," 95–104.
17. Silva, *Secrets in the Fields.*
18. i.e., Johns, "Excavations at Pilgrim's Castle," 145–64.

19. Wilkinson, Hill, and Ryan, *Jerusalem Pilgrimage 1099–1185*, 294.
20. For example, Ash and Hewitt, *The Science of the Gods;* and Mann, *Sacred Architecture.*
21. Roney-Dougal, *Faery Faith, Green Magic.*
22. Irwin and Highfield, *Daily Telegraph,* December 1998.
23. See, for example, Tompkins, *Secrets of the Great Pyramid;* and Lemesurier, *Decoding the Great Pyramid.*
24. Hufgard, *Saint Bernard of Clairvaux,* 148.
25. Charpentier, *Secrets of Chartres Cathedral,* 75.
26. Deroy, *Bernardus en origenes,* 149–54.
27. Ibid.; and cited in Bredero, *Bernard of Clairvaux,* 275.
28. Hopkins, Simmans, and Wallace-Murphy, *Rex Deus,* 113.
29. Luke 8:10.
30. See also Knight and Lomas, *Hiram Key,* 269.

CHAPTER 34. 1159.
CERAS. A PILE OF RUBBLE NEAR
A DILAPIDATED TOWN . . .

1. Guimarães, *A Ordem de Christo,* 12.
2. da Costa, Migueul Manescal, *Definições e estatuto,* 16.
3. Thirty thousand years according to Sousa, João Maria, *Noticia descriptive,* 235–56.
4. Brito, *Monarchia Lusytana,* vol. II, book VI, 231–5.
5. Barbosa, Ignacio, *Monumentos de Portugal,* 141.
6. As defined in Jones, *Dictionary of Old Testament Proper Names.*
7. Sousa, João Maria, *Noticia descriptiva,* 15–27.
8. Ibid., 43.
9. Ibid., 15–27.
10. Brito, *Monarchia Lusytana,* vol. III, book IX, 111.
11. Barbosa, Ignacio, *Monumentos de Portugal,* 130.
12. See, for example, Gardner, *Bloodline of the Holy Grail,* 102.
13. Sousa, João Maria, *Noticia descriptiva,* 175–6.
14. i.e., Zechariah 14:1–11.
15. I Kings 11:5–7.
16. Soural, 177.
17. Vogüé, *Les eglises de la Terre Sainte,* 322.

18. Barroca, "A Ordem do Templo," 157.

19. See Silva, *Common Wealth*, 98; and Titus Livius, "Auspiciis hanc urbem conditam esse, auspiciis bello ac pace domi militiaeque omnia geri, quis est qui ignoret?" *History of Rome*, 41.

20. Reymond, *Mythological Origin*, 35; Silva, *Common Wealth*, 169–87.

21. Silva, *Common Wealth*, 169–87; Miller and Broadhurst, *Sun and the Serpent*; and Burke, *Seed of Knowledge*.

22. For example, Silva, *Common Wealth*; and Reymond, *Mythological Origin*.

23. Brito, *Monarchia Lusytana*, part 1, cap. 2, num. 10, c19; and cited Ferreira, *Memorias e Noticias*, 727–28.

24. da Costa, Bernardo, *Historia da Militar Ordem de Nosso Senhor Jesus Christo*, 27, 40.

CHAPTER 35. 68 AD.
MOUNT SION. MEN IN WHITE,
HIDING SCROLLS AND OTHER IMPORTANT THINGS . . .

1. See Allegro, *Dead Sea Scrolls*.

2. See Eusebius, *Historia Ecclesiastica;* and the writings of Euthychius, Exarch of Ravenna.

3. See Pixner, "Jerusalem's Essene Gateway."

4. Baigent, Leigh, and Lincoln, *Holy Blood, Holy Grail*, 374.

5. See discussion in Knight and Lomas, *Hiram Key*, 54.

6. Hyppolytus in *The Refutation of All Heresies*. See Peake, *Peake's Commentary on the Bible;* and Knight and Lomas, *Hiram Key*, 72.

7. Daraul, *Secret Societies;* and cited Knight and Lomas, *Hiram Key*, 75.

8. Drower, *Mandeans of Iraq and Iran*, 264.

9. Knight and Lomas, *Hiram Key*, 74–75.

10. Schonfield, *Essene Odyssey*.

11. Ibid.

12. i.e., Burke, *Seed of Knowledge;* and Silva, *Common Wealth*.

13. Hooke, *Myth, Ritual, and Kingship*.

14. Allegro, *Treasure of the Copper Scroll*, 33–55.

15. Ibid., 58.

16. Ibid., 107.

17. Ibid., 84.

18. Ibid., 55.

19. i.e., Fagan and Beck, *Oxford Companion to Archeology,* entry on the "Dead Sea Scrolls."
20. Schonfield, *Essene Odyssey,* 162–65.

CHAPTER 36. 1159.
COIMBRA. THE KING OF PORTUGAL'S DESK, PART I . . .

1. Cited Barber, *Trial of the Templars,* 144–46.

CHAPTER 37. 1159.
COIMBRA. THE KING OF PORTUGAL'S DESK, PART II . . .

1. Ward, *Freemasonry and the Ancient Gods,* 286.
2. See, for example, Thomas, *Religion and the Decline of Magic.*
3. Ibid., 190.
4. i.e., Chatwin, *Songlines.*
5. Thomas, *Religion and the Decline of Magic,* 189.

CHAPTER 38. 1159.
COIMBRA. THE KING OF PORTUGAL'S DESK, PART III . . .

1. Allegro, *Dead Sea Scrolls,* 110.
2. See discussion in Baigent, Leigh, and Lincoln, *Holy Blood, Holy Grail,* 330–38; also Gardner, *Bloodline of the Holy Grail,* 53–59, 142–45.
3. Thiering, *Jesus the Man,* 151; and Gardner, *Bloodline of the Holy Grail,* 85.
4. John II: 1–2; and Baigent, Leigh, and Lincoln, *Holy Blood, Holy Grail,* 337.
5. i.e., Begg, *Cult of the Black Virgin,* 103; Baigent, Leigh, and Lincoln, *Holy Blood, Holy Grail,* 334–38; and Gardner, *Bloodline of the Holy Grail,* 102.
6. Harrison, *Prolegomena to the Study of Greek Religion,* 91.
7. I Samuel 14:27.
8. Proverbs 24:13–14.
9. i.e., Baigent, Leigh, and Lincoln, *Holy Blood Holy Grail.*
10. Runciman, *History of the Crusades,* 286–87.
11. Branco, *Ineditos da cronica,* 37–38.
12. Figueiredo, *Historia da Militaria Ordem de Malta,* ii.
13. Brito, *Monarchia Lusytana,* 214–16; document in the Cistercian abbey of Alcobaça.

14. Luke 8:10.

15. i.e., Knight and Lomas, *Hiram Key.*

16. See, for example, Pagels, *Gnostic Gospels;* also Knight and Lomas, *Hiram Key.*

17. See Gardiner, *Egyptian Grammar;* and Jacq, *Magic and Mystery in Ancient Egypt,* 19.

18. Jarman, *Geoffrey of Monmouth.*

19. Knight and Lomas, *Second Messiah,* 103–8.

20. Godwin, *Holy Grail,* 12–20 (Langue d'Oc spelling).

21. d'Albon, *Cartulaire général,* CXCIV and CXCVI.

22. Knight and Lomas, *Second Messiah,* 114.

23. Barber, *Knight and Chivalry,* 126.

24. Anonymous, *Perlesvaus,* 359.

25. Wolfram von Eschenbach, *Parzival.*

26. Gardner, *Magdalene Legacy,* 142–43.

27. Jenkins and Sofos, *Nation and Identity.*

28. i.e., Gildas, *De exidio et conquestu Britanniae;* and Green, *Concepts of Arthur.*

29. Brito, *Primeira parte.* The chronicler Brito dates the battle to 1158, equivalent to 1120 AD.

30. Ussama ibn Munqiah, twelfth century, cited in Maalouf, *Les Croisades vues par les Arabes.*

31. d'Albon, *Cartulaire général,* CXCIV and CXCVI, July 22 and 25, respectively.

32. Thiering, *Jesus the Man,* 151; and Gardner, *Bloodline of the Holy Grail,* 85.

CHAPTER 39. 1160. MARCH 1.
A DAWN CEREMONY ON THE PROMONTORY
ABOVE THAMAR . . .

1. Lawlor, *Sacred Geometry,* 10.

2. Barroca, "A Ordem do Templo, 179, 196.

3. See also Sousa, João Maria, *Noticia descriptiva,* 103–6.

4. Convent of Christ. See Barbosa, Ignacio, *Monumentos de Portugal,* 132.

5. II Samuel 13:1.

6. Thiering, *Jesus the Man,* 151; and Baigent, Leigh, and Lincoln, *Holy Blood, Holy Grail,* 85. See I Kings 9:18.

7. Budge, *Gods of the Egyptians,* 414–15.

8. *Archivo pittoresco,* 346.
9. Ibid., 345; and Santos, José António, *Monumentos das ordens militares,* 141–49.

CHAPTER 40. PRESENT ERA. APRIL.
INSIDE THE ROTUNDA OF TOMAR . . .

1. *Archivo pittoresco,* 345.
2. Bernard de Clairvaux, *Apologia.*
3. Anonymous, *Secret Societies of the Middle Ages,* 308.
4. Schottmuller, *Der Untergang des Templer-Ordens,* 164.
5. Serbanesco, *Histoire de l'Ordre des Templiers,* 259–66.
6. Danby, *Mishnah.*
7. Allegro, *Dead Sea Scrolls,* 113.
8. See Peake, *Peake's Commentary on the Bible.*
9. Pinkerfield, *Bishvili Omanut Yehudit.*
10. Bromiley, *International Standard Bible Encyclopedia,* vol. 2.
11. Markale, *Templar Treasure at Gisors,* 65.

CHAPTER 41. 1865.
THE VATICAN. POPE PIUS IX
GETS ALL STEAMED UP . . .

1. Pope Pius IX, "The Allocution against the Freemasons," cited in Wright, *Roman Catholicism and Freemasonry,* 137–144; and Pike, "Allocution of Pio Nono," 817.
2. Pope Pius IX, "The Allocution against Freemasons," cited in Wright, *Roman Catholicism and Freemasonry,* 137–144; and Mackenzie, Kenneth, *Royal Masonic Cyclopaedia.*
3. i.e., Pike, "Allocution of Pio Nono."
4. Serbanesco, *Histoire de l'Ordre des Templiers,* 259–66.
5. See Bembo, *Letters and Comments on Pope Leo X;* and Bale, *Acta romanorum pontificum,* where the phrase was published as a satire. And yet, far from being a satirical quote, Pope Leo X's phrase was witnessed and recorded by Cardinal Pietro Bembo and Cardinal Paolo Giovio (De vita leonis decimi). The records of Cardinal Caesar Baronius—a former Vatican librarian and the church's most outstanding historian—provide information of falsification in

Christianity. Concerning Pope Leo's declaration, he wrote, "The Pontiff has been accused of atheism, for he denied God and called Christ, in front of cardinals Pietro Bembo, Jovius and Iacopo Sadoleto and other intimates, 'a fable,' it must be corrected" (*Annales Ecclesiastici,* tomes viii and xi). As noted in the *Catholic Encyclopedia* (Pecci ed., iii, 312–14, passim), the church nullified this destructive quote by arguing that what Leo had meant by "profitable" was "gainful," and by "fable" was "tradition." Hence, it was restated as, "How well Christians have gained from this wonderful tradition of Christ." However, Cardinal Bembo, the pope's secretary for seven years, added that Leo "was known to disbelieve Christianity itself. He advanced contrary to the faith and that in condemning the Gospel, therefore he must be a heretic."

6. Pagels, *Gnostic Gospels,* 23, 100.

7. Ibid., 19.

8. Barber, *Trial of the Templars,* 62; and Baigent, Leigh, and Lincoln, *Holy Blood, Holy Grail,* 76–82.

9. Broadhurst, *Green Man.*

10. In Gordon, *Prehistoric London.*

11. Vermes, *Complete Dead Sea Scrolls,* 86.

12. Haskins, *Mary Magdalene,* 35–37.

13. See also Knight and Lomas, *Hiram Key,* 269.

14. See for example, Drower, *Mandeans of Iraq and Iran.*

15. i.e., Roberts, *Journey of the Magi,* 282

16. Baigent, Leigh, and Lincoln, *Messianic Legacy,* 92.

17. Roberts, *Journey of the Magi,* 278.

18. Silva, *Lost Art of Resurrection.*

19. Michael, *Forgotten Monarchy of Scotland,* 61.

20. i.e., Scarre and Lawson, *Archaeoacoustics;* Ostrander, *Psychic Discoveries,* 1070; Silva, *Common Wealth;* Merz, *Points of Cosmic Energy;* and Jahn, "Acoustical Resonances of Assorted Ancient Structures."

CHAPTER 42. PRESENT ERA. APRIL.
BY THE ROTUNDA, AMID THE
SECRETS OF THE BEEHIVE . . .

1. Santos, José António, *Monumentos das ordens militares,* 142; and *Archivo pittoresco,* 345.

2. Santos, José António, *Monumentos das ordens militares,* 142.

3. Sousa, João Maria, *Noticia descriptiva,* 50; and *Archivo pittoresco,* 345.

4. Sousa, João Maria, *Noticia descriptiva,* 180–81.

5. Guinguand, *L'Or des Templiers,* 67.

6. Cited Paraschi, *Portugal magico dos Templarios,* 44–45.

7. Ibid.

8. Ricardo Branco, cethomar.blogspot.com/2007/02/o-tesouro-dos-templrios
-em-tomar_09.html.

9. Wilson, *Ordnance Survey of Jerusalem.*

10. Silva, *Common Wealth,* 219–27, op. cit.

11. For example, Bauval, *Heaven's Mirror;* and Charpentier, *Secrets of Chartres
Cathedral.*

12. Silva, *Common Wealth;* and Lubicz, *Temple of Man.*

13. Silva, *Common Wealth.*

14. Mackey, *Encyclopedia of Freemasonry.*

15. Gardner, *Bloodline of the Holy Grail,* 261.

16. Markale, *Templar Treasure at Gisors,* 66.

17. See Baigent, Leigh, and Lincoln, *Holy Blood, Holy Grail,* 122.

18. Ibid.

19. Oliver, *Historical Landmarks,* 5.

20. IN: *E: M: CL: VIII, era of Caesar 1198 or 1160 AD.* José Hermano Saraiva,
cited in Ricardo Branco, "Descobertas em Tomar," cethomar.blogspot
.com/2008/08/descobertas-em-tomar.html, August 13, 2008.

21. Recounted by Scaliburis and posted in http://cethomar.blogspot
.com/2009/07/porta-do-hades.html, March 7, 2009.

22. Ibid.

23. Ibid.

24. Ibid.

25. Ibid.

CHAPTER 43. PRESENT ERA. APRIL.
MUSING OUTSIDE THE BEEHIVE . . .

1. Stevenson, *Origins of Freemasonry,* 83.

2. Ferris, *Coming of Age,* 85.

3. Ibid., 79.

4. Christianson, *In the Presence of the Creator,* 362.

5. Ibid., 256–62

6. In Newton, *Principia.*

7. Baigent, Leigh, and Lincoln, *Holy Blood, Holy Grail,* 131.

8. Keynes, "Newton, the Man," 27–29.

9. Yates, *Giordani Bruno,* 115.

10. Hourani, *History of the Arab Peoples.*

11. See Bauval, *Heaven's Mirror.*

12. Murray, *Handbook for Travellers in Portugal,* 84.

CHAPTER 44. 1165.
MONSANTO. PECULIAR BEHAVIOR
ON AN UNUSUAL HILL . . .

1. i.e., Lubicz, *Temple of Man;* Bauval, *Heaven's Mirror.*

2. Reid, *Egyptian Sonics,* 16.

3. Jahn, Devereux, and Ibison, "Acoustical Resonances of Assorted Ancient Structures"; Cook, Pajot, and Leuchter, "Ancient Architectural Acoustic Resonance Patterns and Regional Brain Activity," 95–104.

4. Ibid.

CHAPTER 45. PRESENT ERA.
MONSANTO. AND OTHER PLACES FOR MUSING . . .

1. Migne, "Exhortatorius sermo," in *Patrologia Latina tomus,* 185, 320; and Migne, in Upton-Ward, *Rule of the Templars,* 166, 853–76.

2. Cited Barber, *Trial of the Templars,* 8.

3. Also observed by Olsen, *Templar Papers,* 108.

4. See Mackenzie, Donald Alexander, *Wonder Tales.*

5. Sousa, Manuel de Faria e, *Europa Portugueza,* 44.

6. Almeida, Fernando, "Templo de Venus em Idanha-a-Velha," 133–39.

7. Ibid.

8. Boletim da D.G.E.M.N., 25.

9. For example, Burke, *Seed of Knowledge.*

10. i.e., Miller and Broadhurst, *Dance of the Dragon;* Cowan and Arnold, *Ley Lines and Earth Energies;* and Pierre Mereaux, *Des pierres pour les vivants;* and Brooker, "Magnetism and Standing Stones."

11. Howells, *Heathens.*

12. Phillips, Tony, "Magnetic Portals."

13. Reymond, *Mythological Origin,* 35.

14. For example, Silva, *Common Wealth;* and Miller and Broadhurst, *Sun and the Serpent.*

15. Wilhelm, *I Ching,* 39.

16. Brooker, "Magnetism and Standing Stones."

17. Merz, *Points of Cosmic Energy,* 32–33.

18. Ibid., 31.

19. Burke, *Seed of Knowledge,* 129.

20. Pierre Mereaux, *Des pierres pour les vivants,* 138.

21. Devereux, *Earth Memory,* 168; and Burke, *Seed of Knowledge,* 126–29.

22. Burke, *Seed of Knowledge,* 126.

23. Persinger, Ruttan, and Koren, "Enhancement of Temporal Lobe–Related Experiences," 33–45; and cited Silva, *Common Wealth,* 192.

24. Roney-Dougal, *Faery Faith, Green Magic,* 10–40; and May, "Review of the Psychoenergetic Research."

25. Serviço Meteorológico de Portugal, 1962.

26. Murray, *Handbook for Travellers in Portugal,* xxxiiii.

27. Strabo, "Lapides multis in locis ternos."

CHAPTER 46. 1147.
SINTRA. A FUNNY THING HAPPENS
ON THE WAY TO THE CASTLE . . .

1. Juromenha, *Cintra pinturesca,* 134.

2. al-Qazwini, *'Ajā'ib al-makhlūqāt wa gharā'ib al-mawjūdāt.*

3. Account of Abilio Duarte, cited in Adrião, *Sintra, serra sagrada.*

4. *O Domingo Ilustrado* 2, no. 57.

5. Juromenha, *Cintra pinturesca,* 134.

6. Ibid.

7. da Costa, Miguel Manescal, *Definiçôes e estatuto.*

8. *Livro dos mastrados,* fl. 66, Order of Christ, cod. no. 233, fl. CXXXIII, and cod. no. 235, fl. 68, v., now in National Archives of Torre do Tombo.

9. ANTT, gaveta 1, maço. 2, no. 18, Torre do Tombo.

10. Ibid. Undated, but linked to the reign of Afonso II circa 1220. Nearby Freixal was also granted to the Hospitallers in 1195. See *Sintra e Seu Concelho,* vol. 1, 39.

11. *Chancelaria de D. Fernando,* 70.

CHAPTER 47. PRESENT ERA.
SINTRA. IN THE FOREST OF ANGELS . . .

1. Serbanesco, *Histoire de l'Ordre des Templiers,* 300–307.
2. Attributed to Roncelin de Fos, but it was already in circulation by 1240.
3. See also article 29, "Rule of the Elected Brothers," in Serbanesco, *Histoire de l'Ordre des Templiers,* 259–66.
4. Cited Upton-Ward, *Rule of the Templars,* 92.
5. Ibid.
6. Serbanesco, *Histoire de l'Ordre des Templiers,* article 18, 302.
7. Ibid., article 5, 300.
8. See *Cyntrão,* no. 6, 1912.
9. i.e., Silva, *Common Wealth;* Mereaux, *Carnac: Des Pierres Pour Les Vivants;* Miller and Broadhurst, *Dance of the Dragon;* Burke, *Seed of Knowledge.*
10. Gandra, *O eterno feminino.*
11. See, for example, the survey conducted in 1962 by the Serviço Meteorológico de Portugal.
12. Leal, *Portugal antigo e moderno,* 301.
13. Osbernus, account in David, Charles Wendell, *De expugnatione Lyxbonensi.*
14. See Juromenha, *Cintra pinturesca,* 10–12.
15. Strabo, "Lapides multis in locis ternos."
16. Royal charter of August 18, 1281, chancellory of D. Dinis, 1. 1. º, fl. 35.
17. Morgado, Augusto, *Epoca,* August 12, 1972.
18. Associação Portuguesa Para a Investigação, www.gigi.pt (accessed June 9, 2017).
19. Cited David, Charles Wendell, *De expugnatione Lyxbonensi,* 93.
20. Mackenzie, Kenneth, *Royal Masonic Cyclopaedia,* 325, 593–94, 719–22; Tucket, *Origin of the Additional Degrees,* 10; Thory, *Acta latomorum ou chronologie de l'histoire de la Franche-maconnerie Francaise et etrangere,* 52; and Baigent, Leigh, and Lincoln, *Temple and the Lodge,* 194.
21. Pereira, Pereira, and Anes, *Quinta da Regaleira,* 82.

CHAPTER 48. PRESENT ERA. APRIL.
IN THE SHADOW OF A STATUE IN TOMAR . . .

1. Brito, *Primeira parte,* 214–16.
2. Matthews, *Grail,* 12.
3. See study in Pagani, "Ethiopian Genetic Diversity."

4. See Hancock, *Sign and the Seal.*

5. Quadros, *Memorias das origens,* 326–39.

CHAPTER 49. 1153.
GOSSIP IN THE ALLEYWAYS
OF JERUSALEM . . .

1. Otto of Friesing, *Historia de duabus civitatibus,* vol. VII.

2. *Encyclopedia Britannica,* 306.

3. From *Legatio Dauid Aethiopia Regis;* and Góis, *Fides, religio, moresque Aethiopum.*

4. See discussion in Hancock, *Sign and the Seal,* 80–83

5. Pirenne, "Des Grecs à l'aurore de la culture monumentale Sabéenne," AP 257, in Fahd, *L'Arabie preislamique.*

6. *Jewish Encyclopedia,* 497.

7. Hancock, *Sign and the Seal,* 115.

8. Sergew, *Ancient and Medieval Ethiopian History,* 265.

9. Daehnhardt, *Paginas secretas da historia de Portugal,* 54.

CHAPTER 50. 1312.
SOUTHERN PORTUGAL. THE TEMPLARS ENJOY
A SIX-YEAR VACATION . . .

1. Figueiredo, *Historia da Militaria Ordem de Malta,* 116.

2. Inquisitions of 1314.

3. Cardinale, *Orders of Knighthood,* 27. Confirmed in the bull *Ad ea exquibus* by Pope John XXII, March 14, 1319.

4. Ibid.

5. Cited Hancock, *Sign and the Seal,* 168.

6. Prestage, *Portuguese Pioneers,* 170.

7. Baigent and Leigh, *Temple and the Lodge,* 131.

8. See Roux, 1; and Baigent and Leigh, *Temple and the Lodge,* 118–20. A bull of 1178 from Pope Alexander III also officially confirms the Order's possessions. The original charters by the French king are in the town's municipal archives (Archives du Loiret, serie D.357). See also Rey, *Les familles d'outre-mer,* 31ff; and *Le maire, historie et antiquitez,* pt. 2, chap. xxvi, 96ff. See also Charnier, *Guide des archives du Loiret,* 86. The

Order was officially registered with the French police on June 25, 1956, in the *Journal Officiel,* a weekly government publication in which all societies and organizations must declare themselves. The address in the sub-prefecture of Saint Julien-en-Genevois is untraceable. Other documents detailing the factual existence of the Priuré de Sion are found in *Le livre des constitutions.*

9. Baigent and Leigh, *Temple and the Lodge,* 122.

10. Daehnhardt, *Paginas secretas,* 41–62.

11. Prestage, *Portuguese Pioneers,* 215–16.

12. Ibid., 168–70.

13. Ibid., 27.

14. Ibid., 154.

15. Alvarez, *Prester Joam das Indias.*

16. In Ariosto, *Orlando furioso.*

17. Daehnhardt, *Paginas secretas,* 37.

18. Alvarez, *Prester Joam das Indias.*

19. Ibid.

20. Ibid.

21. Alvarez, *Prester Joam das Indias;* and Beckhingham and Huntingford, *Prester John of the Indies.*

22. Alvarez, *Prester Joam das Indias;* and Beckhingham and Huntingford, *Prester John of the Indies,* 226–27.

23. Ibid.

CHAPTER 51. PRESENT ERA.
AKSUM. A FEAST DAY WHEN THE TABOTAT
ARE SEEN IN DAYLIGHT . . .

1. See Hancock, *Sign and the Seal,* 3–8.

2. Dimotheos, *Deux ans de sejour en Abyssinie,* 141–43.

3. West, *Traveler's Key to Ancient Egypt,* 236.

4. Sayce, *Fresh Light from the Ancient Monuments,* 67–68.

5. Morgenstern, *Ark, the Ephod and the Tent Meeting,* 121.

6. Hancock, *Sign and the Seal,* 428–48.

7. Ullendorff, "Hebraic-Jewish Elements," 253.

CHAPTER 53. PRESENT ERA.
A CIRCULAR HALL IN A SMALL COUNTRY
NAMED PORTUGAL . . .

1. Paraschi, *Portugal magico dos Templarios,* 58.
2. Pritchard, *Recovering Serepta,* 314.
3. Paraschi, *Portugal magico dos Templarios,* 59.

EPILOGUE. LUSITANIA.
"A PLACE WHERE THE KNOWLEDGE IS STORED,"
PRESIDED OVER BY A GODDESS WHOSE SYMBOL
IS AN ISOSCELES TRIANGLE . . .

1. d'Albon, *Cartulaire général,* no. 194, 135–36.
2. Sède, *Les Templiers sont parmi nous.*
3. Butler and Dafoe, *Warriors and the Bankers,* 206.
4. i.e., Figueiredo, *Historia da Militaria Ordem de Malta.*
5. Lamy, *Les Templiers.*
6. Guinguand, *L'Or des Templiers.*
7. Seward, *Monks of War,* 205.
8. Stewart, *Forgotten Monarchy of Scotland.*
9. St. Clair, *Histoire genealogique;* and cited in Hopkins, Simmans, and Wallace-Murphy, *Rex Deus,* 108.
10. Ibid.
11. Knight and Lomas, *Second Messiah,* 114.
12. Cowan, Mackay, and Macquarrie, *Knights of St. John,* lxviii.
13. Ritchie, *Crétien de Troyes and Scotland,* 18.
14. Cited Baigent and Leigh, *Temple and the Lodge,* 82.
15. Ibid., 111.
16. See Coppens, *Stone Puzzle of Rosslyn Chapel.*
17. Wallace-Murphy and Hopkins, *Guardian of the Secrets,* 7.
18. Forbes, *Account of Roslin,* 28.
19. Warren, *Temple or the Tomb,* 163–65; and Wilson and Warren, *Recovery of Jerusalem.*
20. Cited Knight and Lomas, *Second Messiah,* 70.
21. Silva, *Common Wealth,* 33–41.
22. Ibid.

23. Baigent, Leigh, and Lincoln, *Holy Blood, Holy Grail,* 241.
24. See Cooper, *Voyages of the Venetian Brothers;* and Andrea, *Irresistible North,* 154.
25. Wilkins, *Concilia Manae Britanniae et Hiberniae,* 380–81.
26. Baigent, Leigh, and Lincoln, *Hold Blood, Holy Grail,* 78.
27. Herculano, *Historia de Portugal,* 201; and Ferreira, *Memorias e noticias historicas,* 800–12, 824–28.
28. Daehnhardt, *Paginas secretas,* 62.
29. Knight and Lomas, *Hiram Key,* 290.

BIBLIOGRAPHY

Addison, Charles Greenstreet. *The Knights Templars*. London: Longman, Brown, Green and Longmans, 1852.

Adrião, Vitor Manuel. *Sintra, serra sagrada*. Comunidade Sintra: Teúrgica Portuguesa, 1994.

Albert of Aachen. *Historia hierosolymitana*. Edited and translated by S. Edgington. Oxford: Oxford Medieval Texts, 2007.

Allegro, John. *The Dead Sea Scrolls and the Christian Myth*. London: Prometheus Books, 1992.

———. *The Treasure of the Copper Scroll*. Garden City, N.Y.: Doubleday, 1960.

Almeida, Fernando. *Pedras Visigoticas em Souré*. Lisbon: Ethnos, number 5, 1966.

———. "Templo de Venus em Idanha-a-Velha." In *Actas e Memorias do 1ª Congresso Nacional de Arqueologia* 2 (1959): 133–39.

Almeida, M. Lopes de. *Ferreira da Costa, and Dinis*. Edited by A. J. Dias and Idalino Ferreira da Costa Brochado. Vol. I. Coimbra, Portugal: Monumenta Henriciana, 1960.

al-Qazwini, Zakaria. *'Ajā'ib al-makhlūqāt wa gharā'ib al-mawjūdāt*. Göttingen, Germany: Wüstenfeld, 1849.

Alvarez, Francisco. *Prester Joam das Indias: Verdadeira testemunha das terras de Prester Joam*. Lisbon: Imprensa Nacional, 1540.

Alvarez, Raquel Alonso. "Los promotores de la Orden del Cister en los reinos de Castilla y Leon." *Anuario de Estudios Medievales* 37, no. 2 (July–December 2007): 653–710.

Anderssohn, John C. *The Ancestry and Life of Godfrey of Bouillon*. Bloomington: Indiana University Press, 1972.

Andrea, Robilant di. *Irresistible North: From Venice to Greenland on the Trail of the Zen Brothers.* New York: Knopf, 2011.

Anonymous, *Perlesvaus.* Charleston, S.C.: Nabu Press, 2010.

Anonymous. *Secret Societies of the Middle Ages.* London: C. Cox, 1848.

Archivo pittoresco. Vol. IX. Lisbon: Castro Irmão & Co., 1866.

Ariosto, Ludovico. *Orlando furioso.* 1516.

Armas, Duarte de. *Livro das Fortalesas, Casa Forte do Arquivo Nacional da Torre do Tombo.* 2nd ed. Lisbon: Edições Inapa, 1997.

Asbridge, Thomas. *First Crusade.* Oxford: Oxford University Press, 2004.

Ash, David, and Peter Hewitt. *Science of the Gods: Reconciling Mystery and Matter.* Shaftesbury, England: Element, 1993.

Auberger, Jean-Baptiste. *L'Unanimite cistercienne primitive: Mythe ou réalité.* Citeaux-Achel, France: Éditions Sines Parvalous, 1986.

Aubert, M., and la Marquise de Maillé. *L'Architecture Cistercienne en France.* Paris: Éditions d'Art et d'Histoire Vanoest, 1947.

Azevedo, R. de, ed. *Documentos medievais Portugueses, documentos regios.* Lisbon: Academia Portuguesa da Historia, 1958.

Baigent, Michael, and Richard Leigh. *The Temple and the Lodge.* New York: Arcade, 1991.

Baigent, Michael, Richard Leigh, and Henry Lincoln. *Holy Blood, Holy Grail.* New York: Bantam Dell, New York, 1982.

———. *The Messianic Legacy.* New York: Delta, 2003.

Bale, John. *Acta romanorum pontificum.* London: John Daye and William Seres, 1574.

Barber, Malcolm. *The Cathars: Dualist Heretics in the Languedoc.* Harlow, England: Pearson Education, 2000.

———. *The Knight and Chivalry.* Ipswich, England: Boydell Press, 1974.

———. *The New Knighthood: A History of the Order of the Temple.* Cambridge: Cambridge University Press, 1995.

———. *The Origins of the Order of the Temple, Studia Monastica.* Vol. XII. Barcelona, Spain: Abadia de Montserrat, 1970.

———. *The Trial of the Templars.* Cambridge: Cambridge University Press, 1989.

Barber, Malcolm, and Keith Bate. *The Templars: Selected Sources.* Manchester, England: Manchester University Press, 2002.

Barbosa, Ignacio. *Monumentos de Portugal.* Lisbon: Castro Irmão & Co., 1886.

Barbosa, J. de Vilhena. *Estudos e archeologicos.* Porto, Portugal: Ernesto Chardron, 1875.

Barroca, Mario Jorge. "A Ordem do Templo e a arquitectura militar portuguesa do Seculo XII." *Portugalia,* new series, XVII–XVIII (1996–1997): 157.

Barthelemy, Edouard de. *Obituaire de la commanderie du Temple de Reims.* Paris: Imprimerie Nationale, 1882.

Bauval, Robert. *Heaven's Mirror.* New York: Doubleday, 1999.

Beckingham, Charles F., and G. W. B. Huntingford, eds. *The Prester John of the Indies: A True Relation of the Lands of Prester John, Being the Narrative of the Portuguese Embassy to Ethiopia in 1520 by Father Francisco Alvarez.* Vol. I. Cambridge: Cambridge University Press for the Hakluyt Society, 1961.

Begg, Ean. *Cult of the Black Virgin.* London: Arkana, 1985.

Bembo, Pietro Cardinal. *Letters and Comments on Pope Leo X.* 1842.

Ben-Dov, Meir. *The Shadow of the Temple: The Discovery of Ancient Jerusalem.* New York: Harper & Row, 1985.

Bennett, J. *Origin of Freemasonry and Knight Templar.* Muskegon, Mich.: John R. Bennett, 1907.

Bernard de Clairvaux. *Apologia.* employees.oneonta.edu/farberas/arth/arth212/Apologia.html

———. *Epistolae.* Vol. III. Paris: Georg Wolf, 1494.

———. *On Consideration.* Oxford, England: Clarendon Press, 1908.

Bernard de Clairvaux, Jean Leclercq, C. H. Talbot, and Henri Rochais. *Sancti Bernardi Opera.* Vol. III. Rome: Editiones Cistercienses, 1957–1977.

———. *Textes politiques.* Paris: Bibliothèque médiévale, 1986.

Biggs, Anselm Gordon. *Diego Gelmirez, First Archbishop of Compostela.* Washington, D.C.: Catholic University of America Press, 1949.

"Boletim da D.G.E.M.N." *Castelo de Pombal,* No. 21, September 1940.

Bordes, Richard. *Les Merovingiens et Rennes-le-Chateau.* Rennes-le-Chateau, France: P. Schrauben, 1984.

Bouquet, Martin, ed., *Recueil des historiens des Gaules et de la France.* Vol. 15. Paris: L'Académie des Inscriptions et Belles-Lettres, 1738.

Branco, Manuel da Silva Castelo. *Ineditos da cronica da Ordem de Cristo de Fr. Bernardo da Costa.* Santarém, Portugal: Edição da Assembleia Distrital de Santarém, 1980.

Brandão, Antonio. *Monarchia Lusitana.* Vol. III. Lisbon: Academia Real das Sciencias, 1806.

Bredero, Adriaan. *Bernard of Clairvaux: Between Cult and History.*

Grand Rapids, Mich.: William B. Eerdmans Publishing Co., 1996.

Brito, Bernardo de. *Monarchia Lusytana*. Vol. III. Lisbon: National Library of Portugal, 1690.

———. *Primeira parte da Chronica de Cister*. Lisbon: Crasbeeck, 1602.

Broadhurst, Paul. *The Green Man*. Launceston, England: Mythos, 2006.

Brochado, Costa. *D. Afonso Henriques*. Lisbon: Portugália, 1947.

Bromiley, Geoffrey, ed. *International Standard Bible Encyclopedia*. Vol. 2. Grand Rapids, Mich.: William B. Eerdmans Publishing, 1982.

Brooker, Charles. "Magnetism and Standing Stones." *New Scientist* 97 (January 13, 1983): 105.

Brownlow, W. R. B., trans. *An Account of the Pilgrimage of Saewulf to Jerusalem and the Holy Land in the Years 1102 and 1103*. London: P.P.T.S., 1892.

Brundage, James, trans. "William of Tyre, Historia rerum in partibus transmarinis gestarum, XII, 7, Patrologia Latina." In *The Crusades: A Documentary Survey*. Milwaukee, Wisc.: Marquette University Press, 1962.

Budge, Wallis A. *The Gods of the Egyptians*. London: Methuen, 1904.

Burke, John. *Seed of Knowledge, Stone of Plenty: Understanding the Lost Technology of the Ancient Megalith-Builders*. San Francisco: Council Oak Books, 2005.

Butler, Alan, and Stephen Dafoe. *The Warriors and the Bankers*. London: Ian Allan Ltd., 2007.

Caesar, Julius. *Incerti avctoris de bello Hispaniensi liber*.

Cardinale, Hygenius Eugene, ed. *Orders of Knighthood, Awards, and the Holy See*. Gerrands Cross, England: Peter Bander Van Duren, 1985.

Carrière, V. *Les débuts de l'Ordre du Temple en France, le moyen age*. Paris: Honoré Champion, 1914.

Cerrini, S., ed., *Regula pauperum commilitonum Christi Templique salominici*. Corpus Christianorum, Continuario Mediavalis.

Chancelaria de D. Fernando, book 1. Arquivo Nacional Torre do Tombo.

Charnier, Henri. *Guide des archives du Loiret: Fonds antérieurs à 1940*. Orléans, France: Archives départementales du Loiret, 1982.

Charpentier, Louis. *Secrets of Chartres Cathedral*. New York: Avon, 1980.

Chatwin, Bruce. *The Songlines*. New York: Penguin Books, 1988.

Christianson, Dale E. *In the Presence of the Creator: Isaac Newton and His Times*. London: Collier MacMillan, 1984.

Chritchlow, Keith. *Islamic Patterns: An Analytical and Cosmological Approach*. Rochester, Vt.: Inner Traditions, 1999.

Cocheril, D. Maur. "Essai sur l'origine des ordres militaires dans la Peninsule Iberique. Collectanea Ordinis Cisterciensium Reformatae, t. XXI, 310.

———. *Routier des abbayes Cisterciennes du Portugal.* Paris: FCG, Centro Cultural Portugues, 1978.

Cook, Ian A., Sarah K. Pajot, and Andrew F. Leuchter. "Ancient Architectural Acoustic Resonance Patterns and Regional Brain Activity." *Time and Mind* 1, no. 1 (March 2008): 95–104.

Cooper, Robert L. D., ed. *The Voyages of the Venetian Brothers Nicolo and Antonion Zeno to the Northern Seas in the XIVth Century.* New York: Masonic Publishing Co., 2004.

Coppens, Philip. *The Stone Puzzle of Rosslyn Chapel.* Kempton, Ill.: Frontier Publishing, 2004.

Coutinhas, José Manuel, *Aproximação à identidade etno-cultural dos Callaici Bracari.* Porto, Portugal, 2006.

Cowan, David, and Chris Arnold. *Ley Lines and Earth Energies.* Kempton, Ill.: Adventures Unlimited, 2003.

Cowan, I. B., P. H. R. Mackay, and A. Macquarrie. *The Knights of St. John of Jerusalem in Scotland.* Edinburgh: Scottish History Society, Fourth Series, 1983.

Cunha, D. Rodrigo da. *Historia ecclisiastica de Braga.* Braga, Portugal: Manuel Cardozo, 1634.

Curzon, Henri de. *La règle du temple.* Paris: Société de l'histoire de France, Librarie Renouard, 1886.

da Costa, Fr. Bernardo. *Historia da Militar Ordem de Nosso Senhor Jesus Christo.* Coimbra, Portugal: Pedro Ginioux, 1771.

da Costa, Miguel Manescal. *Definições e estatuto dos cavaleiros e freires da Ordem do Nosso Senhor Jesus Christo.* Lisbon: Na Officina de Miguel Manescal da Costa, 1746.

Daehnhardt, C. Rainier. *Paginas secretas da historia de Portugal.* Vol. 1. Lisbon: Nova Acropole, 1993.

d'Albon, Marquis. *Cartulaire général de l'Ordre du Temple (1119?–1150): Recuil des chartes et des bulles relatives à l'Ordre du Temple.* Paris: Champion, 1913.

Danby, Herbert. *The Mishnah.* Oxford: Oxford University Press, 1933.

Daraul, Arkon. *The Secret Societies.* New York: Fine Communications, 1999.

Darlington, O. G. "Gerbert, the Teacher." *The American Historical Review* 52, no. 3 (1947): 456–76.

David, Charles Wendell, trans. *De expugnatione Lyxbonensi* [The Conquest of Lisbon]. New York: Columbia University Press, 1936.

David, Pierre. *Etudes historiques sur la Galice et le Portugal.* Lisbon-Paris: Livrarie Portugalia, 1947.

Davies, Daniel, ed. *Celtic Linguistics, 1700–1850.* London: Routledge, 2000.

Delaforge, Gaetan. *The Templar Tradition in the Age of Aquarius.* Translated by John Moyne. Putney, Vt.: Threshold Books, 1987.

Deloux, Jean-Pierre, and Jacques Bretigny. *Rennes-le-Chateau: Capital secrete de l'histoire de France.* Paris: Éditions Atlas, 1982.

Denis, Ferdinand. *Histoire et discription de tous les peuples: Portugal.* Paris: Firmin Didot Freres, 1850.

Deroy, J. P. Th. *Bernardus en origenes.* Haarlem, the Netherlands: De Toorts, 1963.

Dessubre, M. *Bibliographie de l'Ordre des Templiers.* Paris: E. Nourry, 1928.

Devereux, Paul. *Earth Memory.* St. Paul, Minn.: Llewellyn, 1992.

Devereux, Paul, et al. "Acoustical Properties of Ancient Ceremonial Sites." *Journal of Scientific Exploration* 9 (1995): 438.

Dias, Mario Simões. *Os Templarios em terras de Portugal.* Lisbon: Editorial Notícias, 1999.

Didier, J. C. "History of La Roche Vanneau." www.la-roche-vanneau.fr (accessed March 21, 2017).

Dimotheos, Le R. P. *Deux ans de sejour en Abyssinie.* Jerusalem, Israel: Typographie Arménienne du couvert de Saint–Jacques, 1871.

Diodorus the Sicilian. *Historical Library of Diodorus the Sicilian, Valesius, Rhodomannus, and Ursinus.* London: W. McDowell, 1814.

Drower, E. S. *The Mandeans of Iraq and Iran: Their Cults, Customs, Magic, Legends, and Folklore.* Oxford: Oxford University Press, 1937.

Encyclopedia Brittanica. 11th ed. Cambridge: Cambridge University Press, 1910.

Eneix, Linda. "The Ancient Architects of Sound." *Popular Archaeology* 6 (March 2012).

Eschenbach, Wolfram von, *Parzival.* London: Penguin Classics, 1980.

Esquieu, L. "Les Templiers de Cahors." *Bulletin de la Societe des Etudes Litteraires, Scientifiques, et Artistiques du Lot* 22, no. 1 (1897): 147.

Eusebius. *Historia Ecclesiastica.* N.p., 300–325 AD.

Evans, G. R. *Bernard of Clairvaux: Selected Works.* Mahwah, N.J.: Paulist Press, 1987.

Fagan, Brian M., and Charlotte Beck. *The Oxford Companion to Archeology.* Oxford: Oxford University Press, 1996.

Fahd, T., ed. *L'Arabie preislamique et son environment historique et culturel.* Leiden, the Netherlands: Brill, 1989.

Ferreira, Alexandre. *Memorias e noticias historicas da celebre ordem militar dos Templarios na Palestina.* Lisbon: Lisboa Occidental, 1735.

Ferris, Timothy. *Coming of Age in the Milky Way.* London: Bodley Head, 1988.

Figueiredo, Jose Anastasio de. *Historia da Militaria Ordem de Malta e dos senhores grão-mestres della em Portugal.* Lisbon: S. T. Ferreira, 1800.

Forbes, Robert. *An Account of Roslin by Philo-Roskelynsis.* Edinburgh: William Auld, 1774.

Fraser, James. *Proceedings of the Numismatic Society.* London: Royal Numismatic Society, 1837.

Freitas, Bernardino José de Senna. *Memorias de Braga.* Book IV. Braga, Portugal: Imprensa Catholica, 1891.

Freund, Richard. *Digging through the Bible: Modern Archaeology and the Ancient Bible.* Lanham, Md.: Rowman & Littlefield, 2009.

Fulcher de Chartres. *Fulcheri carnotensis historia hierosolymitana (1095–1127).* Edited by Heinrich Hagenmeyer. Heidelberg, Germany: Carl Winter, 1913.

Galvão, Duarte. *Chronica do muito alto e muito esclarecido principe D. Affonso Henriques.* Lisbon: Ferreyra, 1726.

Gandra, Joaquim. *O eterno feminino no aro de Mafra.* London: Thames & Hudson, 1994.

Gardiner, Alan. *Egyptian Grammar.* Westport, Conn.: Griffith Institute, 1999.

Gardner, Lawrence. *Bloodline of the Holy Grail.* Shaftesbury, England: Element Books, 1996.

———. *The Magdalene Legacy.* New York: Barnes & Noble, 2005.

———. *The Shadow of Solomon: The Lost Secret of the Freemasons.* York Beach, Maine: Weiser Books, 2007.

Gerli, E. Michael, ed., *Medieval Iberia: An Encyclopedia.* London: Routledge, 2003.

Gildas. *De excidio et conquestu Britanniae.* http://www.vortigernstudies.org.uk /arthist/vortigernquotesgil.htm (accessed June 8, 2017).

Godwin, Malcolm. *The Holy Grail.* London: Bloomsbury, 1994.

Góis, Damião de. *Fides, religio, moresque aethiopum.* Louvain, Belgium: Rutgerus Rescius, 1540.

Gordon, E. O. *Prehistoric London.* London: The Covenant Publishing Co., 1946.

Graça, Luis Maria Pedrosa dos Santos. *The Templar Castle of Tomar.* Lisbon: ELO–Publicidade, Artes Graficas, 1994.

Green, Thomas. *Concepts of Arthur.* Stroud, England: Tempus, 2007.

Grossman, Heshy, Rabbi. *The Weekly Parsha.* www.shemayisrael.co.il/parsha /dimension (accessed June 8, 2017).

Grousset, Renée. *Histoire des Croisades et du royaume Franc de Jerusalem.* Vol. III. Paris: Plon, 1934–1936.

Guibert de Nogent. *The Deeds of God through the Franks.* Middlesex, England: Echo Library, 2008.

Guimarães, J. Vieira da Silva. *A Ordem de Christo.* Lisbon: Livraria Moderna, 1901.

Guinguand, Maurice. *L'Or des Templiers: Gisors ou Tomar?* Paris: Éditions Robert Laffont, 1973.

Guizot, Michel. *France.* Vol. 1. New York: Peter Fenelon and Co., 1898.

Haagensen, Erling, and Henry Lincoln. *The Templars' Secret Island.* London: Cassell and Co., 2002.

Hagenmeyer, Heinrich. *Le vrais et le faux sur Pierre l'Hermite.* Translated by Maxine Furcy-Raynaud. Paris: Librairie de la Société, 1883.

Hall, Manly P. *Secret Teachings of All Ages.* Los Angeles, Calif.: PRS, 1928.

Hancock, Graham. *The Sign and the Seal.* New York: Crown Publishers, Inc., 1992.

Hancock, Graham, and Robert Bauval. *Talisman.* Shaftesbury, England: Element, 2004.

Harrison, Jane Ellen. *Prolegomena to the Study of Greek Religion.* Cambridge: Cambridge University Press, 1903.

Haskins, Susan. *Mary Magdalene, Myth and Metaphor.* New York: Riverhead Books, 1993.

Hefele, C. J., and H. Leclercq. *Histoire des conciles.* Vol. 5. Paris: LeClare, 1912.

Herculano, Alexandre. *Historia de Portugal.* Books 1 and II. Lisbon: Bertrand & Sons, 1863.

Hill, Rosalind, ed. and trans. *Gesta Francorum et aliorum hierosolimitanorum.* Oxford, England: Clarendon Press, 1967.

Hippolytus. *The Refutation of All Heresies.* Berlin and New York: Walter de Gruyter, 1981.

Hooke, S. H., ed. *Myth, Ritual, and Kingship: Essays on the Theory and Practice of Kingship in the Ancient Near East and in Israel.* Oxford, England: Clarendon Press, 1958.

Hopkins, Marilyn, Graham Simmans, and Tim Wallace-Murphy. *Rex Deus, the True Mystery of Rennes-le-Chateau, and the Dynasty of Jesus.* Shaftesbury, England: Element, 2000.

Hourani, Albert. *A History of the Arab Peoples.* London: Faber and Faber, 1991.

Howarth, Stephen. *The Knights Templar: Christian Chivalry and Crusades: 1095–1314.* New York: Atheneum, 1982.

Howells, William. *The Heathens.* New York: Doubleday, 1948.

Hufgard, M. Kilian. *Saint Bernard of Clairvaux.* Vol. II. Lewiston, N.Y.: Edwin Mellen Press, 1989.

Igrejas, Luis Magarinhos. "Sobre a origem e significado das palavras *Portugal* e *Galiza.*" *Journal Portugaliza,* 2005.

Irwin, Aisling, and Roger Highfield. *The Daily Telegraph,* December 1998.

Isaac de l'Etoile et son siecle, sermon XLVIII, ed. G. Raciti, Citeaux: Commrntarii Cisterciensis, 12, 1961.

Jacq, Christian. *Magic and Mystery in Ancient Egypt.* London: Souvenir Press, 1998.

Jahn, Robert G., Paul Devereux, and Mike Ibison. "Acoustical Resonances of Assorted Ancient Structures." Technical Report PEAR 95002, Princeton University, March 1995.

James, Bruno Scott. *The Letters of St. Bernard of Clairvaux.* Kalamazoo, Mich.: Cistercian Publications, 1998.

Jarman, Alfred Owen Hughes. *Geoffrey of Monmouth and the Matter of Britain, in Wales through the Ages.* Edited by Arthur James Roderick. Vol. I. London: C. Davies, 1974.

Jeantin, Jean Fran L. *Les chroniques de l'Ardenne et des Woepvres.* Paris: L. Maison Libraire, 1851.

Jenkins, Brian, and Spyros A. Sofos, eds. *Nation and Identity in Contemporary Europe.* London: Routledge, 1996.

The Jewish Encyclopedia. New York: Funk & Wagnalls, 1925.

Johns, C. N., "Excavations at Pilgrim's Castle, Atlit, 1932," *Quarterly of the Department of Antiquities of Palestine* III, no. 4 (1933): 145–64.

Johnstone, Paul. *The Sea-craft of Prehistory.* New York: Routledge, 1988.

Jolibois, Émile. *Haute-Marne: L'Ancien et moderne.* Paris: Chaumont Imprimerie et Lithographine Ve Miot-Dadant, 1858.

Jones, Alfred. *Dictionary of Old Testament Proper Names.* Grand Rapids, Mich.: Kregel Academic and Professional Press, 1990.

Jubainville, M. Henri Arbois de. *Histoire de Bar-sur-Aube sous les comtes de Champagne*. Vol. II. Paris: A. Durand, 1859.

———. *Histoire des ducs et comtes de Champagne*. Vol. II. Paris: A. Durand, 1861.

Juromenha, João Antonio. *Cintra pinturesca*. Lisbon: Empreza da Historia de Portugal, 1838.

Kaplan, Aryeh. *Sefer Yetzirah: The Book of Creation in Theory and Practice*. York Beach, Maine: Weiser Books, 1993.

Keynes, John Maynard. "Newton, the Man." In *Newton Tercentenary Celebrations*. Cambridge: Cambridge University Press, 1947.

Knight, Christopher, and Robert Lomas. *The Hiram Key*. London: Century, 1996.

———. *The Second Messiah*. Shaftesbury: Element, 1997.

Konstam, Angus. *Historical Atlas of the Crusades*. London: Mercury Books, 2004.

Lalore, Charles. *Collection des principeaux cartularies du Diocese de Troyes*. Vol. I. Cartulaire de l'Abbaye de Saint-Loup, no. 3. Paris: E. Thorin, 1875.

Lamy, Michel. *Les Templiers: Ces grands seigneurs aux blancs manteaux*. Bordeux, France: Auberon, 1994.

Latrie, L. de Mas, ed. *Chronique d'Ernoul et de Bernard le Trésorier, Société de l'Histoire de France*. Paris: Jules Renouard, 1871.

Lawlor, Robert. *Sacred Geometry*. London: Thames & Hudson, 1986.

Lay, Stephen. *The Reconquest Kings of Portugal*. New York: Palgrave Macmillan, 2009.

Leal, Pinho. *Portugal antigo e moderno*. Vol. II. Lisbon: Mattos Moreira, 1877.

Leclercq, Jean. "Un document sur les debuts des Templiers." *Revue d'Histoire Ecclesiastique* LII (1957): 81–91.

———. *Monks and Love in the Twelfth Century*. Oxford: Oxford University Press, 1979.

———. In *Saint Bernard of Clairvaux, Studies Commemorating the Eight Centenary of His Canonization*. Edited by Basil Pennington. Kalamazoo, Mich.: Cistercian Publications, 1977.

Leclercq, Jean, Charles H. Talbot, and H. M. Rochais. *Sancti Bernardi Opera*. Rome: Editiones Cistercienses, 1957.

Legatio Dauid Aethiopia regis. Bologna, Italy: Giacobo Keymolen Alostese, 1533.

Lemesurier, Peter. *Decoding the Great Pyramid*. New York: Barnes & Noble Books, 1996.

Leroy, Thierry. *Hugues de Payns, chevalier champenois, fondateur de l'Ordre des Templiers.* Troyes, France: Édition de la Maison Boulanger, 1997.

Le livre des constitutions. Geneva: Éditions des Commanderies de Geneve, 1956.

Livro dos mestrados. Lisbon: Torre do Tombo, n.d.

Lizerand, Georges. *La dossier de l'affaire des Templiers.* Paris: Les Belles Lettres, 1964.

Lobineau, Henri. *Dossiers secrets.* Paris: Presses Universitaires de France, 1967.

———. "Généalogie des rois Mérovingiens et origine des diverses familles Françaises et etrangères de souche Mérovingienne d'après l'Abbé Pichon, le Docteur Hervé et les parchemins de l'Abbé Saunière de Rennes-le-Château." Paris: Bibleothèque nationale de France, 1964.

Lubicz, R. A. Schwaller de. *The Temple of Man.* Rochester, Vt.: Inner Traditions, 1998.

Luttrell, Anthony. "The Earliest Templars." In *Autour de la première croisade: Actes du Colloque de la Society for the Study of the Crusades and the Latin East,* edited by Michel Balard. Paris: Publications de la Sorbonne, 1996.

Maalouf, Amin. *Les Croisades vues par les Arabes.* Paris: J. C. Lattès, 1986.

Mabillon, Johannis. *Sancti Bernardi Opera Omnia.* Paris: 1719.

Mackenzie, Donald Alexander. *Wonder Tales from Scottish Myth and Legend.* London: Dover Publications, 1977.

Mackenzie, Kenneth. *The Royal Masonic Cyclopaedia.* Wellingborough, England: Aquarian Press, 1987.

Mackey, Albert. *Encyclopedia of Freemasonry.* Vol. 2. Chicago: The Masonic History Co., 1946.

Mander, Bob. "Balantradoch: The Scottish Temple." In *The Templar Papers,* edited by Oddvar Olsen. Franklin Lake, N.J.: New Page Books, 2006.

Mann, A. T. *Sacred Architecture.* New York: Barnes and Noble, 1996.

Mann, Horace Kinder, and Johannes Hollnsteiner. *The Lives of the Popes in the Early Middle Ages.* Vol. VIII. London: Kegan, Paul, Trench, Trubner & Company, 1910.

Map, Walter. *De nugis curialium.* Oxford, England: Clarendon Press, 1983.

Markale, Jean. *Templar Treasure at Gisors.* Rochester, Vt.: Inner Traditions, Rochester, 2003.

Marques, António Henrique Oliveira. *Historia de Portugal.* 11th edition. Vol. I. Lisbon: Portugália Editora, 1983.

Matos, Leonor Correia de. *A Ordem de Cister e o Reino de Portugal: Mito e raao.* Lisbon: Fundação Lusiada, 1999.

Matthew of Edessa. *Armenia and the Crusades, Tenth to Twelfth Centuries: The Chronicle of Matthew of Edessa.* Translated by Ara Edmond Dostourian. Lanham, Md.: University Press of America, 1993.

Matthews, John. *The Grail: Quest for the Eternal.* London: Thames & Hudson, 1987.

Mattoso, José. *Lusitania Sacra, Centro dos Estudos Historicos.* Lisbon: Faculdade de Direito, 1971.

———. "Perspectivas actuais sobre a nobreza portuguesa 1128–1383." *Revista de Historia Econominca e Social* IX (1982).

———. *Ricos homens, infanções, e cavaleiros. A nobreza medieval Portuguesa nos seculos XI e XII.* Lisbon: Guimarães Editores, 1985.

May, E. C. "Review of the Psychoenergetic Research Conducted at SRI International." *SRI International Technical Report,* March 1988.

McKenna, Stephen. *Paganism and Pagan Survivals in Spain up to the Fall of the Visigothic Kingdom.* New York: Catholic University of America Press, 1938.

Merton, Thomas. *Bernard de Clairvaux.* Alsatia, France: Commission d'histoire de l'Ordre de Citeaux, 1953.

———. *Thomas Merton on Saint Bernard.* London: Cistercian Publications, A. R. Mowbray, 1980.

Merz, Blanche. *Points of Cosmic Energy.* Saffron Walden, England: C. W. Daniel, 1983.

Michael, H.R.H. Prince of Albany. *The Forgotten Monarchy of Scotland.* Shaftesbury, England: Element Books, 1998

Michael the Syrian. *Chronique de Michel le Syrien.* Vol. III. Paris: Ernest Lemoux, 1905.

Michelet. *Histoire de France.* Vol. III. Paris: Librairie de l'Universite de France, 1841.

———. *Le proces des Templiers.* Paris: Librairie de l'Universite de France, 1841.

Migne, Jacques Paul. *Patrologia Latina tomus, S. Bernardi abbatis Clarae-Vallensis, de laude novae militiae, ad militias Templi liber.* Paris: Gamier, 1854.

Miller, Hamish, and Paul Broadhurst. *The Sun and the Serpent.* Launceston, England: Pendragon Press, 1989.

———. *The Dance of the Dragon.* Launceston, England: Pendragon Press, 2003.

Minihan, James. *Encyclopedia of the Stateless Nations.* Vol. IV. Westport, Conn.: Greenwood Publishing, 2002.

Morgado, Augusto. *Epoca,* August 12, 1972.

Morgenstern, Julian. *The Ark, the Ephod, and the Tent Meeting.* Hebrew Union College Annual, vol. XVII, 1942.

Murray, John. *Handbook for Travellers in Portugal.* London: J. Murray, 1855.

Newton, Isaac. *Principia.* Berkeley: University of California Press, 1999.

Niel, Ferdinand. *Dolmens et Menhirs.* Paris: P.U.F., 1966.

O Domingo Ilustrado 2, no. 57 (1898).

Oldenbourg, Zoe. *Massacre at Montsegur.* London: Weidenfelt and Nicolson, 1991.

Oliveira, Nuno Villamariz. *Castelos Templarios em Portugal 1120–1314.* Lisbon: Esquilo, 2010.

Oliver, George. *The Historical Landmarks and Other Evidences of Freemasonry.* Vol. II. New York: Masonic Publishing, 1867.

Olsen, Oddvar, ed. *The Templar Papers.* Franklin Lakes, N.J.: New Page Books, 2006.

Ostrander, Sheila. *Psychic Discoveries behind the Iron Curtain.* New York: Bantam Doubleday, 1971.

Otto of Friesing. *Historia de duabus civitatibus.* 1157.

Oxford King James Bible. Oxford: Oxford University Press, 1769.

Pagani, L. T. Kivisild, A. Tarekegn, R. Ekong, C. Plaster, I. Gallego Romero, Q. Ayub, S. Q. Mehdi, M. G. Thomas, D. Luiselli, et al. "Ethiopian Genetic Diversity Reveals Linguistic Stratification and Complex Influences on the Ethiopian Gene Pool." *The American Journal of Human Genetics* 91, no. 1 (July 13, 2012): 83–96.

Page, Martin. *The First Global Village: How Portugal Changed the World.* Oeiras, Portugal: Casa das Letras, 2006.

Pagels, Elaine. *The Gnostic Gospels.* New York: Vintage, 1989.

Paraschi, André J. *Breve guia da expanção geogràfica dos Cavaleiros Templarios em Portugal.* Lisbon: Sol Invictus, 1986.

———. *Historia dos Templarios em Portugal.* Vol. II. Lisbon: Sol Invictus, 1990.

———. *Portugal magico dos Templarios.* Ericeira, Portugal: Centro Internacional de Estudos Templarios, 1993.

Peake, Arthur Samuel. *Peake's Commentary on the Bible.* Edited by Matthew Black and Howard Henry Rowley. London: Routledge, 2001.

Pereira, Denise, Paulo Pereira, and José Anes. *Quinta da Regaleira: Historia, simbolo e mito.* Sintra, Portugal: CulturSintra, undated.

Persinger, M. A., L. A. Ruttan, and S. Koren. "Enhancement of Temporal

Lobe–Related Experiences during Brief Exposures to Milligauss Intensity ELF Magnetic Field." *Journal of Biochemistry* 9 (1990): 33–45.

Petel, August. *La commanderie de Payns et ses dependences à Messon et au Pavillon.* Paris: Champion, 1905.

Phillips, Jonathan. *Defenders of the Holy Land.* Oxford, England: Clarendon Press, 1996.

Phillips, Tony. "Magnetic Portals Connect Sun and Earth." NASA. https://science.nasa.gov/science-news/science-at-nasa/2008/30oct_ftes (accessed March 28, 2017).

Picknett, Lynn, and Clive Prince. *Turin Shroud—In Whose Image? The Shocking Truth Unveiled.* Toronto, Canada: Stoddart Publishing, 1994.

Pierre Mereaux, Carnac. *Des pierres pour les vivants.* Bretagne, France: Kerwangwenn, Nature & Bretagne, 1992.

Pike, Albert. "Allocution of Pio Nono against the Free Masons." In *Morals and Dogma of the Ancient and Accepted Scottish Rite of Freemasonry.* Charleston, South Carolina: The Council, 1871.

Pinkerfield, Jacob. *Bishvili Omanut Yehudit.* Merhavia, Israel: Sefer Zichron, 1957.

Pinkham, Marc Amaru. *Guardians of the Holy Grail: The Knights Templar, John the Baptist, and the Water of Life.* Kempton, Ill.: Adventures Unlimited Press, 2004.

Pixner, Bargil. "Jerusalem's Essene Gateway: Where the Community Lived in Jesus' Time." *Biblical Archaeological Review* 23, no. 3 (May/June 1997): 22–31; 64, 66.

Prestage, Edgar. *The Portuguese Pioneers.* London: Adam and Charles Black, 1933.

Pritchard, James. *Recovering Serepta, a Phoenician City.* Princeton, N.J.: Princeton University Press, 1978.

Proceedings of the Royal Irish Academy. Vol. VIII. Dublin: M. H. Gill, 1864.

Quadros, Antonio. *Memorias das origens, saudades do futuro.* Lisbon: Publicações Europa-América, 1992.

Raedts, Peter. "St. Bernard of Clairvaux and Jerusalem." In *Prophecy and Eschatology,* edited by Michael Wilks. Oxford, England, and Cambridge, Mass.: Ecclesiastical History Society, 1994.

Reid, John. *Egyptian Sonics: A Preliminary Investigation Concerning the Hypothesis That the Ancient Egyptians Had Developed a Sonic Science by the Fourth Dynasty (Circa 2520 BC).* Ponteland, England: Sonic Age, 2001.

Reilly, B. F. *The Kingdom of Leon-Castilla under Queen Urracca, 1109–1126.* Princeton, N.J.: Princeton University Press, 1982.

Reis, António Matos. "O foral de Guimarães: Primeiro foral português; O contributo dos burgueses para a fundação de Portugal." *Revista de Guimarães,* no. 106 (1996): 55–77. www.csarmento.uminho.pt/docs/ndat /rg/RG106_05.pdf (accessed March 28, 2017).

Reuter, A. E., *Chancelarias mediavais Portugal,* 1, reproduction of the donation in *Livro dos mestrados,* fl. 66; and *Ordem de Cristo,* no. 233, fl. CXXXIII.

Rey, M. Emmanuel-Guillaume. *Les familles d'outre-mer de du Cange.* Paris: Impremerie Imperiale, 1869.

———. *Chartes de l'Abbeye du Mont-Sion, memoires de la Societe Nationale des Antiquaires de France.* 5th Ser. Vol. 8. Paris: N.p., 1887.

Reymond, E. R. E. *The Mythological Origin of the Egyptian Temple.* Manchester, England: Manchester University Press, 1969.

Ritchie, Robert Lindsay Graeme. *Crétien de Troyes and Scotland.* Oxford, England: Clarendon Press, 1952.

Robert the Monk. *Historia Hierosolymitana.* Aldershot, England: Ashgate Publishing, 2006.

Roberts, Paul William. *Journey of the Magi.* Toronto, Canada: Rainbow Books, 1995.

Robinson, John. *Born in Blood.* London: Century, 1990.

Röhricht, Reinhold. *Regesta regni hierosolymitani.* Innsbruck, Austria: Oeniponti, 1893.

Roney-Dougal, Serena. *The Faery Faith, Green Magic.* London: Vega Books, 2002.

Roserot, Alphonse. *Dictionnaire historique de la Champagne méridionale (Aube) des origines à 1790.* Vol. II. Langres, France: Imprimerie Champenoise, 1945.

Rudolph, Conrad. *The Things of Greater Importance: Bernard of Clairvaux's Apologia and the Medieval Attitude toward Art.* Philadelphia, Pa.: Pennsylvania Press, 1990.

Runciman, Stephen. *A History of the Crusades.* London: Penguin Books, 1987.

Saint Bruno. *Lettres des premiers Chartreux.* Vol. I. Paris: Les Éditions du Cerf, 1966.

Salhab, Walid Amine. *The Knights Templar of the Middle East: The Hidden History of the Islamic Origins of Freemasonry.* San Francisco, Calif.: Red Wheel/Weiser, 2006.

Santa Catarina, Fr. Lucas de. *Catalogo dos mestres da Ordem do Templo Portugueses que tiveram ou exercitaram este titulo e carga nesta coroa*

Portuguesa e em outras de Espanha. Lisbon: Pascoal da Silva, 1722.

————. *Malta Portuguesa.* Book II.

Santos, Brother Manuel dos. *Alcobaca illustrada, Apparato Proemial a historia.* Vols. III and VII. Coimbra, Portugal: Bento Seco Ferreira, 1710.

Santos, José António. *Monumentos das ordens militares do Templo de Christo em Thomar.* Lisbon: Biblioteca Universal, 1879.

Sayce, Archibald Henry. *Fresh Light from the Ancient Monuments.* London: Religious Tract Society, 1884.

Scarre, Chris, and Graeme Lawson, eds. *Archaeoacoustics.* Cambridge, England: McDonald Institute for Archaeological Research, 2006.

Schaeffer, Heinrich. *Histoire de Portugal.* Paris: Parent-Desbarres, 1840.

Schmolders, F. A. *Essai sur les écoles philosophiques chez les Arabes.* Paris: Sciencia Verlag, 1975.

Schonfield, Hugh. *Essene Odyssey: The Mystery of the True Teacher and the Essene Impact on the Shaping of Human Destiny.* Shaftesbury, England: Element, 1984.

Schottmuller, Konrad. *Der Untergang des Templer-Ordens.* Vol. II. Berlin: Ernst Siegfried Mittler & Sohn, 1887.

Secco, Pedro Alves. *Escrituras de Thomar.* Book 1. Titulo do Porto, 1568.

Sède, Gérard de. *Les Templiers sont parmi nous.* Paris: Julliard, 1962.

Serbanesco, Demeter Gerard Roger. *Histoire de l'Ordre des Templiers et les Croisades.* Paris: Editions Byblos, 1969.

Sergew, Hable-Selassie. *Ancient and Medieval Ethiopian History to 1270.* Addis Ababa: Haile-Selassie I University, 1972.

Seward, D. *The Monks of War.* St. Albans, England: Paladin: 1974.

Sewter, E. R. A., trans. *The Alexiad of Anna Commena.* Harmondsworth, England: Penguin Books Ltd. 1969.

Shah, Indres. *The Way of the Sufi.* London: Penguin, 1982.

Silva, Freddy. *Common Wealth: The Origin of Sacred Sites and the Rebirth of Ancient Wisdom.* Portland, Maine: Invisible Temple, 2010.

————. *The Lost Art of Resurrection: Initiation, Secret Chambers, and the Quest for the Otherworld.* Rochester, Vt.: Inner Traditions, 2017.

————. *Secrets in the Fields: The Science and Mysticism of Crop Circles.* Portland, Maine: Invisible Temple, 2002, 2014.

Sintra e Seu Concelho. Vol. 1.

Smail, R. C. *Crusading Warfare, 1097–1193.* Cambridge: Cambridge University Press, 1956.

Socard, E., and T. Boutiot. *Dictionnaire topographique de l'aube.* Paris: Imprimerie Nationale, 1874.

Sousa, João Maria. *Noticia descriptiva e historica da cidade de Thomar.* Tomar, Portugal: Conselho Administração, 1903.

Sousa, Manuel de Faria e. *Europa Portugueza.* Book 3. Lisbon: Antonio Creasbeek, 1675.

St. Clair, L. A. de. *Histoire genealogique de la famille de St. Clair.* Paris: Hardy & Bernard, 1905.

Stevenson, David. *The Origins of Freemasonry.* Cambridge: Cambridge University Press, 1990.

Stewart, Michael James. *The Forgotten Monarchy of Scotland.* Shaftesbury, England: Element Books, 1998.

Strabo, "Lapides multis in locis ternos aut quaternos impositos." In *Geographicarum,* AD 20.

Sucena, E. *A epopeia Templaria e Portugal, documenta historica.* Lisbon: Vega, 2008.

Sulpicius Severus. *Chronica II.*

Swanson, Vern. *Dynasty of the Holy Grail: Mormonism's Sacred Bloodline.* Springville, Utah: CFI, 2006.

Terseur, Françoise. *Os Druidas e a tradicão esoterica.* Lisbon: Maio, 1993.

Thiering, Barbara. *Jesus the Man: Decoding the Real Story of Jesus and Mary Magdalene.* New York: Atria Books, 1992.

Thomas, Keith. *Religion and the Decline of Magic.* London: Weidenfeld & Nicolson, 1971.

Thory, Claude-Antoine. *Acta latomorum ou chronologie de l'histoire de la Franche-maconnerie Francaise et etrangere.* Vol I. Paris: Pierre Elie Dufart, 1815.

Tillière, Nicolas. *Histoire de l'Abbaye d'Orval.* Orval, Belgium: J. Duculot, 1967.

Titus Livius. *The History of Rome.* Book VI.

Tompkins, Peter. *Secrets of the Great Pyramid.* New York: Harper & Row, 1971.

Tucket, J. E. S. *The Origin of the Additional Degrees.* Vol. XXXII. 1919.

Tyerman, Christopher. *God's War: A New History of the Crusades.* Cambridge, Mass.: Harvard University Press, 2006.

Ullendorff, Edward. "Hebraic-Jewish Elements in Abyssinian Christianity." *Journal of Semitic Studies* I, no. 3 (1956): 253.

Upton-Ward, J. M. *The Rule of the Templars.* Woodbridge, England: Boydell Press, 1992.

Vallery-Radot, Ireneé. *Bernard des Fontaines, abbé de Clairvaux, ou les noces de la grace et de la nature.* Paris: Desclee, 1963.

——. *Le Prophet de L'Occident (1130–1153).* Paris: Desclee, 1969.

Van Hecke, Lode. *Le desir dans l'experience religieuse: L'Homme reunifie, relecture de saint Bernard.* Paris: Cerf, 1990.

Vermes, Geza, trans. *The Complete Dead Sea Scrolls.* New York: Penguin, 1997.

Vilnay, Zev. *Legends of Jerusalem.* Vol. 1. Philadelphia, Pa.: Jewish Publication Society of America, 1973.

Vincent, Hugues. *Jerusalem de l'Ancien Testament.* Paris: Gabaldi, 1956.

Vincent, R. P. *Histoire de l'anciene image miraculeuse de Notre Dame de Sion.* Nancy, France: n.p., 1698.

Viterbo, Joaquim de Santa Rosa de. *Elucidario das palavras, termos, e frases que em Portugal se usaram.* Vol. II. Lisbon: A. J. Fernando Lopes, 1865.

Vitry, Jacques de. *History of Jerusalem.* London: Palestine Pilgrims' Text Society, XI, 1896.

Vogüé, Melchior de. *Les eglises de la Terre Sainte.* Paris: Librarie de Victor Didron, 1860.

Wallace-Murphy, Tim, and M. Hopkins. *Guardian of the Secrets of the Holy Grail.* Shaftesbury, England: Element, 1999.

Ward, J. S. M. *Freemasonry and the Ancient Gods.* London: Simpkin, Marshall Hamilton, Kent & Co., 1921.

Warren, Charles. *The Temple or the Tomb.* London: Richard Bentley and Son, 1880.

Warren, Charles, and C. R. Conder. *The Survey of Western Palestine.* London: Committee of the Palestine Exploration Fund, 1884.

Webb, Geoffrey, and Adrian Walker. *Saint Bernard of Clairvaux: The Story of His Life as Recorded in the Vita Prima.* London: A. R. Mowbray, 1952.

West, John Anthony. *Traveler's Key to Ancient Egypt.* Wheaton, Ill.: Quest, 1985.

Wheeler, Brannon M. *Moses in the Quran and Islamic Exegesis.* London: Routledge, 2002.

Whitelock, Dorothy, David C. Douglas, and Susie Tucker, eds. and trans. *The Anglo-Saxon Chronicle.* London: Eyre & Spottiswoode, 1961.

Wigoder, Geoffrey. *The Encyclopedia of Judaism.* Jerusalem, Israel: Jerusalem Publishing House, 1989.

Wilhelm, Richard. *The I Ching, or Book of Changes.* Princeton, N.J.: Princeton University Press, 1966.

Wilkins, A. David. *Concilia Magnae Britanniae et Hiberniae*. Vol. II, *Testimony of Walter de Clifton and William de Middleton*. London: David Nutt, 1737.

Wilkinson, John, Joyce Hill, and A. F. Ryan, eds. *Jerusalem Pilgrimage 1099–1185*. London: Hakluyt Society, 1988.

William de Saint-Thierry, Arnald de Bonneval, and Geoffrey de Auxerre. *Vita prima sancti Bernardi*. Books III and V. Parologia Latina.

William of Saint-Thierry, Arnold of Bonnevaux, Geoffrey and Philip of Clairvaux, and Odo of Deuil. *Saint Bernard of Clairvaux: The Story of His Life as Recorded in the Vita Prima Bernardi by Certain of His Contemporaries*. London: A. R. Mowbray, 1960.

William of Tyre. *A History of Deeds Done beyond the Sea*. Translated by Emily A. Babcock and A. C. Krey. New York: Columbia University Press, 1943. Reprint, New York: Octagon Books, 1976.

Williams, Watkin Wynn. *Saint Bernard of Clairvaux*. Manchester, England: Manchester University Press, 1935.

Wilson, Charles William. *Ordnance Survey of Jerusalem*. London: George E. Eyre and William Spottiswoode for Her Majesty's Stationery Office, 1876.

Wilson, Charles William, and Charles Warren. *The Recovery of Jerusalem: A Narrative of Exploration and Discovery in the City and the Holy Land*. London: Richard Bentley, 1871.

Wright, Dudley. *Roman Catholicism and Freemasonry*. White Fish, Mont.: Kessinger Publishing, 2003.

Yates, Frances. *Giordani Bruno and the Hermetic Tradition*. Chicago: University of Chicago Press, 1991.

Zapater y Lopez, M. R. *Císter militante en la campana de la iglesia contra la Sarracena furia. História general de las ilustrissimas, inclitas, y nobilissimas cavallerias dei Templo de Salomon, Calatrava, Alcantara, Avis, Montesa, y Chnsto*. 2 vols. Zaragoza, Spain: n.p., 1662.

Zuckerman, J. *A Jewish Princedom in Feudal France*. New York: Columbia University Press, 1972.

IMAGE CREDITS

All images and diagrams by Freddy Silva except the following:

2.2. Livre des Passages d'Outre-Mer, circa 1490

2.3. Roman du Chevalier du Cygne, circa 1270

2.4. Thirteenth-century etching, public domain

3.2. Byzantine mosaic, public domain

4.2., 5.2., 7.1., 12.2. Gustav Dore, Library of Congress, public domain

6.3. Biblioteca Nacional de Portugal, 1845

7.2. Pedro Augusto Guglielmi, circa 1837

8.3. From *A Pictorial Journey Through The Holy Land*, 1867

11.1. Pamela Coleman Smith, 1909

12.3 Guillaume de Tyr, in *Histoire d'Outre-Mer,* thirteenth century

13.2. 1925 print, anon.

14.2. Vera Effigies, sixteenth century

14.3. Sixteenth-century print, anon.

16.2. Public domain

17.1. Henri Lehmann, circa 1850

19.1. François-Marius Granet, 1840

23.1., 36.1, 38.2. Torre do Tombo, public domain

24.1. Biblioteca Nacional, public domain

27.1., 27.2., 35.1., 35.2., 35.4., 54.2. Warren & Conder, Committee of the Palestine Exploration, 1884

28.3. Jörg Breu the Elder, 1500

30.1. Library of Congress, public domain

32.2., 33.5. Liber Floridus, twelfth century

33.3. Guillaume de Parisiensis, 1539

35.3. From *Jerusalem de l'Ancien Testament,* 1860, by M. de Vogue

40.2. Nineteenth century, anon.

42.1. Bernardino Coelho, Ministry of Public Works, 1934

45.1. Adapted from Charles Brooker, "Magnetism and Standing Stones," *New Scientist,* January 13, 1983

50.1. Bernard Gagnon, Wikipedia Commons, Atribution-ShareAlike 3.0 Unported license, https://commons.wikimedia.org/wiki/File:Bete _Giyorgis_03.jpg (accessed April 20, 2017)

51.1. Tomar archives, c. 1926

54.4. Topographia Helvetiae, Rhaetiae et Valesiae, 1642

NDEX

ABOUT THE AUTHOR

Freddy Silva is a bestselling author and one of the world's leading researchers of ancient knowledge, alternative history, geodesy, and the interaction between temples and consciousness. His other published works include *The Lost Art of Resurrection: Initiation, Secret Chambers, and the Quest for the Otherworld; The Divine Blueprint: Temples, Power Places, and the Global Plan to Shape the Human Soul; Chartres Cathedral: The Missing or Heretic Guide;* and *Secrets in the Fields: The Science and Mysticism of Crop Circles.* He is also a fine art photographer and documentary filmmaker.

Described as "perhaps the best metaphysical speaker," he lectures worldwide, with notable keynote presentations at the International Science and Consciousness Conference, the Association for Research and Enlightenment, the International Institute of Integral Human Sciences, and the International Society for the Study of Subtle Energies and Energy Medicine, in addition to appearances on television, video documentaries, and radio shows.

He was born in Portugal, and holds British and U.S. citizenships. He regularly leads tours to sacred sites in England, Scotland, France, Malta, Ireland, Portugal, Yucatán, Peru, and Egypt.

Website: **www.invisibletemple.com**.

BOOKS OF RELATED INTEREST

The Lost Art of Resurrection
Initiation, Secret Chambers, and the Quest for the Otherworld
by Freddy Silva

Templar Sanctuaries in North America
Sacred Bloodlines and Secret Treasures
by William F. Mann
Foreword by Scott F. Wolter

The Knights Templar in the New World
How Henry Sinclair Brought the Grail to Acadia
by William F. Mann

The Lost Treasure of the Knights Templar
Solving the Oak Island Mystery
by Steven Sora

Templar Heresy
A Story of Gnostic Illumination
by James Wasserman
With Keith Stump and Harvey Rochman

The Secrets of Masonic Washington
A Guidebook to Signs, Symbols, and Ceremonies at
the Origin of America's Capital
by James Wasserman

The Templars and the Assassins
The Militia of Heaven
by James Wasserman

An Illustrated History of the Knights Templar
by James Wasserman

INNER TRADITIONS • BEAR & COMPANY
P.O. Box 388
Rochester, VT 05767
1-800-246-8648
www.InnerTraditions.com

Or contact your local bookseller